PUBLIC OPINION

PUBLIC OPINION

Tracking and Targeting

H. L. Nieburg

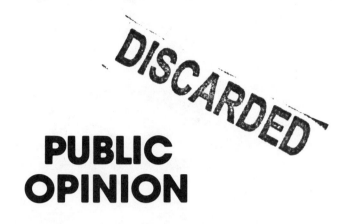

PRAEGER SPECIAL STUDIES • PRAEGER SCIENTIFIC

New York • Philadelphia • Eastbourne, UK
Toronto • Hong Kong • Tokyo • Sydney

Library of Congress Cataloging in Publication Data

Nieburg, H. L. (Harold L.)
    Public opinion, tracking and targeting.

    Includes bibliographical references and index.
    1. Public opinion — United States. 2. Public opinion
polls. I. Title.
HM261.N49 1984   303.3'8   83-24499
ISBN 0-03-069747-6 (alk. paper)
ISBN 0-03-069748-4 (pbk.: alk. paper)

Published and Distributed by the
Praeger Publishers Division
(ISBN Prefix 0-275)
of Greenwood Press, Inc.,
Westport, Connecticut

Published in 1984 by Praeger Publishers
CBS Educational and Professional Publishing,
a Division of CBS Inc.
521 Fifth Avenue, New York, NY 10175 USA

© 1984 by Praeger Publishers

456789 052 9876545321

Printed in the United States of America
on acid-free paper

To Janet

CONTENTS

LIST OF FIGURES

Figure		Page

PUBLIC OPINION

HERBLOCK'S CARTOON

TOTING POLLS

SURVEYS ON 1980 ELECTIONS

©1980 HERBLOCK

- - - - copyright 1983 by Herblock in The Washington Post

INTRODUCTION

"Surveys show the American people don't believe in the press, the government, big business, or surveys."[1] Given the devastation that opinion surveys have brought to the American political process, one writer says we shouldn't be asking how polls can be sharpened, "but why they are endured and how they can be banished." They are, he says, "the life support system for the finger-to-the-wind, quick change politics" of our time and are the "indispensable tools for the ideologically hollow men who work politics like a soap-marketing campaign."[2]

Unlike programs, ideas, and substance, public opinion studies turn everything into numbers, a new species of numerology, a disembodied set of meaningless counters, which are regarded as a special truth but are really just crutches for non-thinking about real meanings. Some experts suggest we are entering a postpolling era, the public having been polled to death all these years, tugged and pulled by too many special-interest claims based on polls, misled by too many wrong predictions, bombarded by too many expert and self-serving analyses. Yet polls are bigger business than ever and, to judge by their ubiquity in the media, are beloved by the people. Or, at least, polls have joined advertising as one of the things the American public loves to hate — and will not be without.

For good or ill, public opinion studies have become the American way and are rapidly spreading across the world. Regardless of what is said in expiation, most politicians, journalists, academics, business people, and the general well-informed public take the subject very seriously indeed!

At their best, attempts to postulate and measure public opinion have proven unreliable and troublesome; yet, even at their worst, they continue to be very meaningful and have been undeniably significant in the social and political process. Even as the misuses, abuses, misreadings, and misunderstandings continue, one thing is unmistakably clear — when all the hullabaloo dies down, the study of public opinion goes on as strongly as ever.

In a modern mass society, there is no escape. Whether as feedback, tea leaves, entertainment, soft news, hard news, prophetic scam, extortionate claim, excuse, scapegoat, whatever, public opinion and its study are ineluctable. Given the mass networks of one-way communication in the modern world, the huge populations that are joined together by pulses of electrons, the nature of the media that make actors and agents out of huge anonymous audiences, there are no alternatives.

Traditional person-to-person networks, common sense, conventional wisdom, personal experience, the views and assessments of friends and associates — all still have significant roles to play. Perhaps these traditional processes remain the most significant. But they are not enough. Inevitably, the means of evaluating mass audiences as voters, citizens, workers, and buyers and consumers of merchandise will match the means of production and distribution of goods and services and information.

In modern societies, everything is professionalized. To err on the side of caution, specialists will seek the best assessments of outcomes they can afford. It is not simply a matter of distrusting personal judgment and experience. The phenomenon of mass societies is beyond personal experience — it cannot be seen or felt or smelled in any form. It is the universal elephant and the seven blind men. None alone can condense it into a mental picture. It would be like the U.S. Weather Bureau doing all of its work out of a single office in Washington. Some form of strategically designed data-collection process is imperative, and with it some intellectual concepts for arranging the data into usable mental images with which specialists can cope.

The never-ending cycles of democratic elections spawn a prognostication industry. We are always moving into a campaign season, living through one, coming out of an election, and at all stages of the ritual, we require a system of information and analysis to feed the persistent appetites. Public opinion studies convert the intangible, airy, and bodiless motions of hypothetical trends into solid monads. Manifested in "Gallup-ing" numbers, the shades created by abstract thought acquire substance and gravity. The apparitions become concrete and visible and are regarded as aspects of a real horse race — with continuous movement and excitement from day to day as they drive furiously into the home stretch.

The horse race mentality is engendered by the relentless cycles of free elections, along with the tipsters, touts, con artists, and pickpockets who inevitably are part of the ritual. Polls may be one of the prices we must pay for the opportunity to live in a democratic society.

The use of the best means available in this process cannot be denied. Preoccupation with the feelings, attitudes, values, thoughts, and reactions of the great mass of people is intrinsic to the same reality that created the modern nation-state. To delve into the subjective dimensions, the volitional reality, of the great audiences assembled in the modern forums of the mass media is to study the real major actors and entities that are part of events. This is an irreversible fact of modern life, a megatrend in itself neither good nor bad, but with whose implications we must struggle.

THE NEED FOR A NEW SYNTHESIS

In all the fields that relate to the study of public opinion, there is today a need for a new synthesis — not only for survey researchers but also for their motivational and market research brethren. All are engaged in the same activity, probing the volitional dimensions of society. All use increasingly the same tools and the same body of theory.

Tracking and targeting are the present state of the art in public opinion studies. Tracking refers to the ability to study with great rapidity the reactions and changes of sentiment of the public on a day-to-day basis; targeting refers to the ability to define the differentiated segments of that public and to communicate selectively with each segment as deemed appropriate.

The segmentation of audiences, combined with the techniques of tracking and targeting, means that survey research is converging with motivational, market, and audience research. Survey methods must count and sort variables by means of probability sampling; and they must give form to large-scale demographics. Motivational studies must delve beneath the surface and profile the subjective dimensions. Market and audience studies put this knowledge together in terms of persuasion and media. It is time to synthesize the theory, knowledge, and methods of all these fields, to reflect in the classroom the actual synthesis that exists in the field among professionals.

Survey research has strengthened all kinds of theory. Based on survey data, "behavioral economics" has provided new answers to basic questions of theory. George Katona, economic forecaster, offers this example: Under classical "law of demand" doctrine, rising prices and interest rates should have indicated a declining housing market in 1977-78. Actually there was a strong upsurge, which could only be explained and verified by survey research, which revealed a significant change in consumer psychology.

In recent years, marketing research has become a model for policy research. In the 1950s, as Irving Crespi points out, the "nose counters" and the "head shrinkers" waged a methodological war against each other. The former wanted to develop reliable, objective measures of consumer behavior — who bought what, where, and how often? They assumed that behavior is unambiguous and readily subject to interpretation. They concentrated on obtaining valid samples of the consumer population. The latter insisted that research should answer the question: Why? As behavioral scientists — mostly sociologists and psychologists — they stressed the necessity to understand motivations and attitudes. "Without such an understanding, the best designed sample . . . would provide information of only limited use for the creation of new products and more effective marketing methods."[3]

The new synthesis needs to take account of the contributions of the last two decades to our understanding of language. Traditional theories of public opinion have tended toward behaviorism and rationalism. But recent theory and research have enlarged our approaches and opened up the new and unfamiliar vistas of transformational linguistics, theories of information, and complex behavioral paradigms.

Opinion measurement depends on words as indicators. Therefore, the researcher must examine the problems of verbal meaning and the relationship of words to acts. Theory of meaning is a vigorous field that has not stood still during the last 20 years — witness the Chomsky "transformational linguistics" revolution and its after-math. The psychology of symbols and behavior, likewise, has seen a revolution that has challenged simple Skinnerian behaviorism.

The relationship of group membership and socialization, media rhetoric, the functions of verbal as opposed to other expressive vocabularies (for example, body language), of attitudes and values to actual behavior — all are areas of important new contributions that must be incorporated. We confront a situation that may require us to redefine our categories, examine new concepts, revise or revalidate the familiar notions — in short we have the obligation to renew the field of public opinion by incorporating the best of the new paradigms into our work.

Of course, this is an ongoing process and has not been neglected by workers in the vineyard. But now and then it is useful to codify the ad hoc process and assemble the prevailing forms into a consis-tent whole.

All the contemporary methods of audience rating are applicable to public policy studies, especially in a nation increasingly frag-mented into "taste publics," that is, groups of people who pay atten-tion only to certain communicators of their choice, excluding others, and thus constituting a "public" only within the network of messages that they in fact actually receive. That which governs us must be able to win our attention first; this may be true of many communication sources, especially in a pluralistic society equipped with mass media networks of all shapes and varieties.

Politics must now be recognized as part of the process of popular culture, as part of the mainstream of the mass marketplace. Every politician and official does in fact act like a salesperson and pro-moter, competing for attention in the exact same marketplace where the people are assembled, that is, where their attention is already focused. Every politican and official must undertake to use the most effective means to win and hold attention for his or her own messages, thereby maximizing chances that messages will be received by the intended audience and perhaps have the intended effect.

Politics is the art of the possible. It is a process of becoming and not a state of being. The boundaries that define the possible are always changing, and the main thing that limits the possible at any given time are the expectations that people hold in their heads about what is in fact possible. This collective set of expectations defines the limits of legitimate political action, institutional and legal change, and the directions and purposes of organized groups. In turn, those expectations can themselves be modified by the same process, making growth and even fundamental transformations possible. The whole is an open system that evolves by inner and outer imperatives.

Easy choices do not become controversies. Only the tough ones are by nature charged with interest and cost, involving choices that will exact a real toll upon the decision makers, regardless of what they do. Those who make the decisions always pay a price. "Every decision creates nine disappointed parties and one ingrate!" Real issues are surrounded by active demands by people and groups that can sting. Those against whom a decision goes are likely to retaliate in some way and erode the legitimacy of the decision maker; more often, they will be propitiated or consoled by a trade-off in another area of policy or by a promise of preferred treatment during the next round.

Consequently, the public opinion researcher can help. While no oracle on policy matters, the public opinion researcher practices the craft of studying the condition of the subjective polity, a dynamic condition that ebbs and flows every moment in the complex bargaining interplays that constitute the real, though often intangible, political system.

In this book we undertake a state-of-the-art synthesis of public opinion study. We will describe and illustrate all of the methods for measuring public sentiment, including instructions for carrying them out, collating, and interpreting the results. We will attempt to consider inherent problems and survey the metaphysical abyss that should trouble the dreams of would-be political consultants, pollsters, and analysts. There are no easy and authoritative escape routes for the ethical and metaphysical complexities of every worthwhile human enterprise.

This is a book primarily for college students. Learning must be active. It must use the whole mind. It must be learning by discovery, in which the student, not the teacher and not the textbook, is the primary agent. The textbook may aid the process, but oftentimes this is done best by riddles and contradictions rather than by didactic instruction. This work will state the hard questions. It will touch upon the pertinent issues of methodology and philosophy that cannot be ignored. It will raise the ethical dilemmas and summarize the historical background of attempts to resolve them by professional codes of practice as well as by government regulation.

This text is designed for use in a course that is devoted at least 50 percent to an active workshop approach, in which the students gain much of their education by conducting surveys in the field, from hypothesis through research design, interviewing, collating data, statistical analysis, interpretation, critique, and proposal of logical follow-up studies.

It is the author's intention, and hope, that students will be stimulated by the multitude of fascinating and creative challenges that this area of study offers, that they will come to it with a playful and adventuresome attitude. Learning should not be an oppressive necessity, like wage labor, but an opportunity to join in the quest for continuous renewal and discovery, which is the essence and the joy of research.

NOTES

1. Robert Orben, *Editor and Publisher*, July 19, 1980, p. 14.
2. Daniel S. Greenberg, "The Plague of Polling," *Washington Post*, September 16, 1980, p. C23.
3. "Modern Marketing Techniques: They Could Work in Washington Too!" *Public Opinion*, June/July 1979, p. 18.

CHAPTER ONE
THIS THING CALLED PUBLIC OPINION

Anything said aloud and heard by anyone — that's a start for a definition of "public opinion." But people use the term to describe all sorts of passive or active expressions, whether verbally or otherwise. People may express by behavior, by body language, by bodily presence, by symbols painted on banners, by their clothing, by almost an infinite number of signs, their preferences, views, values, attitudes, and loyalties.

Everyone knows that "public opinion" is for rough and ready uses. Public opinion may be considered the aggregate of views held by the public on matters of interest, both private and public, upon which they may be expected to act in some way when the matter requires.

We know public opinion is important. Democratic societies presume to serve the "voice of the people." Therefore inquiry into the decent opinions of all the citizens is thought to be the first duty of politicians and governments. That is a fundamental doctrine of any democratic system, however imperfectly achieved by the designs of real-life political institutions.

Regardless of whoever may presume to speak for John Q., and regardless of the transitory rhetoric of political candidates and incumbents, there is a sense in which those who practice the democratic persuasion believe deeply in the underlying force of opinion, as the ultimate measure of the rightness of prevailing collective decisions, as the mysterious but majestic tide that in the end always sweeps everything else away, as the ultimately irresistible manifestation of that impressive and remarkable thing, the voice of the Master, the People!

The Nixon presidency ended, not with a bang, but "in a whimper" (T. S. Elliot, of course). There were no tanks or troop carriers in the streets or very little of anything at all to mark the fall of a leader who had dominated the national elections less than a year before. Gladys and Kurt Lang note that it happened "without any serious political clashes or much visible dissent," without much "joyful demonstration or dancing in the streets. The public response was strangely muted."[1]

They point out that the transition of power would not have taken place this way "had it not been preceded by a dramatic reversal of public opinion." Nixon himself believed that public opinion was the critical factor in what he called this "overriding of [his] landslide mandate." His fight to remain in office, especially after the Friday night massacre, the firing of special prosecutor Archibald Cox in October 1973, when impeachment became a real possibility, was for him a "race for public support," his "last campaign" for survival itself.[2] From his point of view, the main danger lay in the public's getting used to the notion that he was going to be impeached. As the Langs noted: "That was good enough reason for Nixon strategists to keep a close watch on all indicators . . . letters, telegrams, telephone calls, editorials, television commentaries, press reports, and especially, the polls."[3]

The embattled president called forth a media strategy specifically and directly aimed at winning "the battle of the polls" as a means, write the Langs, of rallying support for his stand against further probes into his actions. It was his defeat in this battle for public opinion, as he saw it, that ultimately did him in. He did not accept the cynicism of aide Charles Colson, who is reported to have said: "A good grip on their balls, and their hearts and minds will come too. . . ."

In the confrontation between Lech Walesa and the Polish martial law government, the battle was not of military force and violent confrontations but for the minds and hearts of the people. After releasing him from detention (which had made Walesa a symbol of resistance), the Jaruzelski regime sought to discredit him by filling the media with charges of sexual misdeeds, the accumulation of great personal wealth and material possessions (a Mercedes and fancy apartment, which the government provided), complicity with the American CIA, and so on. None of this worked.

The only thing that might have damaged Walesa was collaborating with the regime, which he steadfastly refused to do. The regime continued in authority but without legitimacy, authority without real power. Unable to induce those with real power (Solidarity leaders) to share it with the government, the regime rightfully understood that it could move only by subtle persuasion, based on the common fear of a Soviet invasion. To use force would be a self-destroying prophecy and might wreck the government completely, leaving in its wake civil war or Soviet occupation, probably both.

In its mysterious and profound way, something called public opinion makes its presence known, intangible and powerful beyond the transitory formal titles of authority. Tenuous and evasive, the decent opinions of humankind cannot be ignored or obliterated. Like the tender violets, they have the power to split the rocks on the hillside. The modern nation-state, splendid in its massive size, its missiles and navies, its vertical cities of granite, its webs of asphalt, its millions of people swarming over its wide land — all of it is held together by tenuous filaments connecting the minds and hearts of its peoples, by subjective feelings and emotions. Enormously potent and yet fragile. Taken for granted and yet its collapse would herald the gravest calamities that humankind imagines. An Ode to Public Opinion: May it shine forever, and most of us serve it one way or another all of our lives!

DEFINING PUBLIC OPINION

It is often useful to consult the derivations of words. At times we discover centuries of wisdom hidden in the roots, which proves that others have been here before us. In Latin, *publicus* means "belonging to the people"; it is a contraction of *populus* and *pubicus*, the former referring to people collectively, the latter to pubic hair (or adult people). *Opinari* means "to think" or "to suppose"; "opinion" includes the root *onis*, for "expectation." The English word "hope" is related, as is the word "option," which comes from the Latin *optio*, meaning "choice or wish."

To mix together all the Latin roots is to come up with a group of meanings surrounding the term "public opinion," which include hopes, suppositions, expectations, predictions, and choices held by people with pubic hair. Current uses encompass all these meanings, refined by such shadings as "beliefs broadly held that are not based on certainty or positive knowledge." Probable, judgmental, and partial truths that people act on in the absence of stronger values or evidence. It also means "passive" or "latent" tendencies that if elicited by approprite stimuli will induce certain kinds of action.

Public opinion is as well a term used to disguise and soften the potential for conflict arising out of different value systems: Opinion implies that in certain areas group beliefs may differ without an inevitability of open warfare. Individual or factional opinions are permissible where a universal consensus (usually called by some stronger word, like "faith" or "commitment") is not socially desirable or has not been found. In this sense, the use of "public opinion" legitimizes a continuation of dialogue and an attitude of openness and tolerance.

There is also an implication that people cannot be held fully responsible for actions and values that are characterized as based on "opinion only." In this usage, the word is an alibi or excuse for mistaken utterance or action, a plunge in the dark, action unilluminated by reason, knowledge, or information.

Strangely enough, it is probably this usage that has led our civilization to term the advice of experts as "professional opinions" rather than as, what it is, special knowledge and skill that the lay person honors and employs to guide her or his own actions. The formal judgments of the people best qualified in recondite areas are termed "opinions," as a way of cushioning their authority and responsibility. The usage warns the people, who are dependent on expert advice or judicial decisions, "you are on your own; we are not sure about what we are telling you."

This incongruity is especially apparent in the formal decisions of judges and juries, which are endowed with virtually absolute power of life and death, creating standards of action that become "truth and knowledge" for others. "And when the physicians disagree?" Medical doctors and auto mechanics do have power of life and death over the rest of us, so that they seek to protect their fallibilities by terming their prescriptions "opinions only" – even though their opinions must be acted upon as though they were natural laws.

It is an anomaly that the people to whom we give such powers over us (in most cases without due process) seek to deserve our confidence in them by repeatedly reminding us that they don't know what they are doing. It is part of the same usage by which doctors and lawyers never learn their crafts and therefore must continue "to practice." The consequences of their advice for good and ill are so portentious that the responsibility is too much for any mere human being. Therefore, they claim only "to practice."

This is a fascinating insight! The problem of Hamlet: the need to reconcile action and imperfect knowledge, to plunge in the dark because of a moral and practical imperative, when the risks are not fully understood and the results may be tragic.

The use of the words "public opinion" has a parallel connotation: the whole polity shares this mortal weakness — the need to act without knowledge, to risk all by living every day. The alternative is quietism and autism, which Western society dismisses in favor of outwardness and activism. The democratic iconography thus tempers the inherent hubris of majoritarianism by tracing its authority to a standard that is modestly tentative and unsure, the opinions of the public.

Other dimensions of common usage need to be explored. Bernard Hennessy adopts the definition: "Public opinion is the complex of preferences expressed by a significant number of persons on an issue of general importance."[4] This is the beginning of a technical definition.

A problem arises from the tendency to treat a number of other indicators — faith, values, knowledge, information, purposes — as synonymous. As always in language, the attempt to be precise often only confuses things and makes well-understood words numb on the brain, like repeating a word over and over again until it turns into nonsense syllables.

Much of the usage reflects different paradigms about human behavior: Are opinions learned responses to symbolic cues? Are they largely induced by group identities? And are they therefore somewhat immune to facts and information? To what extent are opinions part of a rational process and responsive to rational discourse? To what extent does verbal behavior predict physical behavior? To what extent is the opinion process nonverbal?

Many opinions may be regarded as self-markers, like hats, which mainly serve to give a social classification to the bearer. By bearing the marker, a person may assume a set of postures and behaviors toward others, and others will know how to behave in turn.

Opinions may be considered as self-stimulation cues that serve ritualistically to affirm paradigms of reality. They serve to organize and direct the holder's own behavior, giving substance to his notions of reality by supplying routines of action and expression. His actions and expression are palpable; therefore they make palpable the symbolic propositions upon which they are based. Actions dramatize and express opinions; opinions provide the cues and forms of actions.

Opinions may be regarded as bargaining chips: "This is where I stand, what do you propose to do about it?" For both of these functions opinions must be expressed to be socially effective. During an encounter of strangers there is a curious urge that compels them to unload and exchange opinions about a host of topics, as if trying to triangulate their relative places in the universe.

These thoughts lead to the notion of public opinion as a process of interaction, a low-risk, low-energy symbolic substitute for physical interaction. Just as war can be defined as "the continuation of diplomacy by other means," so conversely public opinion can be defined as "measures short of war," that is, social interaction or bargaining short of physical contact, aimed at adjusting relationships in order to maximize mutual need satisfaction and to prevent conflict and disorder.

This suggests a dynamic condition that depends for its efficacy on all the means of social interaction, including leadership, followership, competition and collaboration, bargaining, provisional standards for adjusting conflicts, and the means of creating and constantly revising the main consensual body that holds a healthy society together.

Symbols are signs that stand for things or other signs. They are energy-conserving, highly concentrated tokens of meaning. They are social triggers that, like trigger reactions in nature, enable a small energy input to release or control a larger amount of energy. Like a microchip amplifier (which applies a very weak electrical current to moderate and imprint information on a strong current), symbols release and direct human energy into individual and group activities, both useful and useless.

Symbols, which are the main tokens in the transactions of public opinion, enable society to combat entropy. Entropy is the Second Law of Thermodynamics: All things in nature tend to decay into disorder and lower levels of energy. Symbolic interaction minimizes the energy exhausted by the political process itself, thereby leaving something for all the ongoing day-to-day purposes of social life. This is the reason why symbolic discourse so intensifies during periods of instability, or during civil disorder; the body politic responds to the gravest possible danger by seeking a return to symbolic processes.

The function of distinct words is to denote distinct behaviors. Thus words are not arbitrary signs, but rather represent conventions of social usage.

"Belief" or "faith" is used to characterize commitments to symbols or actions that the bearer wishes to put beyond the arena of opinion; "convictions" are held in a class that will not easily bend and, if challenged, will show little or no change. "Sentiment" is used to characterize an opinion based on personal emotion, which is not to be forcefully impressed on others. A "view" is a personal expression not likely to be supported by future action. "Knowledge" is a privileged guide to conduct, based on evidence and experience; it can only be challenged by similar credentials and evidence.

INFORMATION AND MEANING

"Information" is new evidence with irresistible creditability, whose impact is to force changes in the data base of social and individual memory; it is a primary input that must be dealt with by all who receive it. It penetrates the borders of cognizance, keeping all systems open, even those that are relatively closed. Information may or may not be admitted after being examined — that depends on the individual's screening device — but it is inexorable. It forces itself on consciousness and insists that its credentials be examined.

Information is the means by which an individual's isolated experience at the dangerous frontiers of the society (both geographic and mental) is assimilated by the whole group. It is second-hand experience from afar, transmuted into symbolic forms so it can be readily transported and exchanged. It is the primary means of social adaptation and internal balancing in a social group. It is the means by which a group continually adjusts to new boundary conditions — that is, the group's relationships internally and externally where changes may menace the safety and survival of the group.

Claude Shannon and Warren Weaver have made a central contribution to information theory in their work *The Mathematical Theory of Communications*. Of greatest interest perhaps to computer designers, some of it cannot be ignored by social scientists. "To be sure," they write, "the word information relates not so much to what you do say, as to what you could say . . . that is, information is a measure of one's freedom of choice when one selects a message."[5]

When, in the simplest situation, one chooses between two possible messages, the measure of information (or of choice) is unity (one to one equals one, or $1/1 = 1$). Developing a mathematical algorithm on the basis of this unit becomes possible: "The amount of information is to be measured by the logarithm of the number of available choices."

The information source is free to choose to communicate any one of a discrete set of possible messages — like a person choosing a greeting card. The measure of information is equivalent to the improbability of any one card being selected. Any message contains information only to the extent that it is new; otherwise, it contains, not information, but redundancy — that is, a repetition or recapitulation of previous information. Redundancy is an important part of every communication, but it must be distinguished from information. Shannon and Weaver calculate that the usages of colloquial language constitute redundancy about 55 percent of the time.

This measure of information is found to resemble the concept of entropy in thermodynamics, that is, the degree of randomness in nature and the tendency of physical systems to become less and less organized. By using a ratio of relative disarray to organization, it becomes possible to set up a numerical index of entropy in a system; similarly, the amount of real information can be measured by comparing the actual to the maximum number of choices possible. The converse measurement (turning the ratio upside down) would provide a numerical value for redundancy.

The main contribution of this insight is that information is a message chosen from an infinite number of possibilities, emphasizing its improbable nature.[6] This idea is like Jean Piaget's insistence that human development depends upon invention and creativity. Communication is a constant struggle against chaos, and information is the main tool in that struggle.

Information contains "meaning," one of the most contentious words in the dictionary. What is the meaning of meaning? "Meaning" is more than assigning the correct dictionary definition to a verbal symbol. Meaning is referential, that is, a symbol points or labels real objects in the external world.[7] That is a key function of meaning; but not to be overlooked is the function of symbols to label and retrieve from memory, to point in the subjective world.

Here the symbol evokes emotional potencies from the deep personalities of people; it has the ability to contain and to release energy and put that flow to work in certain directions, both expressive and physical. People generally can define many words which may or may not have meaning for them. Words without emotional reverberations are empty husks, dull and lifeless.[8]

Meaning is always behavioral in that it induces physical effects. It points, it provides procedures for doing and making, for releasing, modulating, concerting individual energies in social enterprises. The process by which emotional bonds are attached to symbols is in essence the same process by which symbols acquire meaning. Meaning and power are synonymous in this sense.

How do certain symbols acquire potency over behavior? Why is that potency fixed in certain directions, inducing only certain specific behaviors and not others? How are such meanings transformed and changed over time? Information and meaning are exchanged through communication, a process that has been defined as "the transfer of meaning or the sharing of experience" among people. Interpersonal communication is between individuals; group communication occurs among specific audiences who have direct means of feedback.

In the past, mass communication was directed at a large undifferentiated audience and had only indirect means of feedback. That is no longer true. Today, and increasingly into the future, modern mass communications and polling are moving toward differentiating between special (or targeted) audiences; mass media accomplish this by programming strategies, allowing the general public to differentiate themselves as separate audiences for different communications.

Audience selection by programming is very important in modern communications and is of great interest to anyone involved in public opinion. Obviously, there is no communication unless the communicator can win and hold the attention of some audience or public (a dimension we will examine in a later chapter). Programming, that is, the arrangement of messages and content to appeal to certain tastes and interests, is in the mass media a reflection of who we are and what we aspire to become.

Our tastes in entertainment, music, or news represent an interior dialogue among ourselves about ourselves. Our tastes represent our real values. They are not always synonymous with professed values. Because programming tends to react with sensitivity to success or failure in winning audiences, it provides an excellent handle on the ways people seek answers to fundamental questions: What's real? What's important? What's next? These are the eternal questions to which a culture continually provides answers.

We will define communications as social linkages that modulate and generate energy flows in certain directions, the social dimension of "meaning." Communication uses symbols as energy valves in the process of social interaction and collective behavior. Communication always requires the attention of the intended receiver or audience to be complete.

Public opinion literature gives great credence to "the funnel of causality," the graphic representation of the process of individual opinion making (see Figure 1). This model attempts to resolve the contradiction between open and closed systems by showing both factors at work simultaneously. Human attitudes respond to a wide variety of inputs (family background, religious training, current facts, and so on), but gradually, as each input is assimilated, the funnel gets smaller, fewer inputs are admitted, and the existing mix of memory acts increasingly as a screening device to limit new entries.

The funnel expresses the need for continued responsiveness combined with some degree of nonresponsiveness to the external world. The shape is increasingly narrowed but still open; the need for stability is expressed by the relative narrowing of the mouth as opinions harden to the extent necessary to make them functional. The human organism requires a high degree of stability and organization. Openness to unlimited quantities of information will destroy it. Information must be admitted grudgingly; each piece must be carefully screened and weighed. Much is rejected because it contradicts the organizational schema, not because it is qualitatively worse than that which is admitted and assimilated.

"Rational" means in common usage "correct," "smart," "right." That's not bad, but technically the word means "in a logical order," and has to do with syllogistical sequence. The common usage is

FIGURE 1.
Funnel of Causality

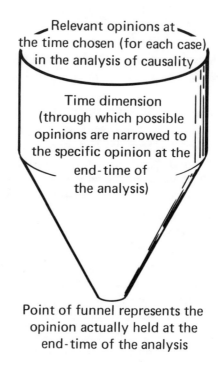

Relevant opinions at the time chosen (for each case) in the analysis of causality

Time dimension (through which possible opinions are narrowed to the specific opinion at the end-time of the analysis)

Point of funnel represents the opinion actually held at the end-time of the analysis

to be preferred for our discussion. We take "rational" as behavioral, not necessarily logical.

Propositions that do not demonstrate a logical sequence may still be associated with behavioral consequences that have other properties that are "rational." Namely, that the means selected are appropriate and likely to achieve the given ends, that courses of action are perceived as cost-effective by some standard of measurement, that benefits outweigh counterbenefits, that indicated courses of action clearly optimize stated values and/or perceived self-interests. All these formulas follow from the normal usage of the term "rational."

PERSONALITY AND OPINION

It is useful to offer a schematic diagram of the personality to illustrate the interrelationship of all these key terms. Picture a triangle with six levels. On the bottom (level 1) is the personality set, the basic underlying structures that are given: physical endowment, health, the biology, and the symbolic and behavioral structures that were acquired by the basic experiences of childhood and family life. This level is like the formal underpinnings of political societies: the physical endowment of land, soil, terrain, and climate, the nature of borders, technology, and human and other biological material, and relationships with other national entities in the system.

Layer 2 is composed of that part of the personality that is shaped by the process of socialization and growing up into the larger world beyond the family; here the entities that influence symbolic and physical behavior are the values that express the individual's place in a complex web of affiliations among secondary groups, including self-conscious memberships, self-conscious identifications (without face-to-face contact), and unself-conscious relationships that nevertheless express themselves in emotional reactions. This level may be likened to the political culture of larger societies, the collection of mental and relational structures that constitute the strongest consensus of values holding a nation together.

On layer 3 we have knowledge, sets of symbolic and behavioral precepts that embody both individual and group learning and experience. This is comparable to the formal constitutional systems of the nation-state that establish positional structures of authority and function, providing the machinery for regulating all the ordinary transactions of the people within its jurisdiction.

Judgment and theories are on level 4, the individual's attempt to apply knowledge to solve concrete problems by assessing the meanings of day-to-day situations and applying the best which his or her knowledge makes available. This is comparable to governments' task of writing general rules of conduct, laws, which the machinery may apply in the process of regulation.

On level 5 we finally encounter the proper and precise realm of opinion, the area where knowledge and information breaks down, where we span the abyss of past and future, where our best judgment contains a frayed and tattered margin, where chance and character become just as important as training and experience. It is here that the virtues of patience and courage take the places vacated by other counsels. This is like what governments accomplish by policies and regulations, attempts to bridge the gaps between general law and the multitude of real events that never entirely fit into the right categories.

At the tip of the pyramid, level 6, we confront the creative principle of the personality, however defined. Whether composed of genius, god-chosen insight, the whim of caprice, dumb impulse, unique position, or the chance trajectory of a cosmic particle, here is the essentially arbitrary input of will and purpose.

This dimension of the personality represents the outpost of behavioral freedom, the ability to say no against all pressures, including self-interest and good sense. It is the existentialist's saving grace of distinct humanness. It makes it possible for people to violate all the structures of determinism, creating a potential for comic or tragic surprise, as well as for the most astonishing feats of individuality. This is like the level of individual choice and discretion for officials of government in their personal performance of duty — the cop who selectively enforces the speeding law, or the clerk who gives confusing nonanswers to inquiries when the social service client has unintentionally offended.

At levels 3 through 5, rationality in the technical sense (the operations of logic) may play an important role; but it is necessary to note that the first principles and the purposeful drive that employ rationality are not by nature controlled by rational processes. Without them, rationality is like a computer without software, a programless computer that is all dressed up with no place to go; it just sits there, warm and humming, spinning its disk drives in a futile search for a role in life.

"Attitudes" are latent behaviors (both verbal and physical), subjective tendencies that will be elicited and made evident by certain stimuli. In response to questions, attitudes become manifest by the choice of symbols that indicate the tendencies toward supporting action. For example, a positive attitude toward the Republican party will be expressed by associating symbols of approval with the symbols of Republicanism; thus expressed, the latency is overcome symbolically. By contributing funds, attending meetings, and voting for Republican candidates, the latency is overcome physically on the occasions of these actions. When not aroused from latency, the attitude may remain as strong as ever in a passive mode.

Although we have labeled level 5 of the personality as the proper sphere of opinion, analysts must deal with the whole personality. Opinion is the probing dimension of behavior. As such it cannot be separated from the entire configuration, which gives it dynamic form and content. Students of public opinion seek to understand the dynamic processes that shape the interacting roles of people, the ways opinions originate, develop, change, and express themselves.

All survey and motivation research attempts not only to count the numbers and directions of opinions but also to gain insights into the linkages among the various levels of causation and personality development.

NOTES

1. Gladys Engel Lang and Kurt Lang, "Polling on Watergate," *Public Opinion Quarterly* 44 (1980): 530.

2. Richard Nixon, *RN/The Memoirs of Richard Nixon* (New York: Grosset & Dunlap, 1978), p. 972.

3. Lang and Lang, "Polling on Watergate," p. 532.

4. Bernard C. Hennessy, *Public Opinion*, 3rd ed. (North Scituate, Mass.: Duxbury Press, 1975), p. 5.

5. Claude Shannon and Warren Weaver, *The Mathematical Theory of Communications* (Urbana: University of Illinois Press, 1949), p. 100.

6. Ibid., p. 104.

7. See Lewis M. Branscomb, "Information: The Ultimate Frontier," *Science*, January 12, 1979, pp. 143-47.

8. See Jerry Suls, ed., *Psychological Perspectives on the Self*, vol. 1 (Hillsdale, N.J.: Erlbaum Associates, 1982).

CHAPTER TWO
PUBLICS, MULTITUDINOUS

In the 1976 presidential campaign, Jimmy Carter's advisers became concerned that the "born again-southerner" image would alienate an important national constituency, upscale males between the ages of 21 and 35. His closest advisers, Jody Powell and Hamilton Jordon, were themselves members of this group. Their peers, like themselves, came of age in the 1960s. As a group, they were thought to be generally skeptical of established institutions, including religion; they tended to cultivate a fast life style from sports cars to women and were readers of *Playboy* magazine. Carter's men knew from the demographics that this group constituted a significant part of the electorate; indeed, that if ambivalence caused them to stay at home, it could well cost Carter the election.

They came up with a surprising proposal: Carter should accept a long-standing invitation for a *Playboy* interview. The danger that it might antagonize other groups was discounted. They had no place else to go and didn't read *Playboy* anyway! Carter was carefully briefed in the argot and symbols of the *Playboy* demographic entity, so that he would be sure to say that Bob Dylan and the Beatles were his favorite singers and that Dylan Thomas was his favorite poet.

When the interview was published and made headlines everywhere, the upscale males were presumably informed that the candidate was really one of them, and the Evangelicals were assured that much of the material was not part of the interview at all. Carter hastened to come out strongly against adultery.

This episode beautifully illustrates what has happened to American society: The mass audience is fractured into demographic entities that represent, not merely convenient theoretical breakdowns, but real groupings that are potent factors in every facet of life, from voting to making choices of jobs, styles of living, furnishing their living spaces, their values in the deepest sense, what media to watch or read, what records to buy, how to spend their money, what and who to believe in, and more.

In a real sense, the old categories of regionalism, urban/rural, religion, ethnic background, and economic/social class have dissolved or become merely sentimental conceits. They are in the process of being rapidly replaced by new categories that have concrete, immediate, and practical impacts on the ordering of human relations; the audience networks respond to increasingly specialized media, age cohorts achieve self-identity by loyalty to certain communicators and styles; and factions of the public act out their internal unities by exclusion of each other's symbols.

The reality of group life in modern mass societies reinforces new bonds of community and new networks of communication. The traditional bonds are vastly weaker and are, to some extent, only paid lip service by those attempting to save them from extinction.

The demographics of marketing and audience rating are emerging as the new mobilization bases for mass societies, real ones, not the wishful-thinking ones. Publicists, promoters, politicians, and pollsters have learned to deal with these entities as fundamental to their work. They have learned to look at what people actually do with their time and money rather than at the claims made by those who try to maintain their own salience by recalling people to traditional loyalties.

WHAT DO YOU DANCE?

Within certain parts of East Africa, various specialized male groups are identified by the dance societies to which they belong; the most important identification they bear is the answer to the question: What do you dance?[1] In the same way, Westerners identify themselves by the things that matter most to them: designer labels, brand names, being "in" rather than "out," filling their living space with a particular idiom of style and music, going to places in leisure time where their cohorts gather, to certain movies, concerts, and bars but not others, following certain sporting events and teams, owning the right cars, and spending vacations at the right spas.

The very embarrassment with which so many educated people talk of these things in their own lives betrays recognition of the reality, though it conflicts with elitist bias. What people do voluntarily, what they do in their spare time, what they do when they say they are "just relaxing a little," what they do with their friends, what they think about when alone, what they look at in the mirror, what they prepare to show others, what they take photographs of, what they do with their earnings for non-necessities — these are the significant things in people's lives. These are the ways people define themselves and express their individual identities. These are the ways people tell themselves and the world who they are and who they would like to be.[2] Why is it that people hate each other's favorite music? Why is catholicity in musical taste for people under 30 treated as déclassé? Each age cohort is recognized as having its own distinct musical styles and tastes.

To a significant degree, the old nineteenth-century class system is dead as a doorknob; an entirely new class system has emerged based on the current alignments of people into value systems that reflect the active organizational principles of their lives, the real structuring processes of mass societies.

Rather than creating undifferentiated globs of people, mass societies create complex and enduring constellations of passive and active affiliation. These webs of relatedness translate into real behavioral classes, possessing considerable uniformity and stability; they can be described, analyzed, located, and addressed in a variety of ways for merchandising goods, studying audiences, influencing voting, or studying public opinion.

These emerging publics have been labeled "taste groups" by sociologist Herbert Gans, emphasizing the fact that they are self-selected by the voluntary choices they make from the overwhelming number of options offered in a pluralistic society. The mass media and the marketplace must structure themselves to serve these groups by means of programming strategies, the presentation of material in styles and forms that succeed in serving or creating appetites among specific audiences. The competition to win and hold attention leads to a lively and sensitive matching between the taste preferences of significant groups of people and the industries that serve them.

Recognition of the new class structure accompanied the revolution of taste that marked the 1960s. A rude surge of energy from below displaced the never-secure high culture forms of decades shaped by immigrants eager to improve themselves and by the centralizing tendencies of heroic wars and economic crises.

Customized Day-Glo motorcycles, ironic "campy" motifs, silk-screened Brillo boxes, pornography and obscenity — all the mass forms, once beneath contempt, achieved a meteoric prestige. Dissident academics and students brought into the universities and museums the cultural productions of all kinds of marginal groups and outcasts. Censorship laws were overturned. Avant-garde this and that became respectable. The world's first television generation grew up at a time when their mere numbers made them the most important demographic ever, demanding and receiving recognition and leadership in every field, opening the way for every taste, exalted or ignoble, to become the basis for new social idioms and new perceptions of group structure.

Less a medium than an environment, television became the common forum, the psychological stage center, culture's dominant mode of communication. Television was probably the great equalizer, a ubiquitous spectacle offering everybody everything in the whole gaudy marketplace of America.

RELATION TO INTEREST GROUPS

It is true that some of older ties still bind — ethnicity, race, language, religion, regionalism — but they are greatly weakened by the universal ties of the mass marketplace. Some of the latter coincide with the former and thus reinforce traditional loyalties, but most of them do not.

What is the relation of audiences or taste publics to interest groups? In the modern world, these are closely connected. The new demographic entities may be considered inchoate or latent interest groups, capable of being mobilized into active organization and self-consciousness by certain events or appeals. The entities are group structures that represent constellations of values, loyalties, attitudes, and behaviors that possess properties of continuity, visibility, and uniformity. From these aggregates may be drawn various group responses, including market and political behaviors, as well as the formation of face-to-face membership groups of many different kinds.[3]

In much the same way as the juvenile hormone acts in the beehive, the spontaneous differentiation of publics acts to create potential new workers, soldiers, kings, and queens.[4] The pheromones exuded by the queen are the mechanism that controls the differentiation of egg protoplasm. If the colony is short on drones, the queen feels queasy and secretes more drone stuff. And more of the eggs strangely decide to grow up and become drones.[5]

The role of attention is the key to human social differentiation. The swarm of communications is not a meaningless jumble, because the individual learns to allocate his attention. He is sensitized to certain messages and communicators only. The organism cannot tolerate an overload of inputs. Symbols, we have seen, acquire meaning in terms of their ability to elicit or block emotional responses, spontaneous flows of energy in certain directions.

Those who seek to earn and hold attention must adopt a programming strategy that maintains their legitimacy in the eyes of their audiences. It is impossible to be all things to all people all of the time, because the functions of group structure are diverse.

Some communicators must aim at the broadest consensus, some at fractional groupings. Competition for the limited resources of public attention leads to a complex and interactive structuring of taste publics. National political leaders must compete equally with other communicators, including pop singers and television programmers. Invention, surprise, drama, humor — all the elements that capture and hold audiences — are used by all to the best of their ability.

National leaders can be viewed as impressarios who watch for opportunities to improve their offerings. Marshall McLuhan says that voting against an incumbent president is "like turning the dial on your television set." Political leaders seek to legitimate their own performances, and in the process they also legitimate the existence of the nation-state. As the subjective collectivity of the society, the nation-state must be not only an administrative entity but also a viable audience. Otherwise, it is merely an empty shell. Both processes require that political leadership constantly validate the communication channels between government and citizens, grabbing the wandering attention of the people by use of every dramatic opportunity that comes to hand.

McLuhan makes the audacious surmise that this syndrome gives rise not only to new and fascinating programs on the tube but also to new and dangerous adventures in foreign policy. In the same mood, hijackers and terrorists are out to steal the show from network executives and the White House.[6]

The psychopolitical vortex of events is one of the frontiers that generate new culture forms. A successful political leader is an artist in a real sense that he invents himself, and in so doing invents a whole culture complex that acquires meaning and emotional power for others. A inputter of new culture forms has a higher specific gravity than other people; he distorts the force fields around him, bending more of the world to his will than seems reasonable. And he must do it without deliberate effort. Political leaders in this sense include all kinds of people outside formal political institutions.

As social inputters, the role of political leader is not unlike that of the artist in any sphere. He must seize and hold the attention of an audience; and in the long term, he must do it noncoercively, by offering something that they want.

ALTERED STATES

"Humans are communications junkies," says Alan Kay, chief scientist for Atari. "Atari's research is woven from the fabric of two themes: fantasy and sharing."[7] The human organism requires sensory inputs, information, as much as food or air; without them, the individual becomes disoriented and confused, soon losing the will and drive to do anything. Even in the poorest ghettos of Mexico, forests of television antennas spring from acres of miserable shacks.[8]

In every situation, the human organism orients itself by some framework or reference point. The outer reality is a chaos until humans begin to inject structure. Such structuring defines a situation and gives it meaning and purpose on a scale relevant to the individual. Its creative or arbitrary character makes it no less essential. Social consensus that supports such structure tends to remove its arbitrary elements and give it authority (even perhaps a sense of inevitability). Like the bull in Ernest Hemingway's *Death in the Afternoon*, which strides into the ring and assumes one area as a base of operations for defending himself, the imposition of structure eliminates disoriented responses and allows all the faculties to function most effectively.

The human organism continuously uses information to orient himself in both the physical and the social worlds. In the social world this happens when structures of friend/enemy, insider/outsider, like me/unlike me, mother, home, and so on can be superimposed on the individual's perceptions of social relationships. The culture is full of cues of this sort that provide a profound cantus firmus to all the surface variations of life. By these cues the individual achieves behavioral orientation.

This happens by means of the most intangible inputs. A large amount of symbolic communication is of this character, able to insinuate itself into memory alongside primary experiences, jiggling around like a first date or a lost love.

This function is performed as richly by "entertainment" as by "educational or informational" programming. In this sense, entertainment maintains the structures of the community and the culture in exactly the same ways as other forms of content that may be regarded as "more nourishing and good for you."

Far from being ornamental, a plaything, a bonus of life, culture is the heart of things, a fail-safe, a repertory of possibility and meaning. Defined as the subjective basis for all doing and making among an organized group of people occupying adjacent space, culture is by nature very difficult to pin down and standardize. It becomes manifest in things, the artifacts of production, hardware, architecture, artworks; and it becomes manifest in action, routines of work and play, ceremonials, the software of all communication.

The most important attribute of culture is the fact that it generates and directs collective energy flows; and it is highly efficient because it produces more energy than it consumes in the process. It enables members of the group to internalize group imperatives, energizing and programming themselves, making the spontaneous release of energy controlled and purposeful in terms of group needs.

What applies to the general culture also applies to the subcultures within it. Because they are self-sustaining, taste cultures (which characterize the various publics of modern societies) must be understood sympathetically from the inside. Culture does make a difference. The question is, To whom? And what difference does it make?

Of every taste culture, the real issue is: To whom is it meaningful? And why? Not, Do I approve of it? Or is it good for people?

Everyone is entitled to his own taste culture. But so powerful is this a distorting lens of all perception and evaluation that it behooves the professional, as the quintessence of professionalism, to develop a point of view that goes beyond his own taste culture, that respects, appreciates, and is sensitized to a pluralistic approach within his own society.

It is amusing to note how anthropology struggled 50 years ago to rise above ethnocentrism and the inherent egotism of modern man, in order to learn something about what modern shares in common with primitive societies. This achievement did not make even a slight dent in the roaring ethnocentrism that thrives among taste cultures within Western nations.[9] Scientists who thrilled at primitive drum dances in Central Africa, finding deep religious significance, could not bring themselves to take seriously the emergence of rock and roll trance states of their own kids at the high school gym. Even sociologists who have finally begun to study taste cultures in their own countries continue to consider some of them depraved and hardly deemed as cultures at all.[10]

Anyone interested in public opinion and politics must study taste cultures because they are the stuff that holds taste publics together; they are the basis for winning the attention of all groups and successfully communicating with them; they are the content of programming strategies that attempt to influence collective behaviors.

It is no longer adequate to use the panoplies of mass communication to address a hypothetical mass audience. There is no such thing; there are only congeries of group audiences. There are lots of specific publics, whose interests are quite various, and who only attend certain kinds of messages and certain communicators.

PRINCIPLES OF TASTE CULTURES

We may state a number of basic assumptions about the subcultures of various taste publics:

- All cultures are valid and self-sustaining for those who internalize them.
- All cultures serve the same functions for individuals and groups.

- All individuals believe that their own taste preferences are superior to all others and have articulate and explicit objections to all the rest.
- All people tend to be relativistic and permissive in terms of taste only in areas they don't really care about.
- Within a given taste culture, program content tends to confirm the reality concepts implicit in the basic belief system of that culture, to reiterate it, to work out new applications and to resolve apparent inconsistencies.
- Within a given taste culture, a constantly recurrent message is the need for group consciousness, intensifying a sense of membership and loyalty, while emphasizing the inferiority of other groups: "We're OK, they're not OK."
- If these principles weaken in the case of an individual or a public, it constitutes a symptom of instability or decline, possibly heralding extinction of some patterns of association, a period of disorientation for one or more individuals, a search mode for collective behavior, and eventually emergence of some new taste groupings.

Young people are socialized into taste cultures as they are socialized into the general culture. The former play a more poignant role, however, because they become the identifying symbols of young persons' first venture outside the family. The young join the "outlaw" band of their peers. Their tastes express separation from the family and a newfound independence. They listen to a particular kind of music, watch particular television shows (that parents are not supposed to like), and begin to dress by the codes of their peers rather than of parents or older siblings. They may engage in behavior that more seriously challenges the family's equanimity.

Young people everywhere find each other by means of the cultural fare of the mass media. They gain identity as a well-defined audience, and a part of the media responds by striving to express and serve their interests. Kids dependent on mom's car to go anywhere, who have never been off the block by themselves, nonetheless discover the existence of a vast cohort of fellow-conspirators out there. They communicate with that support group every time they buy a record or turn on the radio.

Every taste public endows certain individuals with special authority to speak for the whole group. They are authorized implicitly to experiment and adopt new culture forms from time to time, both to refresh excitement and interest and to make the subculture responsive and adaptive to changes made by other groups and in the group's habitat.

The rapid turning of cultural cycles necessitates means of rapid response; the members of the group, in their physical isolation from each other, therefore endow disc jockeys, singers, and TV programmers with the powers of governance. They commence the process of growing to maturity surrounded by their taste-public mates, anxious to discover any late developments in the esteemed body of values and behaviors. The taste culture becomes for its public a complete micro cosmology, with its heroes and martyrs, its fallen angels, its friends and enemies, its sacraments, its sacred places, its routines of worship and celebration.

Robert Pittman at 21 was the highest paid radio programmer in the country. When he was 23, he guided WNBC to the top AM radio spot in New York City. Now, barely 30, he is vice president of Warner Amex, the giant entertainment conglomerate. He is responsible for programming MTV (Music Television), Warner's challenge to Home Box Office.

MTV's target audience is the 14 to 34 age group. It is a classic example of "narrowcasting" (as opposed to broadcasting), that is, it sees its market as segmented and seeks to express and serve only certain segments thereof. "At MTV, we don't shoot for the 14-year-olds – we own them," Pittman declares. "We will reach 90% of them in any given household. You'd have to be a social outcast not to watch it."

> Music tends to be a predictor of social values . . . it symbolizes the culture. To say you don't like somebody else's music is saying, I don't like your dress, your friends, I don't like your life! You tell me the music people like, and I'll tell you their views on abortion, whether we should increase our military arms, what their sense of humor is like, what their favorite TV programs are, their response to political candidates, even their taste in jokes.[11]

Students of political socialization cannot ignore these phenomena. Characteristic patterns of political orientation and values attach to these informal institutions and have profound impact on the adult's political behaviors. The taste publics demonstrate considerable continuity and uniformity over space and time and can be tracked in exactly the same way as they are studied by marketers, audience raters, and serious political consultants.

A taste public, like an interest group, has a kind of latent informal structure that can be represented by a series of concentric circles. At the center are the leaders, spokesmen, role models, taste makers, communicators — whether self-consciously pursuing such roles or having them thrust upon them by the attention of the public and the media. Most of the time, the individuals who achieve these roles soon learn who they are and how they are required to act.

The media amplify their every word and deed, so that with little effort they can playfully or ruefully sculpt a persona that satisfies the needs of their public. They play out a kind of ritual drama in which the reporters represent a Greek chorus that provides them with cues as to the concerns of the audience and the effectiveness of their performances.

Gathered around them are the active workers who serve to create and maintain the public. This includes all the gatekeepers, commercial people and professional communicators (advertisers and advertising people, media people of all sorts). It also includes throngs of volunteers and self-appointed flacks and amanuenses who spend part of their days doing the same kind of work on a freelance face-to-face basis, organizing fan clubs, getting their friends to wear certain symbolic clothing, to get autographs, to cheer plane debarkations, to circulate petitions, to watch certain appearances on video, and so on. The ring of workers includes all the foot soldiers and functionaries that each public requires for the everyday tasks of mobilizing attention in a larger audience.

The third circle describes the attentive public, those members of the taste group who watch all the goings on and who may or may not become active on some of the occasions. They are properly the audience, the readers, watchers, passive believers. They do a little missionary work now and then, and they spread information by continuous gossiping. They buy and wear the T-shirts, and look up their leaders' doings in *People* magazine or the *National Enquirer*. They constitute the troops, the large numbers of people who subjectively identify with the public, whether or not they manifest group-related behavior.

In the fourth circle is the inattentive public, those who mark the vague boundaries of the group. While this audience has not developed a fix on the group, they differ from the rest of the mass public by the fact that they lean in its direction. They are receptive to some extent to its messages and its symbols and are more likely to join the next inner circle than they are to join some other grouping.

The structure of taste publics reflects a volunteeristic, informal universe, and its mechanisms are therefore shaped by the competitive realities of this marketplace. By and large, the inchoate structures are self-sustaining and will exist and operate without paid professionals.

It might be said that the tendency to commercialize the process is driven by the opportunities presented by its spontaneous energy, rather than that the process itself is fabricated by the professionals. Note, for example, how the emerging counterculture of the 1960s was initially ignored and resisted by the commercial entrepreneurs and the media, until they realized its power and sought ways to exploit it for their own purposes.

Mass culture reflects individual and group freedom. It cannot easily be used as a tool of education or indoctrination; that generally doesn't sell. Children's programs especially have to be good, because children have not yet been trained to pay attention to things that are not in themselves rewarding. They are the first to say "the emperor is naked!"

The analysis of interest groups in the political process needs to incorporate the configurations of audiences as important bases of mobilization and political action. Taste publics, highly differentiated and specific, are the underlying structures of a civilization webbed by mass communications.

Too often traditional analyses, colliding with the facts of modern communications, end by deploring the untoward effects upon the old monads: political parties, pressure groups, campaign spending, public opinion, and the process of leadership. The nineteenth-century paradigms of political analysis are clearly breaking down, yet the analysts are loath to abandon them. Instead, they retreat into self-righteous shells of high culture, throwing up their hands in despair.

The older models are still valid if they are interpreted as one of the aspects of the web of affiliations. The taste publics provide pools of potential group members. They may be organized into various kinds of face-to-face action groups for various purposes, including single issue groups, electoral campaign groups, political action committees, public interest groups, and so on.

Often the taste public's very existence is the germ of the attempt to formalize and politicize the group. The notion that publics are generated by the emergence of an issue, that is, the eruption of a public policy controversy that activates opposing coalitions, is not useful. It begs the more interesting questions, namely, Who are taste publics from which they are drawn? And what are the processes that create, maintain, and modify these configurations? Why does a particular issue arise rather than some other? Timing? Why do active political issues rise and fall, like hemlines, usually without necessarily being resolved?

The emergence of computerized mailing lists, of public opinion tracking, of targeted audiences, of motivational research, originally in the commercial fields of market analysis and audience studies, then in the areas of political campaigning and polling, expresses the new basis for the study of contemporary political institutions.

THE POPULAR CULTURE CONTROVERSY

The centrality of popular culture is strongly resisted by the academic world. What is the source of this academic blindness? Like the air we breathe, popular culture is the environment that surrounds us. It is taken for granted. Any reference to it in the classroom elicits laughter and knowing glances. Why? Because it is the primary general culture of the era. It is not something that has to be taught or learned; it has its own dynamism and power and doesn't require additional aids.

Because popular culture has become the real basis upon which the publics of modern society differentiate and mobilize themselves, and because academe must claim a "higher" cultural basis, there is considerable reluctance to formulate theories and practices that treat it seriously. This has been remedied in part during the last decade as counterculture graduates emerged into the academic ranks.

Herbert J. Gans, in his book on the subject,[12] breaks with past notions of the inferior quality of popular as compared with high culture and attempts to develop a model for distinguishing tastes as the basis for other kinds of social behavior. He examines the usual criticisms made of popular culture: It is escapist, encouraging people to avoid their real problems; it is derivative, repetitious, and formulaic;

it ignores the best of the cultural heritage and has no social memory; it is unsatisfying because there is no real discharge of emotions (purgation of pity and fear); it lacks refinement and sublety; it exploits public ignorance and addresses the lowest common denominator of the public; it is consumer, not producer, based; it is transitory and contributes little of enduring worth; it is manufactured on a production line and fails to extend the range of human experience; it is commercially successful.

High culture, on the other hand, is presumed to be the opposite of all these things: It is active rather than passive; it faces and solves real problems; it demands and receives more from its audiences, both in information and attention, and gives back more in turn; it is of higher quality and can do more to improve the society and its people.

Also associated with high culture is the implicit assumption that high culture qualifies people to rule others and to enjoy more privileges than others, while low culture is viewed as cause and justification for the existence of permanent subclasses. In a way, the doctrines associated with high culture have become in democratic societies a substitute for nobility and divine right, a kind of cultural apartheid that is purposefully sponsored by the ruling elites.[13]

In the absence of a system of hereditary ranks and titles, without a tradition of honors conferred by a monarch, and with no "well-known status ladder of high class regiments to confer various degrees of cachet," Americans depend for their "mechanism of snobbery far more than other peoples on their college and university hierarchy."[14]

Gans concludes that almost all of the negative charges made against popular culture are groundless; that popular culture "does not harm either high culture, the people who prefer it, or the society as a whole"; that the differences between cultures "have been exaggerated, and the similarities underestimated." He asserts that, like high culture, popular culture is "a taste culture, chosen by people who lack the economic and educational opportunities of the devotees of high culture"; that America is made up of "a number of taste cultures, each with its own art, literature, music . . . which differ mainly in aesthetic standards."[15]

His clearly patronizing tone squares him with the audience that reads such books, an audience that self-righteously wants to be told they are better than anybody else. At the same time, Gans breaks away from their parochialism to assert the legitimacy of other taste cultures. This is an important transitional work and a hopeful start. He neglects to argue the fact that self-sustaining culture forms are alive, while those that require constant resuscitation from foundations and government are moribund. (The best thing government can do for art, says Senator Daniel Patrick Moynihan, "is to outlaw it!")

In fact, Gans confesses to a high culture bias. If one compared, he writes, the taste cultures alone, "it would be fair to say that the higher cultures are better or at least more comprehensive and more informative than the lower ones." And that American society "should pursue policies that maximize educational and other opportunities for all so as to permit everyone to choose from higher taste cultures."[16]

Gans doesn't remind the reader that virtually every form of art that has endured (without artificial help) started its career as popular culture. Shakespeare was a hot ticket in his own time. Dickens and Dostoyevski serialized their work, like comic strips, in the penny papers. Samuel Johnson was primarily a successful newspaper columnist. Jazz, Charley Chaplin, and Felix the Cat were despised by the intellectuals of their time. Shelley, Keats, and Byron were the Beatles of their day.

There is a vestige of the Protestant ethic in the arguments for high culture: If you don't like, if it tastes bad, if it hurts, *it's good for you*! If it's none of these and you like it, beware! It's self-indulgent, sinful, and probably fattening. Only suffering is virtuous. Sitting through an opera is painful for some of the regular season ticket holders; it is a way of mortifying the flesh for the higher glory of God. It is a trial by ordeal to prove your qualifications to be among the elite of your community.

It is not true that high culture leads and pop follows; more often it is the other way around. Sometimes the so-called masses are a more sensitive barometer to what has enduring worth than the self-conscious elites who are out to impress somebody or to set a good example for posterity.

One cannot, on the other hand, dismiss popular culture as harmless or of no lasting significance. It is very potent indeed. The pols and government leaders are ruled by it to a considerable degree, always attempting to borrow the media attention of the most popular show hosts, actors, and music celebs, and to a considerable extent making the subject matter of successful adventure shows self-fulfilling prophecies by trying to stage public events (government actions, congressional hearings, national debates) in accordance with the same proven clichés.

When CIA plots are commanding the best ratings in the theaters, members of Congress are going to investigate alleged CIA plots in the headlines, just as publishers and TV writers seek to fashion their own successful careers by following any faint clue of what the mass audience will buy.

A main consolation to the dangers raised by the potency of popular culture is the difficulty of anticipating mass tastes. There is something reassuring in the fact that the mass audiences cannot be fed propaganda or nourishment that somebody in power thinks is "good for them." The mental attitude of "nannyism" can never command a mass public, which simply withdraws attention when anything gets boring.

The general audience cannot be forced to watch and listen. What interests them spontaneously, therefore, must reflect deeper currents of social reality and should be studied by anyone wishing to tap into that directional energy. The contents of popular culture should be regarded as an expression of the psychosocial fantasy life of the nation, the archetypal story structures of consciousness that inform the general culture, in terms of which subcultures must be interpreted.[17]

NOTES

1. T. O. Ranger, *Dance and Society in Eastern Africa, 1890-1970: The Beni Ngoma* (Berkeley: University of California Press, 1975).

2. See Tom Wolfe, *The Purple Decades: A Reader* (New York: Farrar Straus & Giroux, 1981).

3. See Yi-Fu-Tuan, *Segmented Worlds and Self/Group Life and Individual Consciousness* (Minneapolis: University of Minnesota Press, 1982).

4. See the important work by Richard A. Easterlin, *Birth and Fortune: Impact of Numbers on Personal Welfare* (New York: Basic Books, 1980). In this work the author, a leading scholar of the relationship between economic and demographic elements, predicts lugubrious and relatively poor lives for the baby boom cohorts of the 1950s and early 1960s.

5. David J. C. Fletcher and Murray Blum, "Regulation of Queen Number by Workers in Colonies of Social Insects," *Science*, January 21, 1983, pp. 312-15.

6. A classic on ritual-theater as part of the process of government, see Clifford Geertz, *Negara: The Theatre State in Nineteenth-Century Bali* (Princeton, N.J.: Princeton University Press, 1981).

7. *Washington Post*, October 25, 1982, p. 22.

8. One can approximate sensory deprivation by the following experiment: Sit in a bathtub filled with tepid water, turn out all the lights and block out cracks of light, and stuff your ears with cotton. A sense of euphoria soon turns to panic as a feeling of turning and drifting into space intervenes.

9. A modern Presbyterian is very tolerant of a Catholic; but a rock music fan cannot bear the presence of anyone who likes John Denver or Barry Manilow (especially Barry Manilow).

10. See Robert Sam Anson, *Gone Crazy and Back Again: The Rise and Fall of the Rolling Stone Generation* (New York: Doubleday, 1977); and Robert Stuart Nathan, *Rising Higher* (New York: Dial Press, 1978).

11. Christian Williams, "Now Music to Their Eyes," *Washington Post*, September 16, 1982, p. E1.

12. See Herbert J. Gans, *Popular and High Culture: An Analysis and Evaluation of Taste* (New York: Basic Books, 1974).

13. See Michael M. Mooney, *The Ministry of Culture/Connections Among Art, Money, and Politics* (San Francisco: Wyndham Books, 1980); also Carl Gardner, ed., *Media, Politics and Culture: A Socialist View* (New York: Macmillan, 1979).

14. Americans are the only people in the world, Paul Fussell notes, "whose status anxieties prompt them to advertise their university affiliations in the rear windows of their cars." "Schools for Snobbery." *The New Republic*, October 4, 1982, p. 25.

15. Gans, *Popular and High Culture*, p. x.

16. Ibid., pp. 127-29.

17. See Leslie Fiedler, *What Was Literature? Class Culture and Mass Society* (New York: Simon & Shuster, 1981).

CHAPTER THREE
THE STRUCTURE OF
THE AMERICAN PUBLIC

Of great importance in recent years to survey, motivational, and market research is the ability to target and track demographically with rapidity and precision the views and behaviors of people collectively and individually. This is a new dimension of capability for all those involved in persuasion and government.

Tracking refers to collecting feedback rapidly in order to measure the moment-to-moment impact of an ongoing campaign. Targeting refers to breaking down the public into its constituent audiences in today's segmented market place, so that campaign strategy and media locations can be most effectively tailored to reach the intended targets. Both tracking and targeting make possible continuous and sensitive monitoring of communications, so that strategy and tactics can be fine-tuned responsively to the opportunities and importunities of events.

What has come to be called market segmentation has changed the nature of American life tremendously. This is because the scientific description of American publics has reversed the notions of anonymity and increasing homogeneity. The fact is that mass media do not create a monolithic audience. Quite contrary to every forecast, the nation is becoming less monolithic and more differentiated.

It is the demographic sciences, including the study of public opinion, that have contributed this central insight. The fact that the media audiences are breaking apart does not mean necessarily that the nation-state is in trouble. But it does mean that efforts to communicate with the nation for any purpose must address a complex set of audiences whose attention and receptivities are complexly focused and structured.

The central change has been qualitative, and not merely quantitative. Today usable information on groups and individuals is readily accessible and can be managed at very reasonable cost and at great speed. This information makes it possible to communicate with the highly segmented audiences of modern media with precision and delicacy. The information can be deployed for timely strategic and tactical use and makes demographic tracking and targeting possible.

The system is usable as a continuous and routine two-way probe of publics and audiences; surveys of various kinds continuously feed back information on the currents of public sentiment, while the most significant strata can be targeted with precision for ongoing efforts to influence and mold that sentiment. The computerized lists make the process of response/action/response virtually simultaneous, and therefore an indispensable capability of all market analysts, advertising account executives, political consultants, and public officials.

A fantastic array of demographic data collections is being spun from every kind of information source. People are classified by sex, age, ethnic background, education, party preference and past voting behavior, responses to previous solicitations, petitions they have signed, volunteer activities, church affiliation, magazines and newspapers they read, income, profession, memberships in professional and interest groups, contributions to political action committees, and so on. The precise targeting data are limited only by the cleverness of the data manager and the availability of lists.

The U.S. Census raw data collections are now being sold on magnetic disks and tapes to entrepreneurs. In turn, these entrepreneurs reduce the contents into precise and instantly accessible targeting and tracking data and make the information available for a fee to all comers.

Tracking and targeting in the segmented marketplace of contemporary America require a structural analysis. The hottest approach today involves using the census data to break down the entire country into postal zip codes. These are classified in accordance with innovative models that bear little resemblance to traditional schemes based on economic class. Important work still remains to be done in the search for more compelling models.

LAYER CAKE MODEL

Herbert Gans follows the traditional structure. He breaks the universe into five categories: high, upper-middle, lower-middle, low, and quasi-folk low cultures. Finding this incomplete, he introduces three more: youth, black, and ethnic cultures. These latter have only provisional standing, "for these may be only temporary offshoots from the others."[1] The five main categories represent traditional sociology, based on economic class, honored in so many nineteenth-century classics.[2] The groups are much less cohesive and homogeneous than would appear, he says, but for analytical purposes, one can treat them as "relatively stable."

High Culture

Dominated by creators and critics, this is the culture of serious writers and artists. Its users are creator-oriented, even if not themselves creators, or user-oriented, like the consumers of other cultures. All are "highly educated people of upper and upper-middle class status, employed mainly in academic and professional occupations."[3] High culture prides itself on its exclusiveness, and its products are not intended for distribution in the mass media. Its art takes the form of "originals distributed through galleries; its books are published by subsidized presses or commercial publishers willing to take a loss for prestige reasons; its journals are so-called little magazines; its theatre is in Europe or off-Broadway."[4]

Upper-Middle Culture

This is the taste culture of the "vast majority of upper-middle classes, the professionals, executives, and managers and their wives who have attended the better colleges." They prefer a culture that is "substantive, unconcerned with innovation, . . . and uninterested in making issues of method and form."[5] *Time, Newsweek,* and *Psychology Today* are written primarily for this public.

They like symphonic and operatic works of the nineteenth century, but dislike earlier music, chamber music, and twentieth-century atonality. This is the fastest-growing of all taste cultures, the boom in college attendance having increased the size and affluence of this public.

Lower-Middle Culture

This is America's dominant public, attracting middle- and lower-class people in the "lower status professions, such as accountancy and public school teaching, and all but the lowest-level white collar jobs." Its members are generally high school graduates, and some have attended small colleges or state universities.[6] It emphasizes an aesthetic of substance: "Form must serve to make substance more intelligible or gratifying. Dramatic materials express and reinforce the culture's own ideas and feelings, and although some questioning is permitted, doubts must be resolved at the conclusion."

Familial dramas deal with "upholding tradition and maintaining order against irrepressible sexual impulses and other upsetting influences." This public is less interested in how society works than in the reassurance that "it continues to abide by the moral values" of its own culture. Its art is romantic, shunning naturalism and abstraction.

Today, Gans says, this culture "appears to be increasingly fragmented; differences among traditional, conventional, and progressive factions seem to be sharper" than in other taste publics.[7]

Low Culture

This Gans describes as the culture of the older lower-middle and of hourly-wage service and factory blue-collar workers, vocational school graduates, and high school/college dropouts. This was America's dominant taste public until the 1950s, but has been shrinking steadily since. Its aesthetic standards emphasize substance and clear-cut definitions of good and evil.

Its characterizations are highly simplified, its stories are morality plays, emphasizing external action rather than the working out of inner conflicts. It is distributed through the mass media, which must share its content with the culture above it. Today, it lacks the purchasing power, Gans writes, "to attract major national advertisers," so that its media can survive economically only "by producing material of low technical quality."[8] The so-called schlock market of tawdry goods of every variety is where these poor souls find beauty.

Quasi-Folk Low Culture

This is the domain of very poor people just emerging from ethnic or rural backgrounds. Data are scarce, Gans points out, because they remain largely oral, tribal, and regional. These people are just awakening to the mass marketplace of America and retain much of the baggage from whence they came. In general, the tastes they are acquiring are those of low culture.

Youth Culture

In the 1980s, Gans's description is a little bit dated — drugs and rock music, communal life styles, sexual experimentation, interest in Eastern religions and far-out cults, and so on — but it is recognizable and can readily be translated into whatever youth are into at any given time. He points out that youth cultures are structured into replicas of the mainstream, with upper-middle youth, low youth, and so on. He emphasizes that strong borrowing exists between all cultures, and that youth cultures have been especially vital and rich in recent decades.

Black Culture

Although with deep roots in Africa and slavery, its rise to visibility in the 1960s was "consciously and deliberately created," and was soon imitated by Puerto Rican, Chicano, native American, and Chinese groups because of the political advantages that accrued to it in terms of the values of the dominant cultures. Despite its growth, it "remains a partial culture. . . . Blacks share the taste cultures created by Whites . . . and consumption habits are little different from Whites of similar socio-economic level and age."[9]

Ethnic Cultures

European immigrants during the last 100 years were mainly uneducated peasants and landless laborers "who spent most of their waking hours at work," whose taste cultures were sparse and dominated by "compensatory content to cope with and escape deprivation." They were based on church and language groupings, and as such were unable to be effectively transmitted to their Americanized and more prosperous offspring.

The revival of ethnicity in the last decade is not a lineal descendant of these groups at all, but part of American upper and upper-middle mainstream cultures.

The attempt to save "economic class" distorts this classification scheme, making necessary all kinds of crisscross distinctions and emendations. Social scientists are loath to give up a paradigm that has served them so well for so long. And the schemata are not without insights. Gans's need to introduce the latter three classes, which cut across everything else, is symptomatic. The pressure to erase the old boundaries and to define new ones is irresistible.

Paul Fussell has offered a system, perhaps ironically, that approximates actual group indicia much closer. He divides America into nine social, not economic, classes — three above and five below middle — and characterizes each by its tastes in language, body weight ("the flaunting of obesity is the Prole sign, as if the object were to give maximum aesthetic offense to the higher classes, and thus achieve a form of revenge"), clothing, food, and housing. Through "facade study," he shows how house-front styles range from the classic middle picture window with a table lamp in the center ("the cellophane on the lampshade must be immaculate"), to high prole ("religious shrines in the garden"), to mid prole ("plaster gnomes and flamingoes"), to low prole ("flower beds bordered by truck tires painted white"). He offers a "living room scale" by which one can rate the status quotient of his own home, for example, for "any work of art depicting cowboys — subtract 3 points." Paul Fussell's tongue-in-cheek essays move us in the right direction.[10]

THE CHOCOLATE CHIP COOKIE

The various forms of audience research in the advertising, marketing, and media industries have evolved complex taste-public schemata that are presently the operational basis for public opinion study.

Characteristics of socioeconomic class used to be closely related to group cultures and subcultures in the literature. Today, such a linkage is still included in the demographic indicators but greatly softened, submerged by the flow of current data that show audience structures themselves have evolved away from nineteenth-century models. The distinctions made by Gans are class-fixed. But they have not proven useful to practitioners who live and die by their ability to assess the real components of the mass audience, who are tested daily by reality principles like "market share" and "Nielsen points."

From Sid Vicious and the Plasmatics to Helen Gurley Brown and the Cosmo Girl, from Old Gold to New Wave, from jogging and high cookery to aerobic dancing and disco — all the spontaneous audience choices that make or break attempts to win and hold attention have become the first concern of trackers and targeters of public opinion.

The relentless churning of formats and styles by the creators does not define the audiences; only the responses to those offerings can have that effect. We can find the most practical schema for defining taste by looking at various media whose audiences tend to differentiate themselves.[11] This includes such audiences as those for specific television shows, those who read regularly certain special-interest magazines, audiences that define themselves by loyalty to certain radio stations and formats, or the group cleavages that are most apparent in the volatile area of clothing styles. There are many other dimensions of the segmented mass audience,[12] but their audiences are relatively stable, and there is a high degree of continuity in their program contents, formats, and focus.[13]

Perhaps Gans's distinctions were true in the past, but today there are creators and users in all the categories; there are mixtures of all socioeconomic groups, wide varieties of professional and work-specialized people, crisscrossed age distributions in all the categories. The mass media have not homogenized the national audience, but they have softened the old parameters and generated new ones. Urban and rural no longer go with clear-cut taste discriminations.

Impecunious members of the lower classes have the same varieties of taste, and the means of satisfying them, as do members of the higher income groups.

BLUE BLOOD ESTATES TO HARD SCRABBLES

Data firms mine gold from census information in supplying the information necessary for all dimensions of targeting. The general Census Bureau overview of state and metropolitan areas is relatively meaningless. What targeters require is the small print, the minutiae of the data, which are mostly unpublished. The bureau has the stuff on its thousands of computer tapes. It tells by census tract how much money people make, what they do for a living, how many are in a family, how many bathrooms, and so on. It is a relatively simple matter to extract from the census tract information the specific demographics and locations by zip code area and city blocks.

The tapes include data by block groups, each of which contains about 1,000 people, or 325 households. There are about 2.5 million block groups in the 1980 figures, as compared with 1.7 million in 1970. The difference is accounted for by expansion of the census tract areas in the methodology. Micro data samples are included. These are individual family census reports, from which all names and other identifying information have presumably been removed to protect confidentiality. The sample of micro data represents about 1 percent of the population, but gives an excellent profile of family statistics, pinpointed by geographic area. Such national data have never been available to public users before the last decade.

With these data, users can create their own sample surveys for unique population segments, or can target their audiences, and can weight the results to achieve the most perfect matches of samples and real world ever. The 1980 census provided income data for the first time for households, as well as by class of individuals and families per census tract.[14]

Direct mailers and credit card companies want to know where their best customers live. Retail chains want to know where to concentrate their sales forces, where to invest, where to build new shopping malls. Media owners want to know what their properties are worth, how to build their audience shares. Arbitron and Nielsen need the means of stratifying and weighting their samples, as do all polling organizations, not to mention political consultants like Matt Reese and William Hamilton.

CACI of Rosslyn, Virginia, offers customers an on-line computer system that spits out the demography and buying power surrounding any particular street corner in the United States. The company spends more than $1 million a year just to update its data banks. In 1982, the three companies (Robin Page, Matt Reese, and Jonathan A. Robbin) mentioned formed a consortium, which bought the 1980 census tapes for $250,000, a real bargain! A host of Census Bureau statisticians have resigned to set up their own data organizations, including in the Washington D.C., area CEC Associates and Cenex, Inc.[15]

Robin B. Page denounces the concept that "all women 18 to 49 in households earning $10,000 a year" are a single market segment. "It's a flat out myth!" Trying to reach them all the same way is extremely wasteful, he says, and may be counterproductive. He calls his system PRIZM, which stands for Potential Rating Index by ZIP Market. "People are tribal, territorial, and socially hierarchical," he declares.

Based in Washington, D.C., Matt Reese uses a similar data base system, Claritas, a technique for pinpointing and contacting supporters and opponents of issues and candidates with great precision. The system was developed a decade ago by Jonathan A. Robbin, strictly for marketing purposes. Claritas categorizes citizens by neighborhood groupings called clusters. Based on the theory that "birds of a feather flock together," it uses census data to define 40 basic clusters. For example, Cluster 25 is defined as "urban/ suburban, older, upper-middle with a substantial Jewish segment." Cluster 38 describes a community of "middle-aged Southern farmers with a Spanish migrant element."

The entire population is broken down in units of 280 households each, which are called block groups. Each unit has a cluster designation from 1 to 40. A fund raiser, salesperson, pollster, or politician can target an appeal, sales pitch, or message to any one of 40 different clusters of demographics, each precisely mapped geographically and accessible separately in the computer.

Reese has been an active political consultant, mainly to Democrats, for two decades. His trademark has been zealous pursuit of two kinds of people: undecided voters who could be persuaded to support his candidate and favorable voters who need to be prodded to make sure they get to the polls on election day. A favorite Democratic pollster, William Hamilton, says the Claritas system has become indispensable to his work, "a highly effective tool for staying in power or knocking off an old curmudgeon." Hamilton uses the data base to poll a sample group in a state and tell candidates what kinds of people — rich, young, or religious, for example — think on certain issues and candidates.

"Polls by themselves are valuable, but inadequate," Reese says. A poll may tell you that working-class Catholic housewives aren't favorably impressed with a candidate, but "the only time you know a woman is Catholic is Ash Wednesday." Now Claritas can specify block groups most likely to contain a high percentage of Catholic working-class housewives.[16]

In 1978, a coalition of Missouri labor unions was hired to help defeat a ballot referendum that would outlaw union shops. The Right-to-Work advocates were riding high. Reese's own poll showed that 69 percent of the voters favored the amendment. Even among labor union members the measure was favored 57 percent to 35 percent against. This was a made-to-order situation for Claritas. Reese recommended that very little money be spent on general advertising; this would only stir up the opposition and give them more exposure. Instead, he concentrated on citizens likely to vote the desired way. They could be readily pinpointed and contacted.

Waves of postcards, telephone calls, and personal visits were directed at such households. Tracking was used to test the effectiveness of various appeals and contacts. The quiet, targeted attack reversed the numbers. Many of the people favoring the referendum didn't bother to vote. High percentages of those leaning the union way did vote. Reese got 110,000 new pro-labor voters registered, and the measure was defeated 60 percent to 40 percent.

Said Hamilton, "Never before has anyone had a situation where a pollster can tell a campaign — Look, we have problems with people who live in new towns, who are white and upper-middle class — then tell the guy that 40 of these people live in this county, 60 here and 120 here. And here are their names, addresses, and telephone numbers."

Claritas is based on the theorem: "The demographic variables which define homogeneous neighborhoods are significantly correlated to resident consumer and other behavioral patterns." Its new buzz word is "geodemography."

Beginning with 300 data tapes from the 1970 census, Claritas essentially went into the list business. It combined the data with all the information on media audiences assembled by the Simmons Market Research Bureau. Each of the 40 area types have been given distinctive names. For example, God's Country refers to exurban towns near oceans or mountains — like the Hamptons on Long Island — which are in Level B (upper-middle class). About 2.07 percent of the nation's households fall into this category. Then there is Sharecroppers, such as Plains, Georgia, on Level D (down-scale) with 1.27 percent of the nation's households, made up of white and black farmers and migrant workers. Some of the other cluster names are Blue Blood Estates, Pools and Patios, Bunker's Neighbors, Bohemian Mix, Downhome Gentry, Hispanic Mix, Shot-guns and Pickup Trucks, Dixie-Style Tenements. Each is given a numerical scale, a weighted composite of education and affluence values. This is how the term "upscale" crept into the nation's vocabulary in recent years. Beverly Hills has the highest scale value — 83; Hard Scrabbles the lowest — 28.

And if the raw census data are available, block by block within each census tract, it is quite a simple matter to break down the demographic abstractions into real households, families, and people. No longer faceless, the national population becomes targettable and trackable in terms of specifics of taste, background, life conditions, and life styles.

MAINSTREAM AND VARIATIONS

We offer for classifying taste publics a tentative schema with four major divisions: mainstream, mainstream variations, status cultures, and special subcultures.

Television is the mainstream today. A recent study reports that 72 percent of the people watch television every day. Only 46 percent listen to radio every day. Yet it is by the latter act that they separate themselves from the mainstream and become separate publics. In breaking down the mainstream variations of American taste publics, different musical styles and radio program formats may provide a powerful analytic system. Music has become a universal sacrament of contemporary taste publics, the means by which the various audiences sort themselves out and assert unique identities.

"Radio is the tribal drum for modern man," declares Marshall McLuhan. Its distant beat tells the isolated hunter in the jungle that he is not alone, that his village lies a certain distance away, in a certain direction. Further, its rhythms keep him informed about the cycles of events when he is not present. He is careful lest he wander too far away, beyond the reach of the drum. In the same way, the Walkman, the car radio, the huge portable stereo studio on a shoulder strap keep young city dwellers connected with their own tribes, even as they pick their way among strangers on Times Square.

These are tied into musical networks, whose distribution systems include record and tape stores, undergrounds of home tape recording and cassette exchanges, concerts and nightclubs, radio, and, to a lesser extent, television. Curiously, music of particular styles has evolved in the mid-twentieth century to become a universal mechanism of group identification – not unlike its role in primitive societies and in sacred institutions. This is true also in the Eastern bloc, where it is perceived as dangerous to the state, and in the Third World, where we have seen tribal dance groups to have an ancient lineage.

Pollsters and marketing experts have long noted this fact and have increasingly used musical tastes as a central morphology for classifying publics; radio has been perceived as one the sharpest, cheapest, and most effective instruments for targeting specific publics, much more saturating than special-interest magazines and much more focused than selected television shows.

Mainstream Culture

This is the most universal bin. Everyone, children and adults of all classes, belongs to it. This is the audience for all communal events, the assassination of a president, the Watergate hearings, *Roots*, early space flights, the "Johnny Carson Show," Who shot JR?, the last episode of "The Fugitive" and of "MASH," the World Series, maybe the Superbowl, blockbuster movies like *E.T.* and *Star Wars*.

Events that command this audience serve to express the broadest consensus of values of the modern nation-state, to give concreteness to the subjective dimensions of the national psyche. Thus all subclasses are part of this audience, including creators/consumers, powerful/powerless, educated/uneducated, work/play, and so on.

Mainstream Variations

This is the breakdown of the general mainstream into some on its important subclasses. Here it is appropriate to note demographic variables and differences in receptivity to mainstream programming. Here is where the differentiation of publics by radio music formats may be useful.

Age groupings are of very great significance, because age cohorts share common cultures in spite of geographic and socioeconomic separation and in spite of the best efforts of upper-middle parents to thwart the effects: preteen, tennybopper (12 to 15), youth (15 to 21), young adult (19 to 30), midadult (30 to 49), older midadult (50 to 70), and aged adult (above 70). These demographics are variously broken down for different purposes, which we will look at in Chapter 10 on sampling frames.

Ethnic, urban/suburban/rural, secular/religious, new/old are still of some importance also, but mainly as aspects of the mainstream, not as traditional aggregates. Radio programming formats offer interesting demographic configurations that enable us to trace the continuities of various latent group loyalties, values, and receptivities.

What communication networks do people actually heed? How do people spontaneously and voluntarily structure themselves into publics? Radio audience analysis provides powerful indicators. Most helpful are the studies done regularly by Arbitron, Inc., the leading survey organization in the radio marketplace.

In 1982, "contemporary" music was dominant, accounting for one-third of the formats of the country's leading stations. This was broken down into its main aggregates: adult contemporary, urban contemporary, and the top-40. All three versions of "contemporary" contain a mixture of musical styles: soft rock, ballads, and dance music. The top-40 limits itself strictly to a play list of 40 current hits, cycling them throughout the day so that the top three or four songs will be heard at least once every two hours.

These three formats conbined totaled 36 percent of the station formats in the top 50 U.S. markets. They zoomed into their present position over the last three years at the expense of disco, rock, and beautiful music, which have been declining. The audience for contemporary is identified as mainly middle American, both sexes, cutting across all socioeconomic and other groups, 19 to 49 years of age.

The next leading contender was album oriented rock (AOR), which came in with 14 percent. This is viewed as a generally younger audience, interested in taping off the albums for their cassette players; this is the major record/tape buying market. "Beautiful music" (Montavani Strings and Percy Faith) and talk/news were in the 12 percent range and attract a mainly midadult and older-adult audience.

Country and western, which has been growing in popularity recently, came in at 11 percent, and although still strong in rural areas and the South, has shown the greatest surge among "urban cowboys." Middle-of-the-road (MOR), Tony Bennett and Nelson Riddle, has been in a long decline, accounting in 1982 for 8 percent; black, about 6 percent.[17]

The short and dramatic life of disco, which came from nowhere and, after the success of the movie *Saturday Night Fever*, knocked every other format into a cocked hat for two years, then disappeared overnight (though surviving in the black market), could be an instructive episode about the behavior of emerging publics in American society. It illustrates the way musical idioms evolve as sacraments of identity. In 1978, the disco industry accounted for $4 billion worth of the gross national product, more than the movies. Half of the hits on the record charts were disco, and all-disco radio stations were dominating their markets.

Andrew Kopkind, writing in Boston's *New Times*, cited disco as "the revolt against the natural Sixties, the seriousness, the confessions, the struggles, the sincerity, the pretensions and pain of the last generation." It is, he wrote, the affirmation of the unreal seventies, the fantasies, fashions, gossip, frivolity, and fun. "The Sixties were braless, lumpy, heavy; disco is stylish, chic, sleek, light. Disco emphasizes surfaces over substance, mood over meaning." The sixties were a "mind trip (marijuana, acid); Disco is a body trip

(Quaaludes, cocaine)." The sixties were cheap; disco is expensive. "On a Sixties trip, you saw God; on a disco trip, you see Jackie O at Studio 54."[18]

With the death of disco came also the end of a 30-year bull market in record sales, as new technologies threatened the role of radio stations and network television, and a further splintering of taste groups into fractionated publics.

Status Cultures

Although parts of the mainstream, these publics make their central concern an attack on the mainstream and its adherents and the development of alternatives to it.

"Formal" high culture vultures assert that anything popular has to be inferior, while anything obscure, remote in time and place, widely overlooked or forgotten, has to be good. Such groups include artists with a capital "A" and those who claim to be avant-garde, most college students going through the rites of passage from mainstream to what they hope will be wealth, power, and knowledge above the mainstream (poor deluded innocents!). This also includes "Geek" cultures, whose devotees deliberately cultivate outrageous and disgusting tastes in order to offend mainstreamers and show their distaste for the latter's cultures.

Special Subcultures

These mobilize and maintain groups that have numerous members engaged in specialized activities, too numerous to have one-to-one communications, but numerous enough to support communication networks that serve their specialized needs and interests. This includes professional groups such as athletes, actors, doctors, lawyers, engineers, Indian chiefs. Also included are voluntary and recreational specialties, such as hunting, skin diving, and furniture refinishing.

The remarkable thing about the new publics is that they are nationally homogeneous, yet broken into all kinds of fragments. Country and western taste groups, for example, share a whole collection of values and receptivities. They are an audience for Willy

Nelson, Dolly Parton, and conservative economic doctrines. They exist in patches throughout the country, as on the South Side of Chicago, in certain working class suburbs in Detroit, and in rural counties in Arkansas. Yet they have uniformities wherever found. They listen to the same kind of radio programming, watch the same TV shows, read the same magazines, admire the same spokesmen and celebrities. The question is to find them.

The model is that of a chocolate chip cookie. The old layer cake of class structure, from low to high culture groups, saw taste preference and audience identification following socioeconomic patterns. Upper-class elite culture was seen as associated with high socioeconomic status. This was the norm, even though there might be exceptions. Working-class people were expected to follow low culture forms and would be attentive to low culture programming. Certainly the class-conscious layer cake doesn't exist in the real world!

Instead, taste publics violate the class boundaries on all sides; but they do not violate the spontaneous boundaries of self-segregation by membership in audience groups. They are media publics, marked by their attention to this or that communicator and medium. Their subjective structures of receptivity identify their inchoate group memberships; and these are highly uniform and visible, whether they are in a ritzy suburb of Washington, D.C., or in a tar-paper shack in Tennessee.

Such extremes of socioeconomic demographics can be part of the same audiences. The characteristics that they share are more important demographically to pollsters, marketing experts, and politicians than the characteristics by which they differ.

The media audience networks are what make tracking and targeting most effective. They are what ultimately must be configured in the new computer data base systems that have emerged as the major weapons of influence and persuasion. Polling is necessary to delve into the content of each taste public. Depth and focus-group interviewing, as well as short-answer survey research, reveal the characteristic structure of every important taste group. Constant research is necessary to track the constant changes of taste. Intrinsic to the process of taste formation is the factor of change.

Events are constant inputs to which existing culture forms react. Central to the dynamics of culture is a taste for refreshment of old forms and the discovery of new ones. Restless as the ever-changing sea, the taste for dramatic events is inherent in the process by which the legitimate forms assert their holds on the attention of their loyal audiences.

In a modern multivariegated society, the communicators and programmers must compete with each other to retain the attentions of their own publics. They daily earn their legitimacy by providing vindication and reassurance for their own audiences against the attacks and blandishments of other taste publics. The whole nation is a chocolate chip cookie, held together by the cookie batter, the mainstream culture, but containing varieties of chips spread haphazardly throughout — some bitter, some sweet, some minted, some flavored with mocha or butterscotch.

In this chapter we have examined the role of publics in American society, the theoretical problems of defining and identifying them, and have assayed the practical applications and implications of these concepts. We have suggested that for the purposes of opinion research and political analysis, we follow the example of marketing and audience studies; that this approach will yield better approximations of group phenomena having continuity, uniformity, and stability in the competitive ever-changing polity. Political realists already do this on a routine basis.

NOTES

1. Herbert J. Gans, *Popular and High Culture: An Analysis and Evaluation of Taste* (New York: Basic Books, 1974), p. 94.

2. See Dennis Gilbert and Joseph A. Kahl, *The American Class Structure* (Homewood, Ill.: Dorsey Press, 1982).

3. Gans, *Popular and High Culture*, p. 76.

4. Ibid., p. 78.

5. Ibid., p. 82.

6. Ibid., p. 85.

7. Ibid., p. 88.

8. Ibid., p. 92.

9. Ibid., p. 101.

10. See Paul Fussell, *Notes on Class* (New York: Summit Books, 1983), quoted by Curt Suplee, "The Slings and Arrows of Paul Fussell," *Washington Post*, September 28, 1982, p. B9.

11. See Gunther Barth, *City People/The Rise of Modern City Culture in 19th Century America* (New York: Oxford University Press, 1979); also Paul Boyer, *Urban Masses and the Moral Order in America 1820-1920* (Cambridge, Mass.: Harvard University Press, 1980).

12. See Alison Lurie, *The Language of Clothes* (New York: Random House, 1981); also Dick Hebdige, *Subculture: The Meaning of Style* (New York: Methuen, 1981).

13. See Andrew Kopkind, "Dressing Up/Mysteries of Fashion Revealed," *Village Voice*, April 30, 1979, p. 1; see also Justine M. Cordwell and Ronald A. Schwarz, eds., *The Fabrics of Culture* (The Hague: Mouton, 1980).

14. See Andrew Radoff, "Census Data, New Studies Highlight NRC Meeting," *Editor and Publisher*, December 13, 1980, p. 19.

15. *Washington Post*, June 7, 1982, p. D16.

16. Rudy Maxa, "Front Page People," *Washington Post Magazine*, July 22, 1979, p. 4.

17. *Broadcasting*, August 30, 1982, p. 68.

18. Andrew Kopkind, "Disco Tech," *New Times*, January 8, 1979, p. 4.

CHAPTER FOUR
POPCORN AND STRAW POLLS

Both qualitative and quantitative techniques are used to study public opinion. The opportunity exists for the researcher to apply a wide variety of methods or to develop new ones. Flexible and creative research design is the key to discovery.

This is an area where the researcher can express his own interests and personality. There is nothing forbidding in methodology. It is the commonsense application of inquiry to resolve hypotheses, the purposeful collection of data that will prove, disprove, or modify the researcher's hunch about what he expects to find.

We will describe and examine all the kinds of public opinion techniques in current use, both scientific and unscientific. Among the latter are popcorn polls, straw polls, and dishonest polls; among the former are long- and short-answer scientific sample studies, depth individual and focus-group interviews, audience testing, and test marketing.

POPCORN POLLS

Popcorn polls are tongue-in cheek indicators of public opinion. During the presidential election of 1964, an enterprising movie theater proprietor placed pictures of the candidates, Barry Goldwater and Lyndon Johnson, one on each of two side-by-side corn-poppers. Then he called the newspapers to report that Lyndon Johnson popcorn was outselling Barry Goldwater 2 to 1. Thus was born the popcorn poll, which has been a regular feature of national elections since.

All kinds of variations have joined the list, vying for free advertising or just for a little comic relief. In Ulster County, upstate New York, five-cent bubble gum cigars with cellophane wrappers marked either LBJ or Goldwater were sold in a kids' candy store; LBJ won 5 to 1. Did some smart aleck son of a Democratic wardheeler rig the count?

Hotdog vendors on the streets of New York joined the gag and were duly covered by the national media. A new version was reported in 1982, when a CBS political reporter set up two identical bowls of jellybeans at a house party of Washington political junkies, one marked "Reagan Won't Run in '84"; the other, "Reagan Will Run in '84." Three times as many negative jellybeans were eaten.[1]

A different implication could be read into two other polling methods that shared a scatological fixation. Bathtique, a specialty chain in suburban malls, sold toilet paper (at $3 a roll) emblazoned on each sheet with the face of either Jimmy Carter or Ronald Reagan. "It's difficult to say who buys the toilet paper and for what purpose. It seems to be selling heavily to accountants and lawyers." Reagan sold out in Syracuse, Carter in New York City. One man came in and sought John Anderson paper. The results in both 1976 and 1980 accurately predicted the election result (inversely of course): "It was more accurate than the polls," the proprietor said.

In Cincinnati, Ohio, a radio DJ invented the "toilet-flushing poll." He called on listeners to report their sentiments in the 1976 election by flushing their toilets on prearranged signals. He had a reporter at the city reservoir measuring the dip in the water level. The drops for both Carter and Ford were about the same: "Too close to call!" was the official verdict.

A similar, but perhaps more serious, measurement was obtained by standing on a corner, or by choosing a parking lot, and counting bumper stickers on cars. In 1964, at the University of Wisconsin, the student newspaper reported that of 356 cars in faculty lots, 25 displayed LBJ and 4 Goldwater stickers. Two ("Bury Goldwater" and "Help Goldwater Stamp Out Peace") were counted as pro-LBJ. In the student lots, Goldwater did much better.

In late 1981, controversial Chicago Mayor Jane Byrne's face appeared on the cover of *Chicago Magazine*, half of the 250,000 copies smiling, half frowning. Newsstands gave them equal rack space. In the center city, the frown won out 5 to 4; but in the grassy suburbs, the grin took it in a breeze, 3 to 1.

People have sought to study issue salience by similar techniques, counting car stickers or logoed T-shirts. Some of the former: Walt Disney World, Animals Have Rights Too, Split Wood Not Atoms, Tennis Is My Racket, Lord Stanley Lives in Philly. Some of the latter: Go Hike a Canyon, It's Better in the Bahamas, I Love John Travolta. Icons of the age.

The choices for magazine cover topics are of considerable moment to editors, because newsstand sales constitute half the circulation, the most volatile part of income. Consequently, good figures are kept on impulse purchases associated with different cover personalities and subjects, figures that may be construed as excellent measures of cultural salience.

The faces of politicians have sold poorly since 1977, Jimmy Carter worst of all — leading editors to ban him from their covers as though he were the plague. Walter Mondale was on the cover of the all-time low sales issue of *People* in February 1978. Henry Kissinger was on the cover of the worst-selling *Cosmo* in 1978. But Joan Kennedy (then Ted's wife, struggling with alcoholism) graced the best-selling issue of *McCall's*.

Elvis was 1977's hands-down winner. Reverend Jim Jones led to best newsstand sales ever of *Time* and *Newsweek*. *Sports Illustrated*'s best — Leon Spinks with a missing tooth; the worst — golfer Andy North. *People*'s best — Priscilla Presley; worst — Ed Asner. *McCall's* worst — Jane Fonda. *Rolling Stone*'s best — Linda Ronstadt; worst — Donna Summer.[2]

Similar indices to the subjective state of the culture have been compiled by measuring the popularity of books on college campuses. *The Official Preppy Handbook*, *101 Uses for a Dead Cat*, and *Garfield Gains Weight* led in sales in 1981; for the entire decade of the 1970s, the leading best-sellers were *Love Story* by Erich Segal and *Jonathan Livingston Seagull* by Richard Bach.

Motion picture box office success can be similarly used to measure the psychological preoccupations of the nation. For the decade, the winners are *Close Encounters*, *The Exorcist*, and *Godfather I*. The choice of names on birth certificates of any given period has been deemed significant by some. In 1900, Mary and John, and in 1978, Jennifer and Michael, were the most popular.[3] Thousands of such measures still remain to be discovered.

Dicksville Notch, New Hampshire, a town with 16 registered voters, becomes once every four years, one minute after midnight on primary day, the harbinger of the presidential sweepstakes and the target of national media attention. Always the first town to report in the nation's first primary, the wily denizens have little else going for them, but become media celebrities on that magical midnight. The media hunger for something to write about during the long day's wait for real returns. This deserves to be treated as a popcorn poll, even though the vote count is real.

Betting odds offered by Lloyd's of London have been used to forecast election results. This is based on the assumption that the odds represent a parimutuel assessment by thousands of observers who are willing "to put their money where their mouth is." Thus the odds represent a measure of intensity, as well as a head count, giving a prediction weighted by the same factor that influences real voting. So good has been this poll that Lloyd's has never lost any money, but of course that is what calculation of the odds is all about.

STRAW POLLS

Straws in the wind — that is the way to tell which way the wind is blowing. The farmer picks up a handful of straw and drops it, watching which way it falls. Straw polls are often called "street corner polls," because they are traditionally taken by standing on a street corner and stopping random passersby. Representativeness of the sample is sought by dependence on sheer accidental selection from the stream of humanity on a well-trafficked downtown corner or at a central shopping mall.

The main characteristic of straw polls is that little further attempt is made to control, to design, or to structure the selection of respondents, the size of the sample, or the method of randomization. Thus there is no guarantee that the sample is truly random, there is no way to estimate the probability of error, and there is no way to stratify the sample in order to ensure that various demographic characteristics get selected at all and get selected in adequate numbers and in rough proportion to the known composition of the target population. In other respects, straw polls can be as scientific as their more respectable counterparts. They can use well-designed instruments (questionnaires), the interviewers can be well-trained, and all other problems of systematic bias can be eliminated. But they do not rise above the limitations of the species.

This is not to say that they are useless. Quite the contrary. Their persistent survival and frequency testify to the fact that they are serving the needs of somebody. They are relatively inexpensive to conduct, anybody can do them, and they can be put together very rapidly. And, in some cases, they are better indications of public opinion than the purely personal and subjective assessments of a reporter or editor who talks to her or his friends or to only a handful of people even less representative of a target audience.

A natural straw poll is the flow of unsolicited cards and letters. Every celebrity and public official receives fan and hate mail, and shows a natural curiosity about whether pro or con is ahead. Until 1933, the White House employed only one person to handle the incoming mail, through a world war and the Great Depression. Woodrow Wilson tried to answer it all himself. Herbert Hoover received about 40 letters a day.

After FDR's first radio address the mail swelled to about 4,000 letters a day, the result of the impact of the medium, which he was the first president to master. Thereafter, the mailroom staff began a growth to its present number of 30. Today the White House receives about 10,000 letters a day.

The pattern developed in the 1930s of counting the pros and cons and subject matter and filing a weekly report with the president's office.[4] Some of the most interesting are extracted to be shown to the president or treated to a personal response signed by him. Ronald Reagan invited people to write to him and promised to answer all cards and letters. After the election that promise proved to be impossible to fulfill, and the mailroom staff now has a backlog of hundreds of thousands of unopened items in storage.

In the same category, most members of Congress solicit mail and advice from constituents, commonly sending opinion polls to every registered voter in the home district. These straw polls are sometimes genuine attempts to gauge the homefolks' thinking; but most of them are poorly drafted, thinly disguised promotional gimmicks designed to flatter the constituents and give them a sense of involvement.

In 1982, Senator Daniel Patrick Moynihan reported in his newsletter that more than 100,000 New Yorkers, out of more than 3 million recipients, returned his preprimary questionnaire. He couldn't collate that many, but his staff drew a "random sample" of 1,000 and collated these, finding that most respondents were opposed to Reaganomics and more concerned about crime than about jobs.[5]

All postcard surveys share some of the limitations of straw polls. Well-designed surveys employing self-administered mail-in questionnaires can be serious polling methods, but may still suffer from the problems of self-selection by the respondents and low returns. Straw polls have recently gotten cheaper and easier through computer automation, so we will probably see even more examples of their use.

The "Telephone Poll" is the name of a compact computer about the size and appearance of a stereo receiver. It can be programmed to dial numbers and ask recorded questions, dutifully recording and collating the answers, or it can be used in conjunction with questions announced on radio, television, or printed in a handout or the newspaper.

> A national lottery. Are you for or against it? Should the National League adopt the designated hitter rule? Yes or No. Give one phone number. The computer does the rest. A synthesized or recorded voice tells the caller how to place a vote. The vote is instantly registered, tabulated, and recorded, and a digital readout shows running total or percentages. How big a staff is needed? None! Zero! Just the Telephone Poll. It accepts 360 calls a minute, per phone line; and is programmed to diagnose its own malfunctions.[6]

This device could also be adapted to scientific sample polls of course, and this has been done. In one version, a recorded voice sounding like a well-known celebrity is used in order to induce a more forthcoming attitude at the other end of the line. The voice of the deceased Elvis Presley was still being used in an afternoon poll of middle-aged housewives concerning a commercial cleaning product. This leads to certain problems, both in good interviewing techniques and in ethics — which will be addressed later.

A two-way cable television experiment in Columbus, Ohio, the QUBE network with 30,000 subscribers, inspired many different uses, including attempts to measure sentiments on public policy issues, feelings toward incumbents, and the impact of specific televised appearances of the candidates. It has been used for such purposes as asking viewers to score the rounds in a boxing match while the bout is in progress, announcing the results, and then comparing them with those of Howard Cossell; asking fans to send in plays during a tense moment in a football game; and so on.

In 1979, after Carter's malaise speech, the Warner cable company asked the QUBE watcher to answer five questions: Did the speech leave you optimistic or confused? Are you more confident now in Carter's leadership ability? Are his plans to deal with the energy shortage tough enough? Did the president convince you to make personal sacrifices? Do you think the country will pull together to solve its problems? The results were largely favorable to the president. In early 1982, 400 households participated in a QUBE evaluation of a President Reagan speech on Caribbean policy, showing by before and after measurements that he had switched about 30 percent to his side.

Ted Turner used the method in a highly dubious way to promote his Cable News Network. Viewers were asked which they preferred, the news product of CNN or that of the other networks. Predictably the respondents gave CNN an 85 percent vote of confidence. (Turner had the refreshing innocence to feature the poll in his promotional advertising.)

Commenting on QUBE, Albert H. Cantril, president of the National Council on Public Polls, chided the news media for treating the results as though they had national implications. "Such a survey cannot even be construed as a measure of sentiment in Columbus." At $10 a month, poor people were not likely to subscribe to cable, skewing the results. Since those who watch and those who decide to respond are self-selected, this presents a fatal systematic error, even if demographic questions are added to see whom they represent.[7]

AT&T established a regular telephone survey service in 1980, mainly for the convenience of commercial survey firms, but soon employed for media political news gathering. The service was designated by its telephone exchange number, 900.

The ABC network decided to use it to get immediate audience feedback to the single great debate in the 1980 presidential election. Two 900 numbers were announced; calling one or the other was the means of casting a vote favorable to either participant. In an hour or so, 727,328 calls were tallied, favoring Reagan's performance over Carter's by 2 to 1. Whether the survey meant anything, and whether the network acted responsibly in conducting it, were issues of considerable controversy afterward. Callers-in had to pay a 50-cent telephone fee for the privilege.

"No credence at all should be given to the figures," said George Gallup, Sr. The procedures used have long since been discredited. It has all the faults, he said, of the Literary Digest poll in 1936, in which postcard ballots were sent to people who had car registrations and were listed in the telephone book. This biased the sample toward people with higher incomes and who have a consistent viewpoint, but represent only a small part of the real public. Albert Cantril said he was concerned that, although ABC disavowed the scientific implications of the stunt, it went ahead with news references to the poll as though it could be taken seriously, "confusing the public about what a poll is and isn't."[8]

Many techniques that must be classified as "straw polls" are very carefully and responsibly contrived. This includes the highly regarded exit polls originated in 1967 by CBS and now widely used on election day. Exit polls survey those exiting selected polling places, in order, not only to make possible forecasts before the polls close, but also to delve into the motivations and reasons for the electoral choices, giving analysts a means of interpreting the meaning of the actual results when they are known.

Every kind of scientific expertise goes into most exit polls. All three of the TV networks have associated themselves with respected polling organizations to carry them out. The polling precincts are carefully chosen to be representative of the total electorate in the district, state, or nation; demographics of regionalism, income, past voting behavior, ethnic background, age structure, and so on are built into the choice; the numbers of respondents are set so as to give significance to the result, to be certain that the breakdown of the sample into subclasses will still give adequate numbers in each. Educated people are recruited, usually members of the League of Woman Voters or active senior citizen groups, to do the work on election day, and to phone in their results quickly to a central collection point.

Yet this method must still be considered in the nature of a straw poll, because at the heart is the rough randomness of self-selection or interviewer selection of the respondents. At the end, exit polls are like street corner surveys, and no matter how well selected the street corners may be, the fact remains that no estimates of sampling error are possible at the level of the actual selection of respondents.

There is no guarantee that voters who respond to the poll are like those who refuse to answer. An interviewer is required to stand a long distance from the exit and may have a difficult time catching the attention of voters, and during busy periods his problems are multiplied. Self-administered secret ballots were thought to have improved the process. But still there is a noticeable bias in favor of younger over older voters, the latter seeming to refuse more readily.

The results may be, and are, interesting and pertinent. They may be considered as valid analyses of motivation. They may in fact accurately foretell the results of the election (their least important purpose). All of these aspects justify their use. But one must also be mindful of their limitations and must not attempt to make them do what they are not designed to do. They are not designed for statistical analysis, and such a use, which sometimes occurs, misrepresents their nature.

In November 1981, CBS, using exit data, projected the wrong winner in the New Jersey gubernatorial race before the ballot counting was finished. This was the first time CBS had used exit polling to project a winner earlier than the rival networks. NBC had successfully used exit data to call the presidential election correctly the previous year, thereby setting a challenge to the other networks. In the 1970s, exit data were used to interpret, rather than predict, outcomes. But in 1980, all that changed.

As early as noon on election day, all three networks reported Reagan getting a large proportion of the popular vote. By supper time, all were suggesting, with appropriate disclaimers, that he might win. Thereafter, NBC abandoned caution and declared a winner. NBC's projection had beaten the others by almost two hours, making it a substantial matter that caused great commotion in the industry. Jealousy was not the only emotion.

Assuming that the methodology was correct, because it had worked that time, NBC received much criticism for the alleged impact on voters in the ten states whose polls were still open at the time of the projection (8:15 P.M. EST). What made it seem even more serious was Jimmy Carter's insistence on making a formal concession while the West had not finished voting. There was talk of Congress passing a law to ban any projections until after all the polls were closed, including those in Hawaii (4 A.M. EST).[9]

Following the CBS fiasco the following year, concern shifted from exit poll forecasts to those based on actual voting data in the East, where careful statistical analysis of structured early returns sometimes makes an early but reliable projection possible, based on very fragmentary returns. Commenting on the egg in the CBS Eye, Warren Mitofsky, director of CBS Election and Survey unit, said he did not know exactly what went wrong. He accepted personal responsibility and declared CBS had no intention of abandoning the use of exit polls: "We will be more reluctant to project a winner," he said, but exit polling is still valuable for answering such questions as How did it happen? What does it mean?

The Associated Press Bureau chief in New Jersey said: "This trend in US political coverage . . . creates substantial pressure. . . . We received calls from member newspapers asking when we intended to declare a winner."[10]

In the 1982 elections, the networks were determined to be cautious in their use of exit polls, to concentrate on the light they cast on the meaning of the actual returns, and to avoid statistical projections based entirely on exit data. All projections would be based on computer-assisted interpretations of structured early returns, and even these would be presented in a tentative way during the early hours after polls closed in the East.

METHODS OF THE SOCIAL SCIENCES

Before entering the domains of scientific polling, discussed in Chapter 5, it is useful to give an overview of all the methods of science that are used in the study of social phenomena. In general, social science methods can be described under five headings; case, comparative, historical, laboratory, and statistical studies.

Case Study

The case study is the basic unit upon which all the rest are built. It takes a single event, example, or episode and attempts to find out as much about it as possible, by every means available. The data are then organized to re-create or describe the case.

The telling has a beginning — What were the antecedents of the event? The origins? The surrounding conditions? What started things in motion? — a middle — What happened? Who were the actors? Who did what to whom? and Why? — and an end — What was the outcome? Effects on conditions and actors? What's next?

The simple case study is usually descriptive; that is, little attempt is made to develop technical terms or measurable indicia; common-use language can be adequate. All the methods of first- and second-hand observation are permissible, including interviews with participants and spectators, participant observation, written reports, and transcripts. The only requirement is thoroughness in collecting pertinent data and fairness toward all the interests and parties involved. Very often the researcher is overly dependent on partial and self-serving sources and has to make a determined effort to balance his or her point of view by seeking a variety of other documentary and personal sources.

In doing a case study, the researcher should be a good reporter, developing the facts and presenting them in an interesting way. Examples include study of how a specific bill became law, the New Hampshire presidential primary of 1980, the OMB and the 1983 budget. Case studies concern unique events, whether on a large or small scale. A more complex case study might use methods other than description for subparts (for example, surveys of voter intention before a specific primary), but the ultimate report will be primarily descriptive and will follow the narrative form.

Like all research, the case study begins with a hypothesis, a proposition that expresses the researcher's best guess. It can be focused on any part of the event: causes, conditions, linkages, personae, outcomes, effects; it directs and contains the collection of data by providing a standard of relevance. A good hypothesis, whether one's own or something taken from the literature, keeps the data manageable and within the resources of time and effort available.

Comparative Study

Two or more case studies can be placed side by side in order to remark their similarities and differences. For example, the legislative cycles of two or more different bills can be compared, to see in what respects the factors surrounding each case differ from each other. This makes it possible to generalize about whatever factors are compared: causes, conditions, actors, interactions, outcomes, effects.

This kind of study leads to a greater concern with precision of language than is required by a simple case study. Whereas an individual case study deals in concrete acts and artifacts, a comparative study begins to abstract entities from among many different categories. This leads to technical language, which is necessary to denote classes of things rather than things themselves. As more and more things of the same and other classes are compared, it becomes possible to report them by counting. Thus, at its simplest level, quantitative begins to support qualitative terminology. The underlying meaning of number is "instances of a class."

A qualitative factor that is found to be uniform or linear can be calibrated into equal units, each with the same qualitative value. Quantification, then, is merely counting the number of units for each occurrence of a factor, to compare qualities in terms of "how many units of each," or to arrange qualitative factors in a numerical order.

By placing comparable events or systems side by side, one can discern resemblances and differences. In real-world phenomena, this may be the only way to try to isolate variables and attempt, by finding appropriate cases, to isolate them.

Hypotheses for comparative studies are more abstract, pulling out classes and categories that apply to many or all cases and trying to discover relationships between them. Grand or modest things can be compared, from whole political systems and institutional categories to specific subclasses. Examples are leadership styles, socialization of ten-year-olds in different schools, democratic systems in Europe, and interest groups in English-speaking nations.

Historical Method

The historical method uses both the case and comparative methods, but considers the dimension of time of central importance. Cases are described or compared in terms of developmental relationships over time, in order to test hypotheses concerned with chains of cause and effect over space and time. Different cases may be taken out of time sequence in order to make possible comparisons that reveal the effects of time itself; that is, to discover whether or not the unique relations of before/after are significant.

The comparative method does not ignore time, but is more interested in the way factors operate universally, outside of before/after relationships. The historian, on the other hand, is interested in unique time sequences and compares them in order to arrive at both specific and general principles to explain or interpret events.

Laboratory Methods

Unlike the physical sciences, the social sciences deal with phenomena that usually cannot be captured and tested in the laboratory. A laboratory is an artificial environment. Its chief characteristics are controlled design and observation of experiments. Each experiment may be likened to a case study; but in the lab every thing that is done is deliberate. All conditions and interactions are controlled. Variables are isolated, so that their effects can be determined, by designing events in which each variable can be present or absent, singly or in combination.

Each event is repeatable so that the observations of one experiment or experimenter can be duplicated and retested many times. Hypotheses state the relationships of variables that can be definitively tested. Quantitative measurement becomes the chief way of describing events because the events themselves are designed in terms of the tools of measurement.

One of the most exciting challenges to social scientists is to find ways of developing and testing hypotheses under laboratory conditions, without, of course, violating the human rights of test subjects. There have been many breakthroughs, but this methodology tends to find only limited applications in areas of social interest.

Much has been done in physiological and psychological studies of individuals. But in the areas of political and group interactions, much still remains to be done. Animal subjects have been used to study human social behavior, but this remains controversial. Many argue that such studies cannot be scaled to human subjects and thus remain merely speculative.

Most successful in the laboratory have been studies of various communication networks, small-group decision making, group dynamics, and simulation experiments or game playing. All of these designs are consistent with humane principles, but do permit the rigorous controls and repeatability of the laboratory.

Statistical Methods

Statistical methods are the counting of many instances of anything, inside the laboratory or in the field. Like the social sciences, modern physics, biology, and chemistry involve dealing with subatomic particles, electrical and magnetic forces, and processes that cannot be directly witnessed or controlled. In these areas, laboratory science resembles social science. It must get data by studying indirect indicators and effects; these are often not uniform and linear, but fall into patterns that can only be described in terms of their probabilities of occurrence.

Control is obtained by clustering large numbers of observations and breaking them down into groups, describing them in terms of the chances that the relationships will be found again under the same conditions of observation. Variables can be isolated by separating the cases in which certain factors or characteristics occur from those in which they do not occur; then measuring, by counting, the total numbers in each class; and then assigning to them a measurement of their comparative frequencies.

This process is bound by the mathematical rules of probability, which, although theoretical, have proven the best available predictors of indirect indicators and large population phenomena.

Statistical methods have proven a godsend for the social sciences. Because of the nature of its subject matter, most social phenomena involve large populations that must be studied in the field under real-life conditions, where controls are minimal. Experiments can be designed based on data collection from manageable sample sizes, and factor frequencies can be counted as they occur in their natural state, with minimum researcher intervention.

Variables can be discovered and their effects isolated by the indirect controls of statistical association and analysis. This is the province of survey as well as aggregate-data research — the former involving asking questions of respondents in order to resolve hypotheses concerning attitudes, values, opinions, intentions, and behaviors, and the latter involving counting and reporting distributions of objective attributes or things: the number of radios per family, number of bedrooms per capita, the amount of iron and steel produced annually, and so on.

Also falling under these five headings are the methods of research that deal mainly with documentary and ideational subject matters: textual analysis, legal and other forms of interpretive commentary, verbal and content analyses, discursive reasoning, theory and meta-theory (theory about theories), bibliographical studies, the examination of ideas and their logical implications. All of these can be designed by the same patterns as fieldwork. The only difference is that the researcher is dealing with documentary records or linguistic relationships.

All of these methodologies can be and usually are employed in combination. Any single research undertaking will try to collect relevant data by all appropriate techniques. In most cases, the nature of the hypothesis, subject matter, available resources of time and money, and the ingenuity of the researcher will determine how various methods will be used.[11]

NOTES

1. *New York Times*, March 11, 1982, p. C9.

2. *Washington Post*, February 6, 1979, p. B9.

3. *Public Opinion*, December/January 1980, p. 43.

4. David Halberstam, *The Powers That Be* (New York: Dell Books, 1979), p. 30.

5. Newsletter, June 1982, p. 4.

6. Manufactured by M. A. Kempner, Pompano Beach, Fla. Call toll-free 800-327-4994; a synthesized voice will answer.

7. *Washington Post*, July 17, 1979, p. B2.

8. *New York Times*, October 30, 1980, p. B19.

9. See Martin Plissner and Warren Mitofsky, "Voting Twice on Election Day," *Public Opinion*, August/September 1982, pp. 14-16.

10. *Editor and Publisher*, November 28, 1981, p. 27.

11. See Albert H. Cantril ed., *Polling on the Issues* (Cabin John, Md.: Seven Locks Press, 1978).

CHAPTER FIVE
SCIENTIFIC POLLS

We now enter the province of science. This means that every available means is employed to eliminate systematic bias and error. This does not mean that one expects always to get the right answers; rather that one expects to get the right answers more often, and that one is able to estimate mathematically the degree of probable error. Furthermore, the scientific method makes possible, with appropriate safeguards, the use of statistical tools of analysis to squeeze all the significance from the data. It permits the requisite skills to be taught to others so that many can practice the craft, and it permits standards of quality to be defined and pursued.

The design of a scientific random sample, and rigorous rules for drawing it from the population, are very important, but they constitute only one of the dimensions of the scientific method. Just as essential are all the others: the self-conscious and deliberate avoidance of bias and imprecision in the overall design of the study, in framing the questions, in selecting and training interviewers, in collating the answers, in reading and interpreting the meaning of the results, in applying the cumulative wisdom of one's own and the discipline's past experience, and in maintaining standards of excellence every step of the way. Thus scientific sampling means applying a method for the selection of actual respondents that will ensure randomness and will protect against both inherent structural bias as well as inadvertent bias.

Under the heading of scientific method must be included a number of quite different techniques: short-answer (using both one-to-one depth interviewing and what is called focus-group interviewing), audience or panel testing, and all forms of test marketing. We will take these up one at a time, looking at the techniques of each, their uses, problems, and advantages and disadvantages.

SHORT-ANSWER POLLS

Scientific short-answer polls are very familiar. The typical instrument (questionnaire, also sometimes called a schedule — to emphasize that it is structured in a certain order to achieve certain purposes) contains perhaps 11 to 20 items, including three or four demographics (age, income, education, and so on).

The questions may be in various forms, but they all share the characteristic of permitting relatively short answers. They can be yes/no, multiple choice, scaled choice (for example, "Rate Bo Derek on a scale of 1 to 10"), or short identification ("What is the name of your state governor?"). There are also closed-ended or forced-choice questions, which means that the answer must be one of the categories offered, including the options of "don't know," "other," and "no opinion."

Short-answer instruments may also use open-ended or free-answer items: "How do you feel about this or that?" or "What would you like to see done to save the Social Security system?" For such questions, the form allows a limited amount of space for an answer, which the interviewer must write down verbatim.

The interviewer is instructed to encourage only a short reply, to avoid probing for elaboration and extension of remarks, to break in at an early pause and go on with the schedule, and to record only a preset portion of the response, for example, the first 25 words, more or less, or approximately the first ten seconds. Short-answer surveys may be done face-to-face, by mail, or on the telephone. Those that are done in person are usually conducted while standing up, at the doorway or out of doors. Such environments tend to work best with short-answer schedules. If the instrument is self-administered, the amount of space available for the response has the same effect.

Based on the theory that whatever a respondent says first is likely to be what is topmost in his thinking, the answer to an open-ended short question can be very revealing, can readily be collated, and will accomplish purposes that forced choices cannot by nature do. Done properly, it has the advantage of testing what is in the respondent's mind, without planting a suggestion there. It permits the respondent to reveal original thoughts, providing a clue to the structure of his attention, and his own priorities of importance.

The open-ended response has several disadvantages when compared with the forced-choice. It is more sensitive to the skills and conscientiousness of the individual interviewer, who must create the proper ambience and who must catch the words and write them down. It is much easier to get a respondent or an interviewer to check off the appropriate square on the questionnaire and then move on to the next item. In the free answer, the respondent or interviewer must write a sentence or two, something many people cannot do, or do with great reluctance. It takes a little longer, and thus costs more. And it is much more difficult to collate.

Because statistical analysis is very important to processing short-answer surveys, open-ended responses must be identified and classified into a relatively small number of categories. And in ten seconds it is possible for a respondent to say things that fall into no recognizable class or into several simultaneously.

Sometimes it is desirable to count different classes of response by content (How many mentions of key words or ideas?) rather than by respondent (How many respondents were positive or negative on a topic?). The project design must include a plan for collating the data, and thus must anticipate and make allowance for these problems. Collation is not a matter of simply counting responses. Open-ended items must first be "coded," that is, categories must be defined, and the contents of each response must be evaluated and assigned to a category. Only then can the work be given to a technician for tallying or be entered into a computer.

With closed-ended items, the designer does much of the hardest work in writing the schedule; with open-ended, much of the hardest work is done in collating and interpreting the answers. Open-ended items are easier to write, but one must be much more resourceful at all the subsequent stages.

Of course, the main considerations are getting the job done, using the method that will work best for resolving a given hypothesis within the time and money resources available. It is not unusual to combine both kinds of questions on a single schedule. Sometimes it is desirable to follow up a forced choice with "Why do you feel that way?" or "Why do you say that?" or simply "Why?" Within the short-answer format, there are no special problems in doing this. Respondents can handle both kinds readily and in the same rhythm and mood.

On the other hand, it is very difficult to mix long- and short-answer items of major substance on the same schedule. The rhythm and social conventions are different. Long-answer is associated with sit-down living room or studio interviews, with many patient probes of the response, sometimes with audio- or videotape recording. An instrument that is predominantly long-answer may include a few short-answer items (including demographics) without disturbing the mood; however, this doesn't work in reverse. If a long-answer item is inserted in a predominantly short-answer interview, the invariable result is that the cues fail to bring forth any but short responses, in spite of the schedule's intentions.

LONG-ANSWER STUDIES

Interviews in depth are psychological tools for probing beneath the surface of verbal statements of opinion. Like Rorschach tests (inkblots), which attempt to read subconscious and unconscious parts of the personality, depth interview techniques seek to reveal deeper levels of meaning, intention, developmental processes, and future behaviors of subjects. The structure of opinion is itself probed in terms of the morphology of the personality, as described in Chapter 3. The six personality levels are set, values, attitudes, knowledge, opinion, and creative will.

Hypotheses tend to be more abstract, involving not only "what people hold what opinions" but also how opinions are formed and how they relate to each other, as well as the dynamic processes at work, both in practical terms of influencing their directions and in theoretical terms of advancing general knowledge of the opinion process. Hypotheses tend to be more exploratory (stated as a question, rather than as a guess of the answer), seeking to discover connections that have not yet been considered by the researcher or the client.

It had been observed that in short-answer surveys, the interviewer tells the respondents; in the long-answer survey, the respondents tell the interviewer. The mood and rhythm of the interviewing must be more leisurely and relaxed, whether on the telephone or in person. Telephone interviewing is sometimes used, but much less than is the case with short-answer techniques. The setting is of extreme importance because it must facilitate an extended and positive flow of thought. Sitting down is essential, not optional, as was true in the previous mode.

DEPTH INTERVIEWS

As noted, this technique can be very similar to short-answer polling, with the exception that the polling instrument primarily involves open-ended questions, eliciting and recording considerably longer answers. The designer must set a rule on length: Record everything the respondent says for at least a minute, or perhaps the first 100 words or so, or let the respondent go on as long as he or she wishes. Probes and cues are suggested to the interviewer in order to encourage a longer answer.

The size of the sample, its design, stratification, and selection can be identical to a short-answer survey. The statistical safeguards and manipulations can follow the same patterns and practices. The same hypotheses can be tested, although the reverse is not generally true; that is, short-answer polls can rarely test the kinds of hypotheses that require long-answer questions.

Depth interviews can be coded (classified and counted) like open-ended short answers, both in terms of number of respondents whose views are distributed among various alternative responses (for example, how many are positive/negative toward an issue, product, personality, program) and/or in terms of number of responses of distinct types (for example, the kinds of first mentions, frequency of mentions, total number of mentions, intensity of mentions, of certain keywords, ideas, and concepts).

Sometimes an hypothesis is aimed more at the discovery of new elements in the public's perception of an issue, candidate, or product rather than at merely counting their distribution in a population. In such a case, the size of the sample is less important than its composition. Statistical and demographic methods aim at structuring and selecting small groups of individuals for depth or focus-group interviews.

Instead of controlling for error by calculations of sample size, small audiences, whose numbers may give unacceptable levels of statistical significance and confidence, are structured to control for certain characteristics especially relevant to the hypothesis. Statistical analysis goes primarily into the design of the experiment and only secondarily into reading and analyzing the results. It is possible to test new hypotheses in the very act of coding the results.

For example, in studying the impact of education on the purchase of foreign cars, a group of representative college graduates will be compared with a group of representative high school graduates, matching other selected variables as closely as possible. Each group will undergo exposure to the same depth interviewing process. The results will be collated, not only to explore for serendipitous discoveries and for testing motivational parameters within both groups, but also for finding differences that can be related to educational achievements.

Depth interviewing strives to combine the goals of standardizing the interview (so that no variables of interviewer ability or rapport will creep in) and allowing the interviewer greater freedom to nudge the respondent into elaborating on the answers. Short-answer polls cannot permit this liberality. They seek to standardize absolutely and hold every interviewer to the prescribed words and actions, no more and no less. Imposing requirements of longer answers, the depth interview technique instructs workers to use a wide variety of probes and cues as the occasion may warrant.

In self-administered questionnaires, adding blank lines or follow-on questions is generally ineffective. Respondents write as much as they want, usually too little, and most deposit the letter in the wastebasket. The low rate of return on mail questionnaires, usually well below 25 percent, is always lower for long and complicated schedules than it is for nice, short, short-answer forms. In telephone polls, long answers often work well, providing there are not too many questions; but there may be a self-selection bias in the kind of people who give long answers on the telephone.

Face-to-face interviewing is always to be preferred when there is enough money available. All depth interviews are more expensive than short-answer interviews by a substantial factor, perhaps ten times as much or more. They take much longer to do (30 minutes per interview as compared with five minutes or less). Better trained interviewers and much more sophisticated coding and counting are required. Cost is one reason why smaller samples are used, but many practitioners claim that is only incidental. They argue that depth interviews are much more effective and provide more interesting and useful data.

In the polling fiasco of the 1948 presidential election, the short-answer pollsters were wrong and two major pioneers of long-answer techniques were right. They were Sam Lubell, political prognosticator, analyst, and columnist, and Leslie L. Biffle, once secretary of the Senate and later press secretary to President Truman. Both were one-man operations from beginning to end, and both used highly personal methods.

Biffle was assigned by Truman to evaluate public opinion concerning the strategies and chances for his reelection. A native of Arkansas, Biffle explained his grass-roots method:

> I never ask anyone how he is going to vote. I wait for people to tell me. And they tell me without my prodding them into political discussions, except by the casual and natural way of talking about things we have in common — the weather, business, how things are going down on the farm or what's happening down the road.[1]

What would people concerned about "informed consent by human subjects involved in research" have to say about Biffle's devious strategem. In 1948, he drove a beat-up chicken truck through areas of the country identified as critical to the outcome of the election. In subsequent years in which he did his unique polling, he dispensed with the live chickens but maintained his credibility as a listener:

> I always put on old clothes and drive a second-hand automobile with a license plate that doesn't tell them I'm from the District of Columbia. I don't intrude on people anywhere by announcing who I am and that I'd like to know what their politics are and how they feel about their congressman or senator or their local political setup. I stop along the road, for example, to check my motor, even though I know it's alright, so that I have an excuse to chat with someone. When I pass a farm I usually ask about the crop I see, and when I'm in a big city I get to talking with the people who work in the factories.

The success of his method in calling state and local, as well as national, elections made Biffle a professional pollster and political consultant to the Democratic National Committee and to the media until his death in 1966. He had an impressive record, calling not only presidential but also congressional seats and state governorships, a notorious graveyard for most pollsters, with remarkable consistency.

Biffle visited key areas, based on his expert evaluation of past voting behavior and a size-up of the issues. "I'm not going to tell you the places I've been," he told a reporter during the campaign season in 1958. "I have made two trips in recent weeks and I'm completing my third and final trip. You can say I've been to certain places in Maryland, West Virginia, Pennsylvania, Kentucky, Indiana, Ohio, Illinois, Iowa, Missouri and Minnesota." He found that the key issues of interest to the people were unemployment in large industrial cities, a revolt of the farmers, the plight of the small businessman, high prices, and the increasing concern about the stability of peace. He foresaw a Democratic tide, and proceeded to name the winners and losers.

President Truman, Biffle said, believed in his kind of polls and "listened with interest when I explained that I engaged people on subjects that interested them and they spontaneously come around to telling me how they were going to vote and why. . . . What I heard indicated victory for him."

> Several magazines and newspapers recently offered to send reporters along with me on my trips. A prominent national magazine wanted to send a special cameraman. Naturally I turned down these offers and suggestions because they would defeat the purpose of my trips. Can you picture my making a casual approach with reporters and cameramen around?

Samuel Lubell, political gadfly, journalist, and kibitzer (author of such books as *Future of American Politics* and *Revolt of the Moderates* and director of the Opinion Reporting Workshop at Columbia University until his retirement in 1972), did more for the technique of depth interview polling than any other person. His method had two major components: scientifically selecting wards and precincts to be visited and conducting only a handful of interviews in each ward or precinct, but what interviews — long and relaxed and deep.

The first component was based on a careful study of past election returns. Though he started in precomputer days, his method of analysis presaged the development of the data base systems that made tracking and targeting possible 20 years later and provided the model for designing computer programs for election night projections. He used the election returns to identify key "swing" precincts — for example, a farm district in Kansas that voted for the winning candidate 90 percent of the time over the last 50 years, or a black precinct in Chicago that had gone the same way as the national urban black vote in the last eight presidential elections, or a blue-collar district in Atlanta that had tended strongly to forecast the vote in all the industrial cities of the South.

"Election returns," wrote Lubell, "are an unusually sensitive locator of significant social currents. Virtually everything that happens to people affects their voting in one way or another. . . . How people vote provides both a time and geographical measurement series."[2] Voting figures, he added, provided a "disciplined framework for research and inquiry, a record the people themselves have made." We know that much voting has nothing to do with campaign slogans; yet by noting changing patterns, we can interpret underlying reasons for a shift over time.

"Any explanation of an election, if it is to be accurate, should correspond to what happened in such shifting communities." For example, election returns can locate exactly where the Bull Moose following of Teddy Roosevelt during the first two decades of the century went over to the New Deal in the 1930s, and where it did not. The contrasting areas can be studied "to reveal the different kinds of supporters that the Bull Moose movement drew, and to measure how much New Deal support came from the old Progressive following, and how much represented new forces breaking with the past."

Lubell discovered in his polls that voting "is almost the last of a person's cultural habits to change." Shifts always reflect other changes that already have registered in the community, such as new population elements, altered attitudes toward issues, or economic developments like industrialization or shifts in the type of farming.

The second component of the Lubell technique is the interviewing itself. Having selected a dozen or so precincts around the country, Lubell would visit each of them several times during a campaign. He would talk to people in their homes, at lunch counters, at bus stations — places where people are sitting down. His interview schedule was loosely sketched in his mind, but he would let the respondent take the initiative and talk freely about anything he had in mind. On return visits, Lubell would look up the same people, add occasional new ones, and visit them like old friends.

Like Studs Terkel, Carl Rogers, and Leslie Biffle, he cultivated the interview method known as "nondirective": The interrogator doesn't ask questions but as much as possible plays the passive role of a good listener. With nods and grunts, and with endless patience and good humor, the pollster "passes the time of day," taking a couple of notes unobtrusively or writing the notes later.

The theory of nondirective therapy was first formulated and practiced by the psychiatrist Carl Rogers in the 1930s. It was part of a revolt against Freudian psychotherapy. Rogers believed that Freud's "directive" approach tended to force the patient's symptoms into a preconceived diagnosis, concealing the real illness and often making psychotherapy unsuccessful. He refused to impose the intellectual baggage of the Freudians on his patients; instead, he scrupulously avoided suggesting any interpretations of symptoms. Rogers discovered that patients invariably diagnosed themselves, and that this process of self-discovery seemed to help patients deal with their symptoms more successfully than was his experience with other forms of therapy. He turned this discovery into a whole school of thought that still plays a substantial role in counseling and polling.

Lubell was an outstanding Rogerian therapist. If his method is judged by results, he was the most successful pollster of the postwar decades. But, obviously, his method was highly personal. Although it may be taught to others, not all people will have the talent to carry it off successfully; more important, few will give it the time and patience and the love of humanity that it requires.

In 1957, the Society of Newspaper Editors brought Lubell together with Elmo Roper and George Gallup on a public opinion panel. Lubell criticized "the pretension of exactness" contained in the short-answer poll methodology: "I do not find that you can rely on percentages with any mathematical precision," he declared. "I would still keep my fingers crossed." Replied Gallup: "One system is impressionistic and reportorial and operated by an extremely able man – a great reporter. I think our system is a scientific one. The proof is that some other person can operate it." Said Roper: "One system is an attempt to create a science. The other is an art run by an extremely able artist." Responding to questions regarding

Lubell's success in 1948, Roper said: "Polls were not designed to predict elections, but to show what the public is thinking."[3]

Time has proven Lubell right about his methods, and they are now considered to be scientific in their own right. His selection of key areas has become the main basis for computer projections of early returns; increasingly, the scientific sample polls have stratified their own sample designs in accordance with similar analyses; and the nondirective interview technique now has a respected place in the panoply of tools.

The long-answer approach has been incorporated into both depth interview and focus-group interview techniques. It has assumed an important place in both commercial and political public opinion analyses.

The industry has become more and more specialized, and the number of firms engaged in studies for private clients has increased geometrically. Depth and group interviews have proven very useful in going deeper into the public's less obvious feelings and attitudes. Some commercial firms do nothing but this type of testing and have built up great resources in skilled interviewers, with the patience and geniality of Sam Lubell, and facilities where such interviews can be conducted.

FOCUS-GROUP INTERVIEWS

Focus-group interviewing is the fastest growing technique in the last decade and involves group discussions under the guidance of a moderator. It is used to explore the attitudes, beliefs, and opinions that people hold about anything, the reasons why ideas fail or succeed.

In test marketing, "before and after" focus groups can provide a picture of advertising effectiveness that can point to the need for different marketing strategies. Analysis of such qualitative data creates a solid basis for quantitative research. For questionnaire development, it provides the appropriate language that the audience uses and understands to describe their ideas.

When speed is essential and large projectable quantitative sampling has to be ruled out, focus groups can often give more reliable results than hastily designed quantitative studies with small samples. There is an ancillary function: Bring the audience or users face to face with each other and with the clients, providing decision makers and creative people a more accurate assessment of the real world. Focus-group research does not preclude obtaining hard data from the respondents who are interviewed. Before or after the open discussion, they can fill out forms to elicit individual opinions, usage, and perceptions.

The technique originated in the 1950s as part of the movement known as group dynamics, a concept that found expression in public education, in psychotherapy, in every variety of counseling from marriage to work productivity. It appeared under names like encounter, reality therapy, T-groups, the Bethel movement, sensitivity training, brainstorming, creativity workshops, and psychodrama.[4]

Psychologist Ernst Dichter pioneered in group interview techniques in the period just after the war. A group of German expatriots rejected Freudian counseling methods as sterile. In the rise of Hitler, they saw people in groups as essentially different from people as individuals. This was the origin of group theory in the modern social sciences. Margaret Mead used it to collect anthropological field data, assembling a group of tribe elders and conducting a round table discussion.

As in an EST session, the personalities of the participants become self-charged power sources that generate their own momentum. The basic idea is that groups of people are capable of tapping hidden forces and revealing deep truths through the interactions of their members; that one-to-one therapist/patient relationships are unreal, removed from the stream of experience and overly dependent on a professional who is not under risk.

Groups, however, when successful, are a focusing lens, bringing together in one burning spot the energies of all participants. Such a critical mass can cause a chain reaction. The physical and mental resources of the moderator may guide the discussion but cannot and should not fully control it. It is possible that the group can penetrate the individual's defense mechanisms and liberate repressed feelings, making it possible to delve deeper and to allow participants to discover new things about themselves.

The relatively unstructured setting allows the surfacing of unanticipated, often highly relevant, feelings that can lead to new insights. The dynamics of a group of people who do not know one another but have much in common permit far greater candor, give support to the timid, and lead in directions that cannot be guessed in advance.[5]

The power of groups has long been recognized. The Jewish minyon (ten men) is necessary in order to worship effectively. The Hindu dharma, the release of sacred power, requires a public gathering. Many modern religious cults emphasize group rather than one-to-one relationships as necessary to achieve ecstasy.

Both nondirective counseling and group dynamics reduce the role of the interviewer/professional, but the latter goes further, giving virtual primacy to the magic of the group and its inner dynamism. Since the 1950s, groups have been applied in many original ways, some highly questionable: nude encounter, Esalen group sexuality workshops, marathon sessions (keeping the group together for days on end, in order, it is said, "to break down" defense mechanisms by fatigue). The process has been subverted by some into a kind of mortification ritual: corporations using it for self-examination by top management groups, like Chinese communist public confessionals; mental hospitals subjecting patients to "reality" sessions, which amount to conditioning them to submit to psychological domination. Remember Nurse Rachit in Ken Kesey's *One Flew over the Cuckoo's Nest*.

Any practice as fruitful and vigorous as this will inevitably become a form of pop psychology and will be criticized. Group phenomena have enjoyed a faddist expansion. Many of the uses have accomplished little beyond momentary sensationalism. However, the trendy period is about over, and we can now put things into perspective. Some uses of focus groups have endured and thrived, most notably as a method of studying public opinion.

One abiding problem of all opinion studies is that of "intensity," the relative strength and stability of an opinion. The nature of human interaction depends not so much on what opinions are given lip service but rather on how intensely different opinions are held. One person with high intensity views on an issue may count as ten in the process by which opinions form; his views will carry ten times the weight of another's low intensity opinion. Opinion is not static. It is a process of interaction among persons with varying degrees of commitment and influence. (Various project design solutions to this problem are treated in a later chapter.)

Statistical studies treat each response as essentially equal to every other response, without regard for the dynamic contexts in which opinions become effective. Short-answer polls are especially vulnerable to this weakness, and so are depth interviews, although to a slightly lesser degree.

The psychic cost of expressing an opinion in confidence and anonymity to an interviewer is thought to be much less than it would be among one's peers. In the real world, psychic cost — that is, the rewards and punishments inflicted in social bargaining (or the anticipation of them) — is an important, if not central, aspect of opinion holding. Therefore any process that tends to relieve the respondents from such effects will distort the result. Group interviews create a microcosm of the real world. Everyone involved is at risk, and there is a tendency for some kind of social/political bargaining to occur in the dialogue. Each participant's ego values are drawn into active commitment; alliances and coalitions form and contend. Psychic costs mimic the larger scale of the mass marketplace. As a result, an automatic measure of intensity emerges from the interaction: What opinions survive the give-and-take? How much consensus develops on what issues? And so on.

On the negative side, it is argued that focus-group interviews generally result in weaker yielding to stronger participants and in an overdependence on too few respondents, who may not really be representative of the desired population. It is argued that the weak role of the moderator invites a member of the group to fill the vacuum, thus turning the session into a personal ego trip, at the expense of the other participants and of the client who had hoped to learn new things about his or her product or advertising campaign.

In addition, it is not easy to induce people to come to a central meeting place and to sit and talk for two to three hours. Consequently, it is customary to pay them for their time, or at least to give them some small premium (such as a selection of the client's products, a coupon redeemable in merchandise, or a nominal honorarium). It is argued that this corrupts the process because it creates an obligation; the interviewees feel a subconscious desire to please, to say nice things about whatever or whomever they perceive to be their host.

Focus groups have been criticized because moderators may be ill-equipped in their knowledge and experience to correct for sessions that are unfocused or otherwise go astray. A famous Boston firm that runs political focus groups in New York State calls upon professors of public opinion at various universities in client districts, who in turn send their graduate students to earn a few extra dollars.

On the other hand, proof is in the pudding. There is no shortage of clients; and many experts feel that this technique is more useful to them than alternative methods. Such sessions give clients a quick qualitative dip into the marketplace. It is also relatively fast and inexpensive.

The focus group is a way to overcome the sense of isolation suffered by people who must address the vast, anonymous publics of mass media. Such individuals are prone to a sense of panic when they cannot reach out directly to that audience and be buoyed and stimulated by its response. People with power suffer from apprehension that the world surrounding them is becoming a hall of mirrors, that the exercise of power in itself tends to dull feedback; most people they deal with are dependent on them and are strongly influenced by the stronger personality's perceptions.

A focus group is a group of people, usually eight to ten, who meet for a couple of hours to discuss a product, an advertising campaign, or a political candidate. They are carefully screened and selected to be representative of various demographic groups. Sometimes, separate groups with differing demographic characteristics, each one more or less homogeneous, are employed as part of a single project. Thus one study may involve as many as six or eight separate sessions and groups. Sometimes it is desirable to put together groups with cross-sectional representation of certain demographic characteristics in order to get a cross fire of ideas and values in the same session. Sometimes both approaches are combined.

Obviously a great deal of scientific analysis goes into designing a focus-group project, recruiting its participants, and interpreting the results. Controls are introduced not by large random samples but by matching and comparing groups in order to make the effects of test variables apparent. Some statistical analysis of separate groups is possible; and the contents of responses can be subjected to extensive quantitative manipulation.

Here it is often more significant to match mentions of keywords or ideas to demographics of age, socioeconomic status, taste group, and so on. The heart of focus-group research, however, is not quantitative — it is qualitative. Its value derives from insight into the untutored natural reactions and thoughts of people. It is a mission of discovery in the "new world." Some examples follow:

• A wealthy and successful businessman is considering running for the Senate. Of course, he seeks information of all sorts before making the plunge, talking to political leaders, his business friends, his wife's professional association, his children. He also retains a political consulting firm that does a number of short-answer telephone polls and focus-group studies.

In both methods the firm tests the public's sentiments toward possible rival candidates, toward the issues, and toward the candidate himself. But in the focus groups they also test themes for promotional advertising, slogans, potential materials for media campaigns, actual TV commercials, display ads, and the details of the candidate's image. By means of focus-group interviews over time, the firm can fine-tune the campaign and can pretest materials before committing expensive and possibly ill-advised efforts.

• A selection of housewives are assembled to discuss hamburger and what products could be developed to make it more interesting. "I don't know where the idea for Hamburger Helper came from," said G. Burton Brown, director of marketing research for General Mills, "but our commitment to it came out of focus group research."[6]

• In Larchmont, New York, handy to both blue-collar Mamaroneck and upper-middle Scarsdale, a dozen men are seated in what looks like a nondescript living room, dominated by a wall-sized mirror. The men are "comfortably polyestered," all talk volubly, responding "to the questions of the one with the pipe and to each other's interruptions." All are over 35 and are clerical, sales, or civil service workers.[7]

In the next room, behind the one-way glass of the large mirror, sit a smaller group whose clothing would suggest about $30,000 more a year. "All lean forward, peering through the glass, listening intently." A television camera in the first room is recording the discussion for future analysis. "My wife was the one who made me use Grecian Formula." In the half-light of the second room, one of the observers shakes his head in disbelief; another replies with a knowing, self-satisfied smile.

• In a classroom on the Binghamton campus of the State University of New York, two graduate students conduct a discussion with ten people about local fast-food emporiums. The Binghamton area is a test market for several firms, including McDonald's and Pizza Hut, and a local advertising firm commissions such focus groups in order to test reactions to products that have not yet been nationally introduced. Chicken McNuggets, McRib Sandwiches, and some other Mcs were introduced in this way, as was the Pizza Hut Salad Bar.

This particular group was recruited by a screener (a telephone poll that sought to assemble a group with specific characteristics) and contains people, half of whom favor Burger King and half McDonalds in frequency of dining. All are between 18 and 39. Sex and other variables of income, education, and family size are represented randomly.

Explored (no back room here, only television cameras up front) were such issues as, Which occasions prompt a visit to a fast-food restaurant? Top of the mind advertising awareness — Which one is thought of first? How do customers feel about relative cleanliness and quality, low prices, new varieties of products? Hot and cold foods? Response to specific advertising? Commercials liked and disliked?

Among the findings: Customers usually do not predetermine which fast-food establishment they will patronize. Traveling distance and accessibility are important, but, being equal, special features (like new products, games, and coupons) are of greater importance. Children are less important as pathfinders than they used to be, and adult tastes must be given greater consideration. The quality of the product is less important than "a sense of comfort and attractiveness." Recommended was more premiums, such as "The drinks are on us!" and special bulk rates: "A bushel of Burgers!"[8]

• In New York's Plaza Hotel, 20 14-year-old girls are sipping Cokes around a table talking about smelling and rock music. A product called Heaven Scent had broken all sales records after its introduction. The right button had been pushed, but no one knew what button it was. The moderator leads the discussion from fragrance in general to the brand in question. The first thing to emerge is that Heaven Scent is easily identifiable on its wearer, that it has an image of innocence and goodness ("My mother likes it") combined with a touch of naughtiness ("The boys know you've got it on"). Next, they discovered that it reminded people of Johnson's Baby Powder. Great for a first perfume for 14-year-olds; deadly if you want to sell it to 16-year-olds.[9]

• Lee Abrams built an empire by compiling music play lists for radio stations. During the last 15 years, he made himself the best prognosticator of what kind of programming will win what kind of listeners, and has controlled the formats of hundreds of stations. Many of today's highly specialized formats were invented by him. But format alone is not enough; it is essential to read the tastes of different audiences daily and weekly, to pick the new record winners as they come pouring from the record companies, to sense a change in tastes or the moment when audiences unconsciously desire a change. Abrams did his early work by the seat of the pants; but as he became successful, he sought more consistently reliable methods.

Without much theoretical knowledge, he invented focus-group interviewing all over again by the logical evolution of his method. He was amazed to learn that the formal methodology already existed. Eventually, he expanded his operation to offer the service in every media market. He called the company Focus Research of Georgia, Inc. (a subsidiary of Burkhart/Abrams/Michaels/ and Douglas), "A 20/20 View of the Future! Conducted in YOUR Market by OUR Researchers." In the 1981 meetings of the National Association of Broadcasters, four workshops on Do-It-Yourself Focus Group research were jammed to the doors.[10]

• Attempting to get a barometer of audience reaction to the Carter-Reagan debate in 1980, the polling firm of Yankelovich, Skelly, and White picked a group of undecided New Yorkers to watch the debate together. Right afterward, the television set was turned off (before hearing any instant analysis by newscasters). The group completed a questionnaire and then held a one-hour colloquy, which indicated a slight improvement in regard for Reagan ("He seemed more relaxed and likeable").[11]

All over the country people are talking in groups about deodorants, douches, dipilatories. They are telling each other what they want from political candidates, newspapers, the movies. People who wouldn't think of discussing their most intimate thoughts in public are doing just that. Women are exchanging views on sanitary napkins and men on condoms in front of videotape recorders, with a sense that they are thereby helping to make a better world. Highly specialized groups such as cardiologists and other physicians are talking about health-care products. In early 1982, the New York Conference Center put together two focus groups of millionaires for a bank that wanted to develop some new financial products.

At the listening end of all these focus groups are the researchers of Procter & Gamble, J. Walter Thompson, Coca-Cola, Quaker Foods, and the Ford Motor Company, not to mention Cambridge Research Associates, the National Opinion Research Center, and every private political consulting firm.

Not that they still don't play the numbers. They continue to rely on the large-scale short-answer sample surveys, the Nielsen, Simmons, and TGI aggregate data reports, and opinion and market studies of every type. But as the cost of large-scale statistical studies escalates, the use of focus groups multiplies. A testing program can be kept within a budget of $1,500 (in 1982) per session, whereas a comprehensive short-answer study done by telephone (the cheapest way) will cost about $25,000.[12]

Apart from cost, they help to answer the creative person's questions: What do the numbers mean? What do people really say and feel? Can I know at the planning stage? At the takeoff instead of after the crash landing? And more important, they are exceedingly useful in tracking and targeting. They provide the interior vision of each demographic entity, giving depth and form to the abstractions, making each part of the segmented market place a full flesh-and-blood person.

COLLATION AND ANALYSIS

Long-answer responses are usually audio and video tape-recorded. In face-to-face situations, this fact has not proven an impediment to good interviews — quite the contrary. The presence of cassette recorders, cameras, and microphones no longer, in this day and age of home equipment, induces stage fright or reticence. The respondent, having been informed that a recording is being made, generally is flattered by the seriousness of the attention he or she is receiving. There is a sense of greater accountability for all participants, as though the world were watching, and a greater effort to express opinions frankly and clearly and to answer the sensitive questions.

These are not the reasons for recording the sessions, but they are now recognized as important bonuses. Much show is made of the fact that inconspicuous mikes and cameras adorn the focus-group studios on Manhattan's Madison Avenue. No attempt is made to conceal the presence of "technicians" behind the one-way mirrors.

The original and main purpose of the recording is to aid in collating and analyzing the interview results. A transcript of the proceedings must be typed; it becomes the basis for analysis. A 30-minute depth interview will produce four or five pages of text; and there are likely to be dozens or hundreds of such interviews.

It is usually better for the interviewer not to attempt verbatim note taking but to listen carefully and respond with probes and cues appropriately. Writing a few notes, to aid in concentration, doesn't hurt, but the audiotape will capture every word for later analysis.

A two-hour focus-group session will produce a 20- to 30-page text, which must be carefully processed and evaluated. In addition, the videotape itself provides an opportunity for the client to witness the expressions and diction of the session, and to show it, or clips from it, to others in later presentations of new marketing ideas.

What to do with the transcripts? Essentially they are subject to scientific content analysis. They are read and reread carefully by several of the researchers, marked up with soft pencils to separate such entities as ideas, concepts, keywords. The researchers discuss the categories they discover and eventually agree on those to be counted and compared. Having reached this point, they go back and mark up the transcripts again, this time looking for and identifying the same items that satisfy the agreed-upon categories. The different markups are compared in order to find and resolve borderline cases.

When this has been done, all the separate categories are listed, and items that fall in each are counted. Generally, the original design of the study was modeled on a set of hypotheses that determined the focus and direction of the sessions. These hypotheses, which established in advance, to the degree desirable and practical, what is sought and what is expected to be found, already lay down many of the categories. But the unique nature of long-answer techniques is that they suggest new and sometimes surprising hypotheses in the subsequent analysis. That is why the reading and rereading of the transcripts can contribute unanticipated finds, which will be worked into the analysis and report.

The final report summarizes the findings in a variety of ways: opinions, attitudes, values, preferences, intentions that relate to the subject in question, arrayed not only in terms of the associated demographic factors but also in terms of their relative intensities (first mentions, second mentions, frequency of mentions), their logical and structural relationships (associational context of different notions, their appearance together in clusters with varying degrees of regularity), and their intrinsic meanings.

Frequently, reports will pass over the population of respondents rather quickly, dwelling instead on the population of responses. The contribution of each respondent will consist of several dozen separable responses in certain orders and frequencies. These become the basic entities to be collated and interpreted, to which demographic complexes are assigned.

The reports identify main responses or themes (those with the highest counts in all categories), secondary responses or themes (those with substantial but lesser representation), and minor responses or themes (those with only isolated mentions). All are weighed for their logical and emotional connections with each other by relating them to the course of the discussion, the cues that prompted them, and the tendency for certain ideas to spontaneously sweep through the group, to strike a resounding chord and lead to a chorus of strong positive or negative reverberations. The raw transcript, of course, is appended to the document, with the breakdowns indicated and the tally sheets attached.

Collation of depth and focus-group interviews is not easy. It requires insight, intelligence, and inspiration. Experience helps to make up for any shortfalls in these areas.

NOTES

1. See *New York Times*, October 12, 1958, p. 3, for all the Biffle quotes and other information.

2. "Voting Records," Eagleton Foundation *Newsletter*, October 1958, p. 3.

3. *Editor and Publisher*, February 2, 1957, p. 58.

4. See Dorwin Cartwright and Alvin Zander, *Group Dynamics, Research and Theory* (New York: Harper & Row, 1953, 1968).

5. See Elaine Cooper Lonergan, *Group Intervention/How to Begin and Maintain Groups in Medical and Psychiatric Settings* (New York: Interscience, 1980).

6. Sandra Salmans, *New York Times*, April 5, 1982, p. D2.

7. Alan Levenstein, "What's Really Bugging You About That Cadillac?" *MORE*, April 1977, p. 33.

8. Study by Roy Harrison and Carolyn Stickley, April 1981.

9. Reported by Levenstein, "What's Really Bugging You?" p. 37.

10. *Broadcasting*, August 10, 1981, p. 66.

11. *Editor and Publisher*, December 27, 1980, p. 14.

12. Salmans, *New York Times*.

CHAPTER SIX
AUDIENCES AND MARKETS

Some of the methods of audience testing:

- Diaries kept by respondents keeping track of day-by-day and hour-by-hour activities of any sort — work patterns, compulsive habits like snacking between meals, nail-biting, smoking, recreational choices, prerecorded music listening on home players, radio listening, television watching, patterns of car use.
- Little black boxes attached to electric appliances to record their use, especially those on TV sets placed by the Nielsen Company to report rapidly on overnight ratings of program offerings by major networks, to provide longer term data for the TV sweep ratings, and to back up the diary method.
- Special studios where test audiences can view programs and commercials and register their responses by pushing buttons during the show, by completing questionnaires afterward, or by being debriefed by depth or focus-group interviews.
- Testing panels, groups of consumers or experts, who try a product and report by means of any combination of opinion measurement methods on their experiences. Taste tests by selected groups are an example. Having a preselected audience at home or in a studio, an audience with desired demographic characteristics, watch shows or commercials, political speeches, debates, and so on, and be measured similarly.
- Test-marketing in a pilot market. Telephone, mail, or person-to-person polls (either short- or long-answer) sample the population

in a special market where a product or a media message has been exposed. This includes taste tests by the general public, as conducted in a supermarket or shopping mall, combined with some form of debriefing instrument.

TIME-DIARY STUDIES

Time-diary studies have been in use since the 1930s, originated by the early media raters Crossley and Hooper. The method can probably be traced back to the turn of the century when Frederick Taylor used time-motion studies to improve worker productivity. Determining how people spend their time has been a subject of considerable interest to social researchers for more than a century.

At the start, time-use figures, including government data on the length of the workweek, were derived by asking people to estimate how many hours per week or month they spent in certain activities. As indicated by John P. Robinson, results from these studies provided "broad insight into how time is spent" but encountered "a host of reliability, measurability, and comparability problems."[1] For example, it is often difficult for respondents to know how to relate the categories in the questions to their actual uses of time. Then memory plays strange tricks. Because of such problems, time diaries took the place of time-use surveys based on unassisted respondent recall.

Time diaries are an important advance in the study of group behavior because "they attempt to record an accurate assessment of a whole day's activities, while still fresh in the mind of the respondents."[2] From studies of time diaries, Robinson drew some interesting conclusions about American life styles since 1965.

Increases in adult education and in magazine/newspaper reading lend support to the theory that postindustrial societies tend to become more "knowledge-intensive." From the increase in crafts, hobbies, religion, and recreation, Robinson infers that we are increasingly interested in self-expression. The use of more specialized and individually oriented contents in records and tapes and books and magazines points in the same direction. Increased reliance on television, travel, eating out, and high fidelity equipment points to the greater integration of technology with leisure time and consumption. Work and housework have been traded for the least demanding free-time activities — television watching, driving, and resting. The diaries suggest an increase in time spent sleeping.[3]

Diaries have been used in conjunction with participant observation, depth interviews, and "beepers" (respondents carry a small beeper and record what they are doing whenever the damn thing beeps). Another variation is the "tomorrow diary," which is kept for the day or week following an initial interview; the interviewer returns at the end of the diary period and asks additional questions based on the diary. Such methods attempt to overcome the unevenness of respondent entries and to circumvent "diary fatigue," thereby lending greater consistency to instrument quality.

Needless to say, the diary method is very expensive and difficult to administer. In its most widely used form, Arbitron derives both television and radio ratings in all U.S. markets — once a year in minor and up to four times a year in major markets, depending on what the economics can support.

LITTLE BLACK BOXES

In the mid-1930s, the C. E. Hooper Company dominated radio audience measurement. Its method was "coincidental telephone" interviews: "Would you mind telling me what station you are listening to right now?" The company's interviewers would call a randomly selected telephone number, ask if the radio was in use, and if so, what program was tuned in and who else was listening and their ages and sexes. Later, as out-of-home listening increased, as number of sets in use multiplied in every home, and as new technologies began to compete, this method became ineffective and was abandoned. Personal interviews and diaries began to be used, and by the close of World War II, the black box audimeter went into large-scale production and use.

Invented at the Massachusetts Institute of Technology in 1936, the audimeter was the means by which the A. C. Nielsen Company of Chicago rode the explosive expansion of television to become the leading rating agency. In 1964, Nielsen withdrew entirely from radio, using the audimeter, combined with diaries, as the basis for its TV audience studies. The black box started as a filmstrip that traveled one inch per hour, while a beam of light left a mark each time the set was turned on or off or the channel was changed.

Once a week the cartridge had to be replaced and mailed to Nielsen for decoding and analysis.

Today, the box is half the size of a small cigarbox. Its central component is a microchip that does the job with no moving parts and can be read at Nielsen headquarters through a telephone line by a computer.[4] Twice every 24 hours, the computer calls and interrogates every box in the 1,200 homes of the sample, all in about one hour's time. The information is analyzed by appropriate software and stored, ready for instantaneous retrieval.

Time series records are available from the beginning of the system, so that longitudinal analyses can be carried out for any time base and for every major market. The current system makes preliminary information available to clients (advertising firms, advertisers, television broadcasters and independent producers, other media) on an overnight basis. These data give average audience ratings (percentage of total potential audience), audience share (percentage of actual homes with sets turned on during any time part), station count, and circulation for each program's duration by each half hour. The national television audience estimates are made available daily to clients via Teletype and a stream of printed reports.

Of course, the boxes tell only when the set is on and to what channel it is tuned. It doesn't tell who is watching or who is paying attention to programs or commercials. As a comparative measure it has been extremely useful and influential. Nielsen attempts to answer these critical questions by means of matched samples drawn from 2,400 households. For every household equipped with a Storage Instantaneous Audimeter, there are two homes in the sample to provide audience composition data. During specified sweep periods, participating households keep diaries of family viewing by each quarter hour.

In addition, a recordimeter is put on each household's set, measuring cumulative set use. When the set is in use, the recordimeter emits a barely audible signal every 30 minutes as a reminder to keep up diary entries. It has been found that the presence of the instrument greatly increases the value of the diary record, like a mechanical Big Brother who gently chides the family to duty. The device is in place all year, but diaries are only kept 34 weeks per year. The rest of the time, the beeper is turned off.

Nielsen issues the National Audience Composition Reports based on the latter data, indicating program performance for the number of persons, by sex and age, who viewed the average minute. Nielsen also publishes for subscribers a Market Section Audiences Report that breaks down the audience in terms of household income, education and occupation of the head of household, number and age of children, and so on for each of the nation's TV markets.

All of the methods for rating media are presently facing the serious challenge of changing technologies and life styles. Television is not only becoming as personal and as portable as radio, but most homes now have as many TV sets as radios; every family member is off somewhere watching a different program. In addition, low-power independent stations, cable superstation networks, original cable programming, video games, videotex and teletex transmissions of newspapers and advertising, all-advertisement stations, discs and tapes, direct satellite-to-home transmissions of programs originating who knows where — all have eroded the old patterns and have made many of the rating systems obsolete.[5]

STUDIO TESTS

Poor Rhoda, going through the agonies of the damned trying to decide whether or not to go to bed with her estranged husband. A dozen people, holding push buttons in either hand, sit in the darkened room watching a TV monitor, occasionally pushing a green or red button as Rhoda agonizes.

This is the Viewer Session Room on the third floor of CBS's Manhattan building, where the research department screens programs for audience response. The 12 people in the room were pulled off the street by a person dressed like an airline attendant with the CBS logo prominently emblazoned on the pocket. After the participants were seated, a member of the research department appeared.

"We all like different things on television," he said, after a brief welcome and a joke about the weather. "We want you to tell us what you like as you watch a program." He instructed them to pick up the two buttons at each seat, holding green in the right and red in the left hand. "Press the green in your right hand if you like what you see; the red in your left when you are uninterested in what you see."[6]

CBS has been conducting audience research since the 1930s. A young psychologist and an eminent social scientist were asked to devise a method of audience testing. Frank Stanton, later to be president of the company, and Paul Lazarsfeld, then professor of sociology at the University of Chicago, devised the method that is still in use (and it is named after them).

The audience pushes the interested/disinterested buttons, and in a back room is a console with rolling graph paper and a stylus. The device yields a polygraph-like squiggly line on a moving coordinate grid, recording all the individual lines, the cumulative negative and cumulative positive lines, and the resultant sum line. The wavy line charts a program's impact moment by moment on the audience.

Data from past tests are used to correlate test results with actual Nielsen/Arbitron ratings of program success so that the results of a specific test can be used to predict performance of the vehicle on the air. Network producers use the data for testing program concepts and for checking their hunches about laugh lines and other elements of a program; executives use the data for testing pilots and making decisions on whether to authorize further production and/or airing; account executives use the data to sell commercial time in advance on untried programs.

At times on-the-air shows are examined when the network wants more data about its audience. Rhoda was clearly in trouble. During the first weeks of the season its Neilsen share lingered about ten points below its average performance the previous season. CBS had made it the linchpin of its Monday night schedule − 8 P.M., the beginning of prime time, a time slot intended to lock in the viewers for the rest of the evening.

Were Rhoda's marital problems turning off the audience? MTM Productions had decided after an agonizing debate to begin Rhoda's third season with a separation from her husband, Joe. "Rhoda is an underdog battling her way through life armed with wit and tenacity," an MTM exec said. "In marriage, she was becoming a wholesome, upbeat, totally-integrated lady." Making her single gave more story opportunities, but it also forced her heavily female audience to confront the reality of failed marriage and divorce. And the ratings tumbled.

In the Viewer Session Room, the lights were turned on and questionnaires distributed. What did you think of the show in general? How would you describe Rhoda? Joe? How would you compare this show with, say, "All in the Family"?

The forms were collected and a group interview commenced. One woman said it reminded her of her daughter's problems and was heartbroken that two nice, intelligent people like Rhoda and Joe couldn't work it out. Another said that characters on the show were taking the separation too lightly. "I don't like to see divorce flaunted." After about one hour, the woman in charge thanked everyone and told them to keep the CBS ballpoint pens used to fill out the forms.

The next day, the whole episode was repeated with 12 new recruits. Grant Tinker, then head of the MTM, commented: "Television executives are in a nervous business and audience research probably helps them make up their mind, but suppliers have to go with their own creative instincts."[7] From the network's point of view: "Our product is people looking at programs and commercials," and the job of research is to determine what people want to look at.

Arnold Becker was the director of CBS research. He started out in 1954 at ABC in similar work. In 1976, he directed a staff of 50 people at CBS, twice as large as the in-house staffs at the other networks. The business of programming all the day parts of a network is the heart of success or failure. If there is a better way than the hunches and tastes of advertisers and executives to select programs, nothing will be stinted in using it.

For the 22 hours of weekly prime time to be filled, each of the three networks originates five to ten new series each season. These are selected from more than 2,000 story ideas, 125 scripts commissioned, and about 40 pilots actually produced. A half-hour pilot costs about half-a-million dollars, and three-fourths of them are scrapped. Putting a show on the schedule involves millions of dollars in production costs. Now that the "season concept" has disappeared, and new competitive vehicles are introduced and withdrawn at any point in the year, the intensity of audience research has increased. As Shister says, "Television remains a showman's medium but, more and more, the objective facts proffered by the research departments are influencing what gets aired."[8]

Long before a pilot shows up in the Viewer Session Room, professional polling organizations have thoroughly tested the probable appeal of a variety of concepts — situations, characters, settings, plots — using both focus-group and depth interview techniques. Those elements that test well are developed into trial scripts.

The bulk of the research department's work used to take place during the first three months of the year, after commissioned pilots had been completed and before the networks must decide in April on the fall lineups. That is no longer true. The Freddy Silverman effect has destroyed that neat arrangement. Now counterprogramming and audience flow control are permanent facts of life every week and month; and research departments now are at it without respite throughout the year. Becker's staff writes a four- to ten-page report on each pilot, predicting that a show will "against average competition" do average, above average, or below average. "We're right about 85% of the time," he claims.

ABC and NBC test their pilots with a Los Angeles-based service, Audience Studies, Inc. (ASI), which has been in business since 1965, originating as a division of Columbia Screen Gems to test motion pictures. ASI developed for this purpose a dial-operated indicator, rather than buttons. On the dial are calibrations marked from "very, very dull" to "very, very good." While watching a movie or TV show, the participant keeps adjusting the dial to whatever point expresses her or his response. This is considered superior to the Stanton-Lazarsfeld system, because it requires continuous reporting by the audience and because it provides a measure of more or less pleasure for every member of the test audience at every point in the show.

ASI puts emphasis on structuring the audience by screening and recruiting in advance on the basis of predetermined demographic data. CBS does its demographic analysis after the fact, exercising rough control in picking the public off the street (a straw poll?), but then rigorously using the data on the questionnaires to correlate responses in terms of such variables as age, sex, and socio-economic status.

ASI uses audiences of about 400 ("larger audiences react more spontaneously") at its Sunset Boulevard theater called Preview House. Like CBS, however, many previews are conducted around the country in order to tap regional and national preferences. ASI likes to warm up the audience and train them in using the dials by starting with a Mister Magoo cartoon. This is really a control test, to make sure the audience is reacting "to visual stimuli" within average parameters. The audience should be neither too hot nor too cold or it may make subsequent responses to the pilot statistically unreliable. ASI claims to be able to predict a show's Nielsen shares to about .9 percentage point.

In the late 1970s, NBC, trying to get out of the basement, began testing pilots on cable systems in ten major markets. "We contact [a sample of] the audience, tell them about the pilot and then call them back for their response after airing. That way, we select the sample. They don't select us."[9] This is considered more accurate because the viewing situation is realistic, avoiding any contagion effects of co-presence in a theater or studio audience.

"We're better as a negative than a positive indicator." It's easier to pick out the clinkers than the superstars. Often a pilot will test well because of a strong story line, but there is no guarantee "that subsequent scripts will be as good or that the author of the original will be available for the ongoing series." There are always scheduling factors, causing a good show to die in a certain time slot against impossible competition.

There is something of a conservative bias in TV audience testing. Executives and researchers tend to lean positively toward things that are already succeeding in the real marketplace and tend to play it safe with new and original material. Becker admits that "All in the Family" probably would never have made it to the air if it had been up to his department: He had predicted a "less than average" performance. "The people who tested it didn't know they were allowed to like it. . . . To this day we have never got people in a test to say they like 'HeeHaw' even though it continues to be a ratings hit."

Research generally shows the importance of character in the success of a sitcom. "What counts most," ABC research director Marvin Mord says, "is the empathy that develops between the public and the character. The more the pilot sample likes the characters, to relate to them as recognizable types . . . and the more they care about their lives, the greater the chances that a series will catch on."[10]

In the last decade, audience studies have been moving into new areas of technology. Musicologist Thomas Turicchi used measurements of the electrical conductivity of the skin as an index of emotional responses to music. This is exactly the same principle that underlies one part of the polygraph (lie detector). Turicchi's mathematical scale was put to use by a San Francisco research group, ERA Research, Inc., in the mid-1970s. Termed GSR (gradiated skin response), the scale is used by the firm on a portion of respondents in a depth interview poll. About 10 percent of the total sample are invited to a banquet hall or theater, there to be wired to galvanometers and exposed to the televised material to be tested. The responses are rated on a 50-point scale.

Turicchi started his own company, Program Data Sales, Inc., and sold his service to record companies eager to pretest new record releases. He claimed a 91 percent accuracy in predicting which would make the top 40 on the charts.

For a time, he succeeded in applying the technique to testing TV news formats. During the hectic local news competition for audiences in the mid-1970s, when fast-paced "Eye Witness" reports, with lightweight ENG (electronic news-gathering equipment) remote teams ranging the city, were first coming into vogue, there was considerable interest in testing anchorpersons and news topics. The galvanic index was used to read audience scores for attention, reactivity to specific ingredients, and integrating them into a single score for a given format.[11]

The networks have shied away from this technique because they are unconvinced that it tells them what they want to know. Positive and negative reactions appear identical; and some engineers believe that variations in skin conductivity are really related to sweating, and not necessarily to emotional levels.[12]

An ingenious use of audience testing was developed to test hypotheses about body language and crime. A professor of communications isolated five body movement characteristics found to be "more typical of potential assault victims," hypothesizing that these unconscious signals were interpreted as indicating vulnerability to potential muggers – for example, walking "gesturally," moving just the limb, hand or foot, instead of "posturally," moving a large portion of the body in an integrated fashion.

The study was done by surreptitiously videotaping 60 persons walking in a high-crime area of New York City. The tapes were shown to 12 prisoners convicted of assault against unknown passersby. From the inmates' descriptions, a rating scale of vulnerability was devised, ranging from 1 for "a very easy mark" to 10 for "would avoid it." Other sets of prisoners then rated the videotaped persons in terms of muggability. By careful examination of the differences in characteristic body movements between muggable and unmuggable persons, the five typical movements were isolated.[13]

TEST PANELS

Test panels need not detain us long. Like audience testing, this technique submits materials to a sample audience to be rated by them in some fashion. However, this variation appoints a special audience to be impaneled on a continuing basis for various comparison tests to be done at their homes.

Arbitron, for example, recruits small groups of people representing certain demographic categories to self-administer questionnaires on products and advertising. By agreeing to join the consumer panels, the respondents can expect to get questionnaires in the mail several times each month, on a variety of subjects. If they are prompt and conscientious, they receive small gifts and premiums; and they have the satisfaction of sitting in judgment on attempts to market new commodities.

Sometimes a panel may be composed of experts with special credentials or people with special occupations and professions. A manufacturer of drawing pens commissioned a test of a new line. A group of architects and engineers, users of such products, were sent a free set of pens and questionnaires to be completed after using them for a while. The return ratio of the users' evaluations was high, because of a sense of obligation created by the gift and also because professionals have a sense of obligation toward the quality of tools of the craft.

Such a technique can have many applications. During the 1980 primary campaign between President Carter and Ted Kennedy, pollster Pat Caddell wired up more than 100 volunteers across the country to read about and watch the campaign events, ads, commercials, speeches, and news programs and to call in their reactions immediately to a central recording device whenever they witnessed something that they thought worthy to report. He used the same method for comparing the effectiveness of Carter's and Reagan's acceptance speeches at the nominating conventions. Not satisfied with this, he also used himself as a test audience of one, and was seen circulating in the crowds at events where Carter's rivals were greeting the public.

The Public Broadcasting System introduced the concept of "reaction line programs," inserting announcements before and after certain programs and asking viewers to call a number and record their reactions. A secretary audits the phone tape regularly and counts the positive and negative comments, extracting any remarks of interest for the station managers to share.

This yields, at very moderate expense, a method of comparing audience response to different kinds of programs. True, self-selection makes it a form of straw poll, but the absolute numbers are less significant than the relative numbers. And the data are useful in programming the stations. PBS was forced to this expedient because it is not a client of commercial rating services and is not included in the market rating instruments.

CBS-TV, in 1981, used the same technique to test a new vehicle for young audiences. Developed by the Children's Television Workshop ("Sesame Street" on PBS), the pilot, called "Sign On," was the first new concept in many years aimed at kids. This involved a format that aimed "to guide children through the puzzling and often turbulent years of adolescence," to be "a grownup show for kids," using comedy, music, documentaries, interviews, health, news, and consumer information.

Before committing itself beyond the pilot, CBS wanted a test run. This was accomplished by announcing the time and day and inviting parents and children to watch and call in their opinions. In addition, the Parent-Teachers Association and Action for Children's Television, two active pressure groups in this field, were recruited to organize their members to alert children and parents and get them to phone in responses.

Whether the "taste test" is a promotional gimmick or a real means of research is questionable. In the case of Budweiser Beer and Pepsi Cola, the use of roving test teams at county fairs, college campuses, and shopping malls, and the commercials based on the results, probably belong in the former class. Negative advertising and the trend to openly identify competing brands in making invidious comparisons reflect a more cutthroat struggle for market share than has been acceptable in the past. It has something to do with our more open and cynical folkways, and less with the collection of scientific data.

Heublein winemakers joined the mode in 1982 with a campaign to boost its Colony Classic Chablis against the market leader Almaden

Mountain Chablis. "Take the Colony Taste Test" the TV spot said, offering an official wine-tasting party kit for $6.99. Tough advertising was not new to this national market. Gallo has its campaign featuring well-known wine experts taste testing a variety of leading wines and confiding to the public their professional judgment as to the best. Taylor has been reenacting award ceremonies in which its product wins 11 gold and silver medals. Sales themselves have been the taste test as the American public during the last decade went from 85 percent sweet to 85 percent dry wine preferences.[14]

TEST MARKETING

Test marketing differs from audience testing in that it studies human behavior by using the natural processes of the marketplace. It applies techniques in a real market, where actual market conditions prevail and where the spontaneous behaviors of people acting alone, buying and selling, reading and watching, coming and going provide indices for the evaluation of public motivations and opinions and for measuring the relative influence of the various advertising media.

It offers a powerful set of tools for market segmentation, that is, for breaking down the audience into segments so that promotional efforts can be targeted where they will be most effective. In some of its more ingenious applications, test marketing approaches the rigor of laboratory methodology, turning the real-world marketplace into a giant lab.

The most common technique is to locate certain communities that are microcosms of the national marketplace and to introduce new products there with the full treatment. Survey and motivational research, as discussed above, are used in conjunction with test marketing to enrich the yield of information. Product concepts, packaging, scents and colors, advertising mixes and strategies can be sharpened in the natural habitat. Political campaign materials and candidacies can be given an out-of-town tryout, so to speak.

In his 1982 Senate reelection campaign, Ted Kennedy commissioned Pat Caddell to do a series of studies in New Hampshire that have to be considered test marketing. Not lacking campaign funds and considered a shoe-in in his own state, Kennedy was urged by his staff to use the opportunity of the campaign to evaluate his ability to overcome "the character issue" in 1984. The ads were designed to overflow into New Hampshire, rather than to convince Massachusetts voters.

Three different, intensely personal ads, each five minutes long, portrayed Kennedy as a compassionate man who has suffered much. They showed him with his son who lost a leg to cancer and with the families of his slain brothers. "He's not a plaster saint," one ad noted. Caddell's interviews showed that the ads were having a significant impact in New Hampshire, where both Republicans and Democrats reported themselves as more positive in their regard for Kennedy. The staff used the study in an effort to keep him in the run for 1984, in vain, alas.[15]

Couponing is another popular method of test marketing. Cents-off discount coupons are circulated in print media to induce people to try new products or to remember old favorites. Coupons test the comparative drawing power of the media in which they appear. The response of the public, that is, the number of coupons redeemed, provides quantitative measures of media audiences. These data permit targeting special appeals and special products by allocating the promotional dollar strategically among competing print media and among specific newspapers and magazines.

For example, Information Research, Inc., of Chicago uses newspaper coupons and cable technology to reach targeted TV households for different kinds of market research. By means of an addressable converter, a device that inserts commercials only on the 2,500 home sets of specially selected samples, the firm is able to introduce control groups into marketing tests, thus isolating variables. This makes it possible to see the effects of independent variables such as timing and nature of the appeal.

At the same time, the sample households subscribe to the local newspaper. The cable TV ads are backed up with targeted newspaper ads, containing coupons for the same products, delivered only to the same households (that is, special inserts go into these 2,500 papers that are not in those received by other subscribers).

Grocers in the vicinity redeem the coupons in the usual way, returning them to the research firm, where they are collated and analyzed. Cable's "closed environment" makes it easier to keep track of the test TV ads and "to assess changes in product movement." Various segments of the 2,500 households can be compared with each other and with nonsample households.[16] This is an elaborate and expensive sytem, but it makes feasible a truly scientific, almost a laboratory methodology.[17]

The Nielsen Company makes more income in this area of consumer studies than in its TV ratings business. You might say that coupons are its cents-off bread and butter. This increase in couponing, said Nielsen's director of market research, "provides dramatic evidence of the American consumer's love affair with refunds and rebates."[18]

A related technique is to use different return box numbers or different telephone numbers in different ads or commercials. Thus the responses to each box or telephone number can be readily tallied to give a measure of the drawing power and the audience attention to the particular medium, or issue, in which the number was used.

Some market analysts hold that the combination of advertising and couponing is a form of synergism, boosting newspaper readership (studies by Larry Starch Inc. show that ads containing coupons were remembered twice as often as ads without coupons), as well as increasing sales at the grocery, and making possible the sensitive and continuing feedback that marketing experts use to discover and serve their markets.

Becoming an unavoidable part of the American way of life, coupons have been used as a method of political polling. Early in 1982, the *New York Post* ran a pro-Koch couponing campaign to convince the mayor to enter the primary for the Democratic gubernatorial nomination. Following his *Playboy* interview remarks about upstate living the *Syracuse Herald-American* ran "Dump Koch" coupons, urging clippers to send them in and get as a premium a chance at derailing the Koch campaign for governor.

In the same manner, special promotions carried by nonprint media can be used, not only to promote the products involved, but to rate the drawing power and audience receptivity to the stations, time parts, and programs on which the advertising appears. This kind of test marketing permits, as a main or as a subsidiary goal, evaluation of audience attention, intensity, loyalties, tastes, and interests, not unlike the analyses made possible by previously discussed techniques.

Thus test marketing has dual purposes: first, to develop and promote products, and second, to develop and test promotional strategies — by testing the means of communication with general and segmented publics.

Market segmentation means discovering the most likely customers for a product or service and the most effective means of communicating with that public. As we have seen, mass media have not homogenized the American public. Quite the contrary, there has been a complex process of differentiation going on. This process has broken down or softened the traditional distinctions of the publics by socioeconomic class, by ethnic background, by region, and so on, and increasingly replaced them with distinctions based on cultural taste preferences and on differentiated media attention.

Practitioners of politics and public policy have learned the same lessons and followed the example of the business sector. The same consultants and analysts who work for commercial clients put their capabilities to work for political clients as well. All publicists, promoters, politicians, and pollsters have some sort of audience in mind when they plan and execute a strategy of persuasion or analysis. The model may be researched and formal, or it may be based on casual observations. The general public is thought of in terms of the separate publics that compose it. Persuasion, analysis, and marketing are matched to each segment in terms of its common interests and by means of the media to which it attends as well as to the general public through the most universal media.[19]

CANVASS OR CENSUS

Counting the whole population of anything, from artifacts to attitudes, constitutes the technique of census, or canvassing (covering the whole thing). The word "census," Latin from the root "to enroll, tax, assess," is defined in the dictionary as the act of counting the people and evaluating their property for tax purposes; hence, any official count of total populations. This is not strictly scientific, although systematic methodology is needed to ensure a total count, to design the kinds of indicators to be included in the count, and to evaluate the results.

The official U.S. Census every ten years, with special counts in between, tries to be a true universal count and relies heavily on scientific demographic analysis both in designing and in deriving useful data collections. Government uses all kinds of other census counts in carrying out its responsibilities, including all the economic data collected by canvasses, setting agricultural crop quotas under price support programs, or reports of "leading indicators" — business starts and failures, trends in the money supply, and so on.

As a methodology, a total canvass may be deemed useful in studying opinions and motivations of populations of moderate size where the mechanics of a total count are not prohibitive and where scientific sampling would be useless because of the small numbers involved. Hypotheses about opinions/motivations of small groups can be best resolved by interviewing all members of the population. Any of the techniques reviewed above — short- or long-answer, open or closed questions, depth or group interviews, audience testing, and test marketing — can be used in any combination.

For example, a hypothesis about the educational views of parents having children in kindergarten: In a small or medium-size school district, it is practical to canvass all of them; several dozen or even several hundred parents may be interviewed. Of course, one might determine to sample them instead. Pick 25 by some rough or controlled random method. That would remain a straw poll, and no quantitative projections could be made from it.

Perhaps all that is needed is some rough estimates without careful measurement. In that case, any sample will do. But in populations too small to be reliably sampled, only a census will provide authoritative data. If the teacher wants to poll parents on a trip to the zoo, a canvass of the whole population, and a lopsided result, may give her the necessary authority.

In the chapter on sampling, we will further examine the issues involved in deciding between sample and census surveys. Many of the modern data banks used for tracking and targeting are based on U.S. Census data. It has been proposed that the U.S. Census should abandon a universal count in favor of sample surveys. Population size not only makes scientific sampling practical but, some say, would make the count much more accurate, as well as much less costly.

We have attempted to summarize and describe all the methods used in opinion and motivation research, areas of applied social science methodology. Our emphasis has been on illustrating each technique in both traditional and innovative forms. The latter examples should point the way to the open frontier of new possibilities that beckons as invitingly today as ever in the past. The well-tried methods should not be neglected. They retain their vigor and usefulness, and there are always new opportunities to apply them in the continuing enterprise of discovery.

NOTES

1. John P. Robinson, "Toward a Post-Industrious Society," *Public Opinion*, August/September 1979, p. 46.

2. Ibid.

3. Ibid.

4. See A. C. Nielsen Company, *Everything You've Always Wanted to Know About TV Ratings* (Northbrook, Ill., 1976).

5. See Elizabeth J. Heighton and Don R. Cunningham, *Advertising in the Broadcast Media* (Belmont, Calif.: Wadsworth, 1976), pp. 171-202.

6. Neil Shister, "Polygraphs and Wires: TV Research Guys Mean Business," *MORE*, December 1976, p. 36.

7. Ibid., p. 37.

8. Ibid., p. 38.

9. William Rubens, NBC vice president for research; quoted in ibid., p. 39.

10. Marvin Mord; quoted in ibid., p. 40.

11. *Broadcasting*, November 17, 1975, p. 36.

12. See Richard Zoglin, "Program Testing — Support or Scapegoat?" *New York Times*, July 23, 1978, p. D25.

13. Betty Grayson reported her study in the *Journal of Communications*, Winter 1981; cited in *New York Times*, February 3, 1981, p. C4.

14. Philip H. Dougherty, "Advertising," *New York Times*, April 14, 1981, p. D12.

15. Martin Schram, *Washington Post*, November 8, 1982, p. A1.

16. *Editor and Publisher*, June 27, 1981, p. 15.

17. In 1981, manufacturers distributed a total of 102.4 billion coupons, according to Nielsen Clearing House estimates, up 13 percent from the previous year. Newspapers accounted for 78.5 percent of the total; the redemption rate rose slightly to 5 percent. *New York Times*, February 19, 1982, p. D10. The rate of household participation (those who clip and use some coupons during the year) has been climbing rapidly, from 27 percent in 1977 to 45 percent in 1980.

18. Richard H. Aycrigg, *New York Times*, October 16, 1980, p. D7. Studies show that the medium carrying the coupon affects both its rate of redemption and the length of time it takes to be redeemed: comic sections, 1.6 percent redemption rate; in regular newspaper ads, 2.9 percent; newspaper magazines, 2.1 percent; on-page in magazines, 2.5 percent; magazine pop-ups, 4.8 percent; and direct mail, 10.5 percent. The best redemption was for coupons included on or in boxes of the same product: 17.6 percent. As for time of redemption: newspapers, 48 percent in first four weeks, 20 percent in the second month, and 12 percent in the third. Freestanding inserts take longer; and direct mail takes longer still.

19. See Larry J. Rosenberg, *Marketing* (Englewood Cliffs, N.J.: Prentice-Hall, 1977), one of the best texts on the evolving segmentation of the American public.

CHAPTER SEVEN
INTERVIEWING

Talking to people is something we all do every day of our lives. Sometimes we do it well; sometimes not so well. Interviewing is talking to people, but it implies two different roles: interviewer and interviewee. In the spontaneous conversations of life, the roles of aggressor and victim fluctuate between the parties. In public opinion research, the interviewer is stuck with the aggressor role and must simultaneously pursue that function, while overcoming its inherent disabilities. Thus interviewing requires a high degree of art, skill, and experience. It can be learned and taught, but some always do it better than others.[1]

Short-answer surveys can be prescribed and controlled to the highest degree, standardizing the way questions are asked, including timing, expression, and wording. This is one of the leading advantages of the form. Workers are carefully briefed to avoid contaminating the answers by adding personal color or their own explanations in the course the interview.

But even here the idiosyncrasies of interviewers do affect the results. It would be desirable to have enough variety of interviewers to randomize this effect or to have the same person do all the interviewing, so as to consider interviewer loading as a constant. Usually, the route chosen is to write the questionnaire so clearly and with such adequate instructions to the interviewer that variations can be safely disregarded.

Automated telephone interviews with recorded or synthesized interviewers, and with intelligent built-in machine collation, are being used for some limited purposes. It is not considered a real substitute for live interviewers, although it reduces the costs of telephone polling almost as low as that of mail. For very short instruments with very short-answer questions, it provides a realistic capability. Do you own a hair dryer? What is the brand name? How many hours is it used a week? With the advent of automatic telephone answering devices in many homes, we face the alarming prospect of tape recorders interviewing each other.

Interviewing in person is generally a more satisfying experience than the heavy duty of repetitive telephone calls. In journalism, the use of the telephone threatens to replace shoe leather; editors are wary of this and see it as dangerous to the quality of news gathering. There is a consensus that news sources find it easier to evade answers and give reporters the runaround; reporters can miss the nuances that would be apparent in personal interviewing.

Face-to-face interviews are the best. People tend to relate to real people in their presence, to feel a normal obligation to the requirements of courtesy and hospitality. Thus the rate of refusals is usually below 25 percent; the interviews are generally of good quality; and, with well-trained interviewers and refinements in the instruments, questions structured to achieve special purposes are feasible. Visual materials (artwork, products, ad copy) and fairly long lists printed clearly on cards can be examined by respondents as they consider their responses.

But this method is costly, and because of the life styles of Americans in recent years, it has developed its own shortcomings. In the last 20 years, response rates of face-to-face interviews, which used to average 80 to 85 percent, have dropped, even with callbacks.

A committee convened by the American Statistical Association studied this problem in 1973 and concluded that the soaring number of not-at-homes was caused by the increase in working spouses; the trend toward urbanization, which led to more recreational and leisure activities out of the home; increased geographic mobility, which means that people are moving around more (nearly one-fifth of the U.S. population moves in the course of an average year); and the tendency of young people to leave the nest earlier and to maintain more unstable addresses.[2]

These problems, combined with the practical difficulties of hiring, training, and supervising many part-time interviewers and the very high costs, have led to quality compromises in the use of the method. "Populations of less scope and significance are often studied," Don Dillman points out. Instead of sampling school-teachers of an entire state, "those in one city are studied." Instead of carefully selecting a city whose characteristics correspond with the average profile of the state, "the handy university city is chosen," in which usually the education and income distributions are extremely atypical.

In other cases, the researcher may use university students, or even students in a single classroom, stretching the bounds of scientific creativity completely askew. Or the sample sizes can get so small as to make statistical projection dishonest; and the number of callbacks (very expensive, but very essential to the design of a scientific sample) can be reduced to save money, thereby nullifying the value of randomization.

To some extent, the switch to depth interviews, in which large numbers of respondents and careful sample designs are less emphasized, is partly a result of these problems and may represent a compromise in research purpose. Sometimes the hypothesis is molded by the availability of resources, rather than by the limits of imagination and intellect. Thus face-to-face interviewing as a preferred method ends up by limiting the value of the project in the first place. It seems likely, Dillman concludes, "that alternate data collection methods will experience increased use, regardless of their projected adequacy."[3]

MAIL AND TELEPHONE SURVEYS

Mail and telephone interviews, which used to be considered the stepchildren of survey research, have been coming into their own in the last decade. It might be said that telephone polls, which typically show response rates about 25 percent less than face-to-face interviews, have virtually taken over the field of survey research.

Use of the mail, the cheapest of all — in which the respondents are their own interviewers and is a method that typically yields returns about 50 percent less than face-to-face — has also become a workhorse. Much effort has been invested to overcome the limits of these methods, and considerable success has been claimed.

Of those to whom mailed questionnaires can be delivered, the best educated are far more likely to respond, tilting the bias seriously. Even completed schedules leave much to be desired: They are always incomplete and spotty; with open-ended items, answers are short and vague, and probes and cues are ignored.

Yet the cheaper methods do have advantages. The lower cost makes possible larger and more complex sample designs, expanding the theoretical horizons and facilitating the use of statistical tools. In personal interviewing, sample sizes are often based on time and money, rather than on what would be ideal for the project. This can be a severe limitation when it comes to generalizing about subsamples of the population. Adjusting the results or oversampling subcategories of special interest are solutions that introduce new margins of error. With face-to-face methods, it often is impossible to say in advance which subclasses will turn out to represent significant variables, so the project may come up short.

Enlarged samples and more sophisticated sampling designs are the best approaches; telephone and mail interviewing makes this possible with minimal costs. As the volume of survey research increases and as budget constraints tighten, telephone and mail methods receive attention as the practical alternatives.

Some of the improvements for mail surveys are advance notification by letter, telegram, or telephone that a questionnaire is being sent; special, personalized stationery; using air mail, special delivery, or registered letters to create a sense of importance; inclusion of stamped return envelopes; sending cash, checks, coupons, or premiums with the questionnaire; attractive layouts; careful composition of the cover letter; pleas for help rather than offers of reward; stress on social and scientific values to be gained; and use of repeated follow-ups.

In telephone surveys, the research potential has been overshadowed by the 1936 Literary Digest disaster, when Landon was forecast the winner over Roosevelt on the basis of very large samples drawn from telephone listings. It was presumed that a clear economic class bias was associated with having a telephone in 1936, when fewer than 35 percent of Americans had phones. Today that association is almost completely nullified. All social welfare agencies recognize telephones as necessities of life and include them in recipients' subsidized budgets. So even the neediest have telephones.

The 1970 census showed 23 states in which at least 95 percent of households had telephones. The average for the nation was 94 percent. For many groups (architects and ministers, for example), telephone coverage is virtually 100 percent.

However, for the many poor and young who do not receive aid, the phone may be in the hall, next door, or on the sidewalk, a fact that perpetuates a more limited sampling problem. This can be dealt with by, for example, asking for the youngest adult male in the house and adjusting the sample later to represent the correct proportion of this group in the total sample. Telephone directories also have an opposite bias; the absence of unlisted phones, usually in high-status homes. But this presents no special problems because the telephone numbers are generated randomly from lists of all possible numbers in use in each exchange area.

Telephone interviewing has been further facilitated by the technical improvements of generating random numbers and dialing them by computer. Long distance rates have come down dramatically over the years, so that it is an equally simple matter to call around the corner or from coast to coast. Voice quality is excellent regardless of distance, and a taped record can be made readily if that is desirable. It may be done routinely as a means of quality-checking interviews, and may be an essential means of getting long-answer responses. In general, the courts have found it legal to tape with knowledge and permission only at the calling end, although that is still an area of legal development.

The 1936 taint limited systematic study of the uses of telephone polls, while not limiting use itself. Telephones have been used to complement other methods: prodding the return of mailed materials, arranging personal interviews, reinterviewing people in person (producing response rates from 84 to 100 percent), and so on. The pioneers in this area were once again the market researchers, whose cold-eyed concern for the bottom line led them to depend on telephones as their principal interview device.

By the 1960s, dozens of specialized "boiler room" operations were selling their services to the pollsters, advertising agencies, and advertisers. A typical boiler room is in a rundown office building, furnished with eight or ten cubbies, each with a chair and telephone, or with a large table with eight or ten chairs and phones. It is usually dark and dingy, smelling of spilled coffee, cigarettes, and spoiled lettuce. The supervisor oversees the place, dealing with problems and keeping the interviewers busy and their random number assignments in order.

The private pollsters and market researchers have acquired much expertise and experience, which is proprietary and consti- tutes their stock in trade. The boiler room operators are not dum- mies. They too become adept practitioners of their arts. The spread of these specialized facilities was predictable. Because they contract to do the actual phone interviews for many research organizations, they can afford to maintain permanent facilities with full-time employees. The owners and operators have pretty good ideas about the design of telephone polls, how respondents should be approached to maximize responses, how long they can be held on the line, how best to phrase questions, and how to train and manage interviewers.

It is clear that mail and telephone communications are different from personal interviews. Each system has a grammar and a code of its own. Interview forms and techniques cannot be blithely trans- ferred from one to another. The proliferation of commercial solici- tations on the telephone has tended to stimulate more guarded and defensive telephone behavior. This will doubtless have a negative impact on future response rates and will further complicate the lives of opinion pollsters.

THEORY OF SOCIAL EXCHANGE

The approach to interviewing in different contexts must be based upon a theory of social exchange. Broader than economic exchange, in which money serves as the common denominator of values, social exchange involves obligations incurred among people to act toward one another so as to satisfy each other's expectations in relevant areas of a defined relationship.

There are three things that must be done to maximize survey response: Minimize the costs, maximize the rewards of responding, and establish trust that either the rewards will be forthcoming or a general sense of debt exists. These calculations need not be based on material or immediate transactions. They appear to be most effective when, rather, they involve intangible psychic values.[4]

One of the most effective psychic rewards is to explain to respon- dents the use that will be made of the information they are asked to provide; to tell them that their input can make a real contribution to public policy or a marketing decision. Treating the interview as an opportunity for respondents to support their own values in a larger social discourse tends to induce cooperation. This approach makes cooperation itself an indication of the salience of the issue (that is, the degree to which the issue is part of a conscious dialogue in the society), so that the refusal to cooperate can itself be incorporated into the design as a social indicator.

Of course tangible rewards are also used. However insignificant they might be (Arbitron offered "glow in the dark stickers" in one of its mail marketing polls), and whether enclosed with a questionnaire or promised by return mail, a sense of obligation and a desire to be forthcoming are established for many people.

Initial impressions are often determinative. A questionnaire that looks formidable may be rejected out of hand. Yet the same respondent, once involved, may disregard the time and energy invested in the task. Indicating that a telephone interview will "only take a moment of your time" may have the same salubrious effect. The delicate balance between getting the necessary data and keeping the form clear and concise, with lots of space between rows of intimidating print, with short and nonambiguous questions, must be sought at all times.

Dealing with possible embarrassment and anxiety may, after all, be more important than accuracy. It is the niceties of manners, of the polite exaggerations of normal usage, that are effective. In normal relationships, people are accustomed to indirect and softened approaches, especially from strangers. Too much conscientiousness in preparing them for the interview may be read, not as honesty, but as a hostile and aggressive display. The result will be disastrous to the interview. This is one of the unanticipated counterindications resulting from the rules of "informed consent in advance" propounded by the government in the 1970s for the protection of the rights of human subjects in research.

All of the softened verbal formulations are appropriate: Would you do me a favor? Would you be so kind? Could you see your way to take a few minutes to help? Such circumlocutions are valuable social facilitators, although a balance must be struck. Overdoing it becomes facetiousness and mockery.

The element of trust is probably the most important. Token financial incentives gain their value as symbols of trust, as expressions of good faith. A good interviewer approaches every telephone call as though one were planning, after the formalities, to ask to marry a daughter. The presence of a supervisor in a boiler room helps to spot problem calls when the interviewer feels out of sorts and is getting a lot of refusals. Such problems can undermine the sampling design; and polling organizations, which need to know who and how many incomplete calls were encountered, will change contractors if the rate is consistently high.

These principles must be implemented somewhat differently in mail and telephone environments. Contact by phone is concentrated in a few short minutes, the respondent usually receiving little forewarning. The mail instrument must avoid immediate destruction, but then can do its work gradually and at greater length. In the former, it is important to avoid surprise, which will bring an immediately negative reaction; in the latter, surprise is effective in holding attention long enough to get any hearing at all.

The consistently higher response rate of the telephone depends on the tendency in a direct communication for people to linger out of curiosity and politeness: "OK, it's your dime." Thus, if the interviewer can avoid offering any provocation or excuse for a negative response, he or she can depend on a continuation of the conversation. In a letter, the opposite is true: If the missive fails to get to the point immediately, it loses the opportunity forever.

Nondirective interview techniques can rarely be practiced except in face-to-face situations. Long pauses on the telephone are usually interpreted as signaling the end of the conversation. If the respondent doesn't spontaneously rush to fill in the spaces, the caller must do so or lose the rest of the interview.

How does one decide when to use face-to-face, telephone, or mail interviews? There are advantages and disadvantages to all three. In some cases, the resources available dictate the method.

For example, to survey all trial lawyers in the United States, one would draw a random sample from a legal directory and would need to interview subjects scattered all over the country. To get decent numbers at least 1,200 names are necessary. Face-to-face is out of the question; that would cost a fortune.

Telephone interviews would be nice, but that would require six to ten interviewers working over a period of three to six weeks. With callbacks and overhead, $20,000 would not be too much to spend. If the funds were in hand, telephone interviews might be the preferred method. Given well-trained workers, one could expect a handsome enough response rate (say, 85 percent, about 1,000 good interviews) to yield acceptable numbers, without skewing the sample seriously by a possible hidden bias separating the refusniks from the others. One could safely operate on the assumption that failure to cooperate was associated randomly with other parameters.

If you don't have $20,000, then use the mails. One might conduct a survey of the same audience with two people, the principal investigator and a secretary. You might want to increase the sample size, allowing for a greater refusal rate. The difference in costs for large increments in sample size is very moderate. The sample might be doubled for only a 5 percent increase in costs.[5] Most of that additional cost would be in processing time, not in mailing and secretarial. Of course, the large number of nonreturns would sharpen the danger of a self-selection bias, and one would have to be prepared for that possibility.

With overhead (salaries, facilities, heat and light) and direct costs (postage, office supplies), the mail survey could be pulled off for under $3,000, most of which would be salaries for the two people prorated to the proportion of the time spent on the project. If both are collecting their salaries whether or not they do the survey, then the overhead costs can be discounted, and the direct costs would be quite moderate.

Telephone surveys can be much faster. Simply by increasing the number of workers and telephones, one can do the whole job, if there is a reason for doing so, in a week or less. There is not much that can be done to speed up a mail poll. Both respondents and the post office move in mysterious ways their wonders to perform. With follow-ups, one cannot hope to get back an optimum number of responses in less than six weeks. With processing time, three months would be a fair interval from start to completion under the most favorable conditions.

Decisions on survey type involve, in Dillman's words, "finding the most desirable . . . or least objectionable balance among sampling methods, survey costs, allowable complexity of questions, and a host of other factors."[6]

The rule for good sampling is "every member of the defined population has an equal opportunity of being included." When one looks at the response rates of any survey type, one has to ask whether the nonresponders represent a systematic bias in terms of the hypothesis being tested. For example, if trial lawyers were being asked about their work loads, among other things, and if only the ones that were not busy responded (by mail or telephone), it wouldn't matter what were the total number of good interviews, or how well the sample was designed. The survey would be worthless. In such a case, a design is necessary that goes after the very busy lawyers aggressively in order that they will be included in the sample in the same proportion as they exist in the total population. Possibly, a mail poll could be followed up with telephone calls or by face-to-face interviews.

Using an initial sample size that is larger than needed, presumably so that anticipated nonreturns will not prevent achieving desirable numbers for statistical reliability, can be a treacherous process. Such substitution procedures are not recommended, even if the names substituted are selected by the very same random design. Self-selection bias is introduced and is magnified by this procedure. "Substitution does not help; it is only equivalent to building up the size of the initial sample, leaving the bias of non-response undiminished."[7] The bias is only concealed and exaggerated by the numbers and is thus doubly dangerous. The correct solution would be the reduction of nonreturns, by all the means that imagination can invent, including spending more money and possibly changing the method of interviewing.

If a complete listing of the population is available, as in the case of trial lawyers, it is easy to draw a representative sample, but harder to ensure a representative cross-sectional response. If, as is the case with many categories of people, there is no enumeration of names within the categories relevant to the polling purpose, area samples must be drawn — that is, samples based on geographic data, such as census tracts or crisscross block listings for urban neighborhoods, or by telephone area codes and exchanges.

The problem of nonreturns continues for all sampling and interview methods, including face-to-face. It is the scale of the problem that might make it a serious concern. If the refusal rate does not go much over 25 percent, substitution will not present insurmountable problems. If the refusal rate goes over 50 percent, there is a real question of whether those included can really be regarded as a scientific random sample. With this in mind, one can determine to what extent special exertions are required to reach the reluctant, and to what extent interpretation of findings and the report of statistical confidence must be explicitly qualified.

Dillman believes that substitution of households in telephone surveys has more serious consequences than in face-to-face interviewing, because in telephone surveys the households are less likely to be similar. There is some assured homogeneity in the physical proximity of households; less in the leaps possible in telephone sampling.

"The nature of the implementation process" also works adversely in telephone sample substitution, he says. "Typically, a considerable number of calls are conducted in a very short period of time. Considerable bias may result when substitution is used freely" after making only few attempts to get a number and "if the calls are all made during specific hours." Households containing older people and women are most likely to be reached regardless of the time of the calls. Thus such households tend to be greatly overrepresented by substitution.[8]

In mail polls, a nonreturn is counted as a refusal; other interview methods can break down refusals into a variety of categories (not home, don't know, haven't made up mind, and so on), which can also be counted as significant returns. Questions designed to force a substantive response (How are you leaning? If you had to vote today, how would you vote?) cannot be used in mail instruments at all and are more effective in person than on the phone.

It has been observed that telephone election polls tend to produce higher rates of "undecided" than face-to-face polls taken of the same population at the same time. Apparently, the personal element induces a stronger tendency to give concrete answers. This, together with the higher rate of completed interviews, may well justify the higher expense.

THE HEISENBERG PRINCIPLE

Named after the German physicist Werner Heisenberg, this principle states that it is impossible to measure with accuracy the position and mass of subatomic particles because the measuring device distorts the phenomena. It loads the circuit in arbitrary ways. This is also known as the principle of indeterminacy, and can be similarly applied to the study of public opinion. The interviewer and the questions seriously load the circuits, providing data that may be distorted by the means for their collection. In operant conditioning experiments with animals, psychologists have begun to understand that many of the patterns described in classic learning studies "appear to have been caused by the mere presence of the experimenters."[9]

The concept of "rapport" between interviewer and interviewee refers to the achievement of easy and relaxed interplay, which presumably leads to a cooperative and forthcoming attitude and to rich and accurate answers. How is rapport to be created? Start with the most superficial things – in person, the dress, the demeanor, the voice of the interviewer, and the vocabulary of the questionnaire. A hip dresser might have no trouble creating rapport in a neighborhood of upwardly mobile young adults. A dark polyester three-piece suit might facilitate rapport in a business setting. A black person might do poorly in a white working-class neighborhood or in a tense, newly integrated suburb. On the telephone, the audio aspects take the place of the visual, with the same strong effects on the respondent.

In general, it is thought that interviewers should be as invisible as possible. They should blend with the environment. They should look as much like the people they are interviewing as possible, in age, life style, grooming, appearance. And this should probably not be faked. Appropriate emissaries should be dispatched to the different taste group camps. This should be true for telephone interviewers as well. But, you say, on the telephone, who knows? There are subtle clues that identify people to each other. A false note or a glimpse of the class enemy, and the call goes down the drain.

Honesty and directness are the best policies. Deviousness takes too much energy and, once detected, destroys any chance of rapport. Older persons should interview older persons, Republicans Republicans, males men, alcoholics alcoholics. The wide use by the syndicated pollsters of retired people and housewives, and of college student interviewers by academic polling organizations, may have some deleterious effects, but they are considered mild.

In this best of all possible worlds, where everything in it is a necessary evil, these are probably the blandest three groups of any. And even within these groups, some matching is possible. An alternative approach is to depend on chance to randomize interviewer effects. Use a wide variety of interviewers and deliberately disregard mismatches, expecting the various possible distortions to cancel each other out.

The use of polls to test communications media where the polling instrument is part of the medium itself is all too common. Television uses phone-in polls to compare itself with competing media. Ted Turner uses his Cable News Network on QUBE cable to rate CNN against the news programs on the three major networks. In-paper newspaper and magazine polls undertake to study such things as where readers get most of their information and in what media they place the most trust. Radio stations do on-the-air polls on whether they should change their formats.

These are obvious straw polls and cannot rise above their poor sampling frames. But it should be noted that the Heisenberg effect is also at work. "Readers who are motivated enough to cut out, complete, and return in-paper questionnaires . . . tend to be regular, interested readers. They are not representative of the very people you want to attract" by changing the product to meet their needs.[10] People tend to be supportive of what they voluntarily attend, as though they feel a need to justify and rationalize their own behavior.

The same effect occurs in scientific sample polls, where its presence may avoid detection. If a respondent stops to talk, opens the door, stays on the phone, or reads the cover letter on the questionnaire, this very act is a commitment. He feels an unconscious urge to rationalize what he already has done; this he accomplishes by being supportive of any implied purpose of the study.

Vacuum-cleaner salespeople are very conscious of this effect and use it to insinuate themselves into a sale, by a series of imperceptible degrees of early commitment. Students of public opinion must be sensitive to this effect and strive to avoid planting in the research design, unconsciously, a suggestive purpose that the respondent may endeavor to support.

Studies have demonstrated that student opinions of teaching can be strongly influenced by the way the polling instrument is presented to the class. "I walked into the classroom and brusquely handed back an essay assignment . . . chided them on their apparent lack of effort. Next I handed out the evaluation forms and told them it was their chance to get even." A week later, in the same class room: "I was sunny of disposition. I joked with them. I told them what a great class they were . . . and, oh, by the way, I had misplaced those faculty evaluation surveys. Would they be so kind as to do them again?" Between the two runs, improvement in perceived teaching performance went up on all items, from a low gain of 17 percent to a high gain of 46 percent.[11] Because of this effect, most schools look for more controlled methods administered by third parties.

In public opinion and motivation studies, most of which involve short-term contacts with respondents, the Heisenberg effect may present real problems. Consider, the Nielsen and Arbitron TV and radio studies based on time-diary techniques. There is a clear short-term tendency for people in these tests to alter their listening/viewing habits toward high culture norms. There is an increased interest in news and documentaries, shows that are "good for you," educational specials, and, on radio, toward middle-of-the road and beautiful music.

If the families stay in the sample, the effect tends to subside after a while; but unfortunately, there tends to be turnover in the sample. Just as the predictable effect wears off, so does the novelty of the extra tasks imposed in keeping a record of family patterns. So just as the indicators begin to give a more normal account, they get turned off. The little black boxes face the same effect. When first installed, family television watching is influenced. For a time, the family watches out of a sense of duty — not what do we like, but what is good for the country. The boxes have the considerable advantage that families soon disregard their presence, and the sample remains fairly stable.

This is closely related to a tendency in all kinds of polling to get socially desirable answers, that is, to have questions answered in a way that conforms to dominant belief patterns. People show a distinct tendency to court popularity with an unseen audience or with the audience of the interviewer, or to give the predictable safe answers. This tendency tends to reduce the significance of the poll considerably.

Curiously, this tendency is reinforced by the physical presence of the interviewer. This is one parameter in which mail and telephone methods may be superior to face-to-face questioning. In a study of physicians' reading of medical journals, one researcher found that the latter method produced twice as many socially desirable answers as did telephone interviews from the same population. On questions concerning abortion and marijuana, the same pattern was identified.[12]

Socially approved answers tend to reduce psychic costs to the respondents. In the case of low intensity opinions, many people will take refuge in what they perceive as socially approved. This tends to overrepresent attitudes that support the status quo. A wide variety of positive symbols can be counted upon to elicit supportive responses, which probably should be classified as "don't knows."

Questions containing clearly loaded language, of course, are avoidable; but the researcher may not be sensitive to words that are loaded for others. In some cases, there is no unloaded word with the right meaning. "Education," "human rights," "equality," and other such words are sometimes indispensable to the purpose of the poll. How to ask people about women's rights without using positively charged words? There are also negatively loaded words, among them "advertising," "TV sitcoms," "bankers." These always give enhanced negative responses, however used. Apart from obvious words, sometimes one only discovers that a word is charged when it is too late to change it.

The only solution is to pretest the questionnaire on a wide variety of people to eliminate the offending terms. Where that is not feasible, then the same question can be asked more than once in different words and contexts to check on coloring caused by predictable social approval or disapproval. Another safeguard is to measure the intensity of the opinion, so that the collator/interpreter can discount or qualify many low intensity responses. We will examine this approach in the next chapter.

Interviewer distortion and subversion are real threats to all research that depends on a large staff. Therefore, the smaller the staff, the easier it is to control quality at this critical interface. Thus, because mail polls depend on respondents to interview themselves, a carefully designed questionnaire must receive great emphasis. Telephone surveys can be monitored very effectively; the dangers of interviewer fatigue or indifference can be avoided or checked by a sensitive on-site supervisor.

Face-to-face interviewers in large sample polls present the greatest challenge. Here advanced training, high morale, good supervision, and good quality control are important. Of inestimable value is having experienced regular interviewers close to the areas where the samples can be drawn. Large polling organizations that do regular face-to-face polling (a declining industry) pay close heed to maintaining such a capability.

In 1968, the Gallup organization scrapped a poll of Harlem black attitudes on public and personal problems of the minority community because at least two interviewers had "falsified part of their data." This is the first time, Gallup said, "we have ever thrown away a complete study" out of 8,000 polls taken since 1935. Checking the raw interview data, it was found that no buildings existed at some of the addresses; and a spot check revealed that some of the respondents, noted by address in the area random sample design, could not be located.

The inaccuracies first came to light, not because of internal quality control, but embarrassingly because the *New York Times* sent a photographer and reporter to get comments and illustrations to go with the statistical report of the survey.[13] Gallup said that "in regular survey work, most cheating comes from an overload of work." To avoid that, each interviewer is limited to five respondents, he said, but there are occasions when that number is increased. "It shows up in control questions."

Reached by a reporter, one of the deviant interviewers said all the interviews were genuine. He had done them on the street, but made up names and addresses. "I was uptight to get it in." The racial tension in Harlem at the time made it dangerous to send in regular white interviewers. Trained blacks were not available, so ad hoc interviewers were hired. Ripping off Whitey was much more honorable than doing his spying in your own community.

As preparation, new interviewers are admonished to read the questions exactly as worded, without adding or subtracting verbally or otherwise. In probing, they are instructed simply to restate the question in the same form, deflecting requests for clarification with the stock phrase: "We would like you to answer in terms of the way the question is stated."

Whether that practice is honored in the field is always a matter of anxiety to researchers. Specific words may be accentuated. Voice inflections and timing may give additional information to the respondent, telling him how to respond. People tend to edit their lines when forced to repeat them over and over again, a problem more difficult to prevent than deliberate subversion, against which a number of steps can be taken.

Gallup includes in election polls a request for optional names and addresses to be used "only for administrative checking," it carefully tells the respondent. A surprisingly large number of people willingly supply the information, people who at the start of the interview would probably refuse to participate if their names and addresses were requested. Supervisors use the data to spot-check whether the reported interviews actually took place and whether some key questions were answered the same way both times. (Variations are discovered even in honest interviews.)

Another trick is the control question embedded in the poll. It looks like just another question but instructs the interviewer merely to insert a certain mark on the answer form, and the instruction varies on different interview sheets. Consequently, the interviewer (who is told nothing about it in advance) must read every sheet in order to mark the right item in the right way. If the control question is incorrectly marked, the polling organization knows that the interviewer faked the interviews, not even bothering to read each form.

"These cheater questions are put on the ballot to the specific purpose of tripping him up," Gallup said in a 1964 interview, "and they can be pretty devastating. When we find one, all the interviews of that worker will be thrown out, and sometimes redone. It rarely amounts to more than a fraction of one percent of the interviews."[14]

True, a conscientious faker would be more careful and would sit down and interview himself many times, reading each sheet. But experience has shown that people who are unscrupulous enough to take their pay under false pretenses are usually unwilling to do the work required to cover up the fact. Thus most fake interviews can be readily identified, even without the more expensive means of spot reinterviews.

Open-ended short answers are harder to counterfeit and easier to detect; long answers even more so. Of course, a counterfeiter really devoted to his craft might spend a couple evenings inventing open-ended responses or interviewing his dormmates; but that is usually harder work than going out and doing authentic interviews. Also, a sharp collator can detect the slip into repetition that characterizes such counterfeiting and can make deeper inquiries which will usually expose the deception.

Monitored telephone calls have the advantage here. Some boiler rooms have a listen-in capability provided for the supervisor (at the very least, she or he can hear one side of the conversation when in the same room). This can be used not so much for policing as for assisting the interviewers to improve their skills. The major problem is tedium arising from making a large number of calls during an eight-hour work shift. The supervisor can detect fatigue and boredom and make sure that interviewers get ample and timely rest periods, as well as shift them from one project to another now and then.

CONTAMINATION

With self-administered surveys (whether by mail or in person) there is danger of contamination by people other than the respondent selected by the sample design. The most extreme case is where somebody else completes the form. More frequent is for respondents to consult their friends to seek advice on how to answer the questions. The face-to-face interview is not entirely protected against contamination. If other members of the household are present, they may exercise the perfectly normal prerogatives of kibitzers everywhere. The respondent may accept cues from them, or their mere presence (without obvious cues) may constrain the subjects from answers they might otherwise make. Telephone interviews have been found to work best in controlling contamination.

However, as Dillman points out, contamination can be a desirable means for obtaining accurate information. This can be true when the survey is designed to reveal the normative tendencies of a group or class of people. The respondent therefore may need to check his own impressions of the information with members of his own group. He, in effect, is broadening the sample, within the limits of the original sample design. In addition, where the survey seeks behavioral information (as well as opinions), such as, How many times did you watch a news program during the last week? consultation with a spouse may be the best means of ascertaining the facts.[15] The individual supplying the data may be less important than the information itself.

In face-to-face interviews, the person who has the necessary knowledge may not be home at the time of the visit. Mail interviews have the potential advantage of permitting respondents to check their memories with others, to become more aware of their own behavior after looking at the survey form, to check records, and to consider their responses more carefully. Whether a significant number of them will actually do these things is not known; but, in general, with highly specialized audiences (for example, a study based on county executives sponsored by their own professional organization) many of them will do so.

On the telephone, there is generally a sense of urgency to finish the call and get off the phone. This is not conducive to getting corroborative information from any source but the respondent's memory. Of course, callbacks can aid the process, if the design insists on this kind of data collection.

TO TELL THE TRUTH

The twin issues of validity and reliability are omnipresent dimensions in all public opinion research. The former is the test of whether the respondent reveals his "real" opinion. Surprisingly, for some purposes this is not of critical significance. Because all kinds of people have all kinds of motives, it can be safely assumed that the amount and directions of invalidity tend to cancel themselves out if, and this is an important requirement, the study avoids other systematic sources of error. As Bernard Hennessy points out, "The first practical test for the political meaning of public opinion is not the ultimate truthfulness of inner conviction, but the internal consistency of public behavior."[16]

In the 1950s, the Gallup organization began experimenting with "secret ballots" in election polls. The ballots would be given out by a interviewer, marked by the respondent, and placed in a box that resembled a ballot box. Half of the sample would be interviewed in the traditional way, the other half asked to vote a secret ballot. The samples would match in every other respect, so that the impact of secrecy on the nature of declared voting intentions might be gauged. It was thought that the principle of the secret ballot was so important to Americans that it should be respected in polling as well.

The findings have rarely shown significant differences between open and secret responses. In the 1964 presidential elections, it was feared that many Goldwater voters would come out of the closet on election day. The large number of "undecideds" seemed to point in that direction. The use of split open/secret ballots was expected to reveal the fact. But it didn't, and the world found out why on election day – when the Goldwater phantom vote didn't materialize.

The closet vote theory reemerged in 1980. Pollsters Caddell and Gallup found that Reagan's support tended to be lower in face-to-face interviews than in telephone interviews taken at the same time. After the election, the returns showed that Reagan had made substantial gains among "weakly identified Democrats." These may have been unwilling to admit their switch in a personal setting but were less inhibited on the telephone.[17]

Any substantial trend of lying to pollsters would undermine the whole enterprise. Some researchers have suggested that the problem of "volatility" of recent years is really a case of voter distrust, not only of political leaders, but also of all American institutions. "Don't bother me!" rather than "I haven't decided yet."

Saturated by polls and pollsters, as well as by all the other busybody intrusions on privacy, people are irritable and testy. They want to withdraw from involvement in any public matter. Attempts to draw them back are resented in sufficient numbers to increase "don't knows" to a point that jeopardizes the findings; and a large proportion of responses are impulsive and shallow, just to get rid of the questioner, without regard for the truth of the matter.

Were this to be a general trend, the entire justification for public opinion studies would evaporate. Fortunately, this doesn't seem to be happening. Most polls continue to yield reasonably accurate results because most people are willing to tell things – their incomes, political preferences, and so on – to strangers that they might not tell to friends and relatives. There is still a wide reservoir of decency in the public, an impulse to react to friendly overtures with friendly responses.

Polling is generally recognized by people as an aspect of mass communications. They feel like they are on "Candid Camera." They know how to react and what manners are appropriate. They readily distinguish the approach of a pollster from the approach of a masher or a panhandler, and still are flattered to be asked their opinions. People readily adapt to the conventions of polling, almost as if they were being offered an opportunity to pass through the looking glass into the remote worlds of media and news.

"Pollsters feel safe in assuming that most people do not lie, simply because there are no compelling reasons to lie." In the absence of sanctions against lying, people show "an inherent moral and psychological predisposition to tell the truth."[18] The main incentive to shade their true feelings arises from the impact of social approval.

They like to be regarded as "good citizens" who espouse desirable opinions, such as "I voted in the last election" or "Racial discrimination is wrong." A poll is often regarded as a "test," in which one strives to give the "right" answer. "This impulse," Lewis and Schneider point out, "can lead respondents to express an opinion about an issue they know nothing about, simply because they do not wish to appear empty-headed or uninformed." This is not the same as lying, and the poll design can seek, through identification type questions and reports on actual past behavior, to put this into perspective.

The cheater item has often been used to test honesty. One researcher surveyed college students to gauge prejudice against various ethnic groups. One of them was "Danireans," entirely fictitious; yet many respondents rated them carefully as a recognizable group. The German weekly *Der Spiegel* did a rating of cabinet members, including the name of a nonexistent person, who came in sixth, ahead of ten other names.[19]

It needs to be pointed out that the pollster is actually lying to the respondent when she or he asks a fictitious question. For example: Samuel Johnson: "Now in so far as you approach temptation to a man, you do him an injury; and, if he is overcome, you share his guilt."[20] The authority of the interviewer legitimizes the question. One might conclude that the tendency to answer fictitious questions doesn't prove anything about real questions, except the predisposition of respondents to cooperate.

Respondents will always answer questions on their own terms, whatever the intentions of the research design. The best to be hoped for is that the degree of error arising from these sources will be more or less constant, so that "trends can be assessed and comparisons made."[21] The results of survey work are useful and informative in spite of the many known sources of error.

Survey and market researchers continue to look for ways to enhance the validity of interview data, as well as — a related matter — new methods to measure opinion intensities. One wag suggests asking respondents to take an oath on the Bible as a required screening question. Others have more seriously suggested finding ways to use the new technologies that aver to induce or weigh truthfulness in people.

Truth serums, lie detectors, voiceprint analysis, and hypnosis have been suggested and used and even defended as both proper and productive. Truth serums are drugs that appear to weaken the defensive functions of the ego, enabling an interrogator to impose his own will, forcing disclosures and admissions that the subject would otherwise edit out. Alcohol and hallucinogens have been widely used by police agencies and the CIA, not to mention market research organizations and psychotherapists.

Some of the many interaction groups of the last 20 years have advocated the use of drugs during sessions as making possible grand liberating experiences. Similarly, hypnosis, transcendental meditation, and marathoning enjoyed (or suffered) brief vogues in individual and group therapy, aimed at achieving the same goals. Fortunately, most extreme practices die of their own inutility. Once the novelty wears off, people are no longer sustained by the fascination of singularity.

Focus-group interviews, without special gimmicks, are thought capable of enhancing validity through the process of group interaction itself. By imposing the normal psychic risks and ego reinforcements of group interplay, a process is produced that is closer to reality. After the initial familiarization period, individuals in the session cannot resist the truth-seeking importunities of their peers. Consequently, a successful focus-group interview veers toward truthfulness as the spontaneous and intense chain reaction catches fire.

Generally, survey reliability is more important than validity. The former refers to "the reproducibility of the results" if the same parameters of survey design are implemented in the same environment. Thus, an aptitude test is said to be reliable "when it measures the same dimensions of the intellect of all children given the test at any single time and when successive measures of individuals show consistently similar results."[22]

A large number of polling experiments have been designed to test reliability by, for example, repeating the exact same survey design more than once, each run-through completely independent of the others — drawing a separate sample by the same methods from the same sampling frame, assembling a separate staff, and so on. The reproducibility of results is remarkably consistent, well within the limits of predicted sampling error.[23]

The best reliability test would be to interview the whole population while simultaneously doing a scientific sample survey. This is approximated by election forecasts, allowing a test of reliability every time. We know that most such forecasts are successful, but that the dramatic impact of the small number of mistakes tends to outweigh greatly the record in the public mind. In fact, this is not a good empirical test. Between the cup and the lip there is many a slip. People who vote in the survey may not get to the polls, people change their minds before election day, and so on.

The time dimension and the imponderables of events cannot be duplicated by any reproducibility testing. Polling organizations love the chance to test their research instruments in the electoral furnace, because it provides one of the most ready methods to improve their work in all areas. But they are very careful to remind the press and the public of the differences between a series of surveys and the one that counts on election day. The discrepancies, which sometimes occur, do not invalidate well-designed preelection polls at all, if the limits of the enterprise are clearly understood by all.

In conclusion, it should be clear that the dimensions of interviewing are as multivariate and intractable as human beings themselves. The tenuous and exasperating interplays between humans can never be reduced to a precise science. The purposes of the study, the resources available, the experiences of the researchers, and various intangibles go into the decisions. For better or worse, with our fingers crossed we persevere with our commitments and projects, collecting data and writing reports, and hoping there will be a next time when we will do even better.

NOTES

1. See Raymond L. Gorden, *Interviewing: Strategy, Techniques, and Tactics*, 3rd ed. (Homewood, Ill.: Dorsey Press, 1980); and Gerald R. Pascal, *The Practical Art of Diagnostic Interviewing* (Homewood, Ill. : Dorsey Press, 1983).

2. American Statistical Association, Conference on Surveys of Human Populations, "Report," *The American Statistician*, February 1974, p. 31.

3. See his excellent discussion of these issues : Don A. Dillman, *Mail and Telephone Surveys/The Total Design Method* (New York: Wiley, 1978), pp. 2-12.

4. See Peter M. Blau, *Exchange and Power in Social Life* (New York: Wiley, 1964).

5. Everett Carll Ladd recommends that mail surveys should strive for a sample size of about 4,500. Then "you look at the patterns of response. That's where you get important information." Quoted in *Chronicle of Higher Education*, January 23, 1978, p. 7.

6. Dillman, *Mail and Telephone Surveys*, p. 40.

7. W. Edward Deming, "On a Probability Mechanism to Attain an Economic Balance Between the Resultant Error of Response and the Bias of Nonresponse," *Journal of the American Statistical Association*, no. 18 (1953): 743.

8. Dillman, *Mail and Telephone Surveys*, p. 48.

9. Bruce R. Moore and Susan Stuttard, "Tripping over the Cat," *Science*, September 7, 1979, p. 1031.

10. C. G. Russell, *Editor and Publisher*, April 7, 1979, p. 7.

11. Paul Rice, "How to Get High Marks," *Chronicle of Higher Education*, October 7, 1981, p. 20.

12. John Colombotos, "Personal Versus Telephone Interviews: Effect of Responses," *Public Health Reports* 84 (1969): 773-82.

13. *New York Times*, November 1, 1968, p. 33.

14. George Gallup, Sr., *U.S. News and World Report*, October 5, 1964, p. 59.

15. Dillman, *Mail and Telephone Surveys*, p. 65.

16. Bernard C. Hennessy, *Public Opinion*, 3rd ed. (North Scituate, Mass.: Duxbury Press, 1975), p. 101.

17. See Patrick H. Caddell, "The Democratic Strategy and Its Electoral Consequences," in *Party Coalitions in the 1980s*, ed. Seymour Martin Lipset (San Francisco: Institute for Contemporary Studies, 1981), pp. 274-75.

18. I. A. Lewis and William Schneider, "Is the Public Lying to the Pollsters?" *Public Opinion*, April/May 1982, p. 42.

19. Ibid.

20. James Boswell, *Life of Samuel Johnson* (Boston: Little, Brown, 1959), p. 440.

21. Lewis and Schneider, "Is the Public Lying to the Pollsters?" p. 47.

22. In 1944, Hadley Cantril collected the results from comparable studies obtained by four independent polling organizations, discovering very minor variations of result. "Do Different Polls Get the Same Results?" *Public Opinion Quarterly*, 9, 1945, p. 62.

23. Ibid.

CHAPTER EIGHT
QUESTIONING

The way people react to an issue can depend on how pollsters phrase their questions. Quite apart from any margin of sampling error, there is the margin of uncertainty implicit in the qualitative ambiguity of verbal prompts. This can be minimized by well-crafted questions; but, let's face it, language by its nature is fuzzy, metaphorical, and subjective. There is no escape from the lack of precision even in the best-crafted instrument. The professional goal of writing questions is to achieve the optimum precision, to capture the substantive truth.

THE ART OF WRITING QUESTIONS

We have seen that interviewing is as much an art as a science. Writing good questions in the first place takes skill, experience, and lots of prayer. It has been shown that results can vary by as much as 20 percent merely by rewording questions. Different sampling designs seldom produce findings that vary by half this amount.[1]

In rating the sources of poll error, experts agree that the imponderables of question wording are by far the most serious, followed far behind by faulty interpretations and inadequate sampling. The importance of wording applies equally to every method of interviewing — face-to-face, telephone, and mail — and to both long- and short-answer studies, although in the latter, wording is somewhat more critical. In open-ended, both long and short, the researcher fudges some on the difficulties, but faces them again in the coding and collating process.

"Wording and testing," Stanley Payne reminds us, "necessarily go hand in glove. . . . It should not be overlooked that pre-testing is far from being fully developed and that even the most elaborate pre-tests may be restricted to a few areas and a few hundred cases."[2] The worth of questions cannot be judged by a low number of "don't knows." It all depends on the purpose of the poll, the hypothesis that is being tested.

The writing of questions can be divided into three distinct parts: the kind of information sought, the question structure, and the choice of words.

On the first of these, the touchstone is the hypothesis that is being tested. A hypothesis is a question in the mind of the researcher combined with the best guess as to the correct answer. For example: From which media do people get most of their information about current events? It is my guess that people will rank sources of news in descending order: television, radio, newspapers, the grapevine. The best guess includes any data that become available to refine the hypothesis, including past studies and pretests, before the project is frozen into the form in which it will be administered.

The hypothesis can be anything of interest: a ridiculous proposition made of thin air, a solid hunch, a textbook theory about human behavior, somebody else's conclusion from another study, an original theoretical proposition about the impact of any class of variables on resulting distributions of opinions, a structural or institutional description of political inputs/outputs, the verification of factual statements about human attitudes, beliefs, behaviors, and attributes, or a search for factual information for any applied use. Here the originality of the researcher can enjoy the fullest range.

Often, the hypothesis says as much about the mind of the researcher as it does about the minds of the people who are subjects of the study. Take, for example, the evaluation of teaching, mentioned earlier. If one hypothesizes that teaching quality is the main factor in education, then one devises a survey that asks students to describe and rate various elements in the teacher's performance. If one hypothesized rather that learning is the main factor, regardless of the teacher's skills, then one would attempt to evaluate a class experience in terms of the study habits and motivations of the students. This, essentially a difference in hypotheses, is a lively controversy in teaching evaluation.

The same principle underlies all survey and motivational research. What do you want to know? What is your best guess as to what you expect to find? The whole research design springs from the researcher's answers to these questions.

Designing a poll is like painting a picture. The researcher is like an artist, attempting to give flesh and substance to her inner visions of reality. Like an artist she is free to offer her private world to an audience. She is willing to take chances because that makes it more engaging for everyone. There is virtually no limit to what can be expressed by the medium of poll taking.

Don Dillman makes the useful distinction among beliefs, attitudes, behavior, and attributes. Beliefs are "assessments of what a person thinks is true or false." Typical choices embodied in belief questions include whether or not the respondent thinks something is correct/incorrect, accurate/inaccurate, what happened/what did not happen. "In all cases, belief questions are designed to elicit people's perceptions of past, present, or future reality."[3] An example: In your opinion does getting an abortion prevent someone from having another child?

Attitudes have to do with how people evaluate things, their preferences, positive or negative, toward an object, person, or course of action. Do you agree or disagree with the statement, Anyone who wants an abortion should be able to get it? Reports on intentions, that is, future behavior, should be considered as attitudes, because the circumstances of implementation are still hypothetical. Predicted behavior is a present preference, not an actuality.

Behavior questions aim at reporting actual behavior patterns. Do you know anyone who has had an abortion? Have you ever recommended an abortion to a friend? Of course, memory plays tricks. Answers to such questions may be distorted. Belief about one's own behavior is really being reported. Attributes are concerned with demographic data that characterize respondents, such as home ownership, political party affiliation, and so on. This kind of information is very valuable in that it permits the manipulation and interpretation of opinions in terms of hard and pertinent variables.

Keeping these distinctions in mind enables a researcher to clarify the project design, to translate the hypothesis into useful questions.

All the different types of questions can be modeled to elicit data about attitudes, beliefs, behaviors, and attributes.

RULES OF THUMB

"Half the battle consists of putting the issue in a form that we can understand ourselves. We need first and foremost to define the issue, regardless of the understandability of the words."[4]

- Use simple words. Don't talk down. Be colloquial. If correct grammar sounds artificial, be ungrammatical. Split an occasional infinitive and end a sentence occasionally with a preposition. This is the way people actually talk.
- Keep questions short. Keep questionnaires as short as possible. Try to eliminate what Payne calls "blab" words, those that don't say anything but sound important: American, government, society, citizenship.[5]
- Watch out for unintentionally loaded terms: status quo, prestige, pride pricking, stereotyping, dead giveaways.[6]
- Stick to items that bear on the hypotheses; don't overdo the fishing expedition.
- Don't be afraid to repeat important things. People forget things that everybody knows and even what they have just recently heard.
- Screen for knowledge and information. Have you ever heard of such-and-such? What would you say such and such is? What examples can you give me of such and such?
- Beware of implied alternatives. The negative side cannot be considered obvious; it should be stated. And half of the interviews might reverse polarities – a question stated positively should be restated negatively to check the differences. Similarly, the options should be stated in different orders in roughly equal proportions, so that the systematic impact of the first and last things in mind can be eliminated.
- Three little words – might, could, should – are full of infinite treachery! They should be separated and used with deliberation and care in accordance with the purpose of the study.

OPEN-ENDED, BOTH SHORT AND LONG

Accepted theory holds that it is best to proceed from the general to the specific. Openers can be of the open-ended short-answer variety, moving later into more structured and specific questions. Although screening questions need to come early, specific demographics (age, education, income, marital status) work better at the end. By that time some degree of rapport exists, and the respondent may be more willing to give sensitive information.

A number of introductory questions may appear in a single instrument as the conversation moves from one topic to another. They should be very free-form, general, and relaxed. Payne gives these examples:

In a community relations survey —

When you think of the three or four leading manufacturing companies here, which ones come to mind?

If a friend of yours who knew nothing about X Co., asked you to describe the company, what would you tell him?

Survey for the oil industry —

What kinds of activities and businesses do you think of as being included in the oil industry?

What do you think happens to the money that is collected in gasoline taxes?

In consumer market studies —

What's your reaction to this product just from seeing it and smelling it?

What does good quality in an alarm clock mean to you?

What things in particular would you look for in buying a toothbrush?

How did you go about buying your last pair of shoes?

Various other surveys —

If you had a half hour to talk to the president of your company today, what things would you most want to talk to him about?

What comes into your mind when you hear the term "advertising"?

Asking for general suggestions works well in getting into an interview: What conditions do you feel could be improved in this plant? What would you suggest to the president to improve his image? Direct conversational wordings are necessary in the openers; they can become more technical and artificial later when the structured questions demand it.

Don't be afraid to write logical step-by-step follow-up questions as the schedule moves from general to specific. Would you tell me just why you say that? What was the result? In what way? Would you mind telling me what you know about it? Can you give any examples of that? Anything else? What else?

Asking about the reason why is the most common type of open-ended short-answer question. Draft them in the most natural way. Why do you say that? Why pick that one? What caused you to change your mind? Closely related to reason-why questions are argument questions, which tend to be less personalized: What things would you say are good about a library as a place to work? What are the disadvantages? In what ways is that good? Bad?

Precoding means asking a general open-ended question, not suggesting any answers to the respondent but including on the interview sheet a breakdown of possible answers. The interviewer classifies the answer on the spot and enters a checkmark on one of the options (including, sometimes, "other"). This can save a lot of work later, but it may also conceal or distort important differences in the responses.

Open-endeds are good for a variety of purposes, as we have seen. Now we discover new ones: as openers in moving an interview along while building and maintaining rapport and as an initial venture to learn something about drafting closed-ended items for a follow-up poll.

IDENTIFICATIONS

The simplest questions are used for knowledge/familiarity checks. Do you know the name of the congressman from this district? What do the initials FCC mean to you? How many of these brand names do you recognize? Such questions are something like a quiz and must be presented in a way that softens the schoolroom atmosphere. Better defer such questions for later in the schedule, so that a few real opinion questions come earlier and some reliable rapport will be established. These should be phrased to permit concise answers.

DICHOTOMOUS QUESTIONS

The most commonly used questions are dichotomies, intended to suggest only two possible alternatives, sometimes with the third way out of "other," "don't know" (henceforth abbreviated DK), or "no opinion." Such questions typically call for answers of yes/no, approve/disapprove, for/against, favor/oppose, this/that proposition, Democratic/Republican, Reagan/Carter.

Ordering decisions as a series of left/right turns gives clarity to what is essentially a confusing melange. The proverbial housewife goes to buy a frying pan: large or small? deep or shallow? low- or high-priced? cash or charge? The decision is arrayed by the same principle as any classification system, enabling the mind to find the right file drawer rapidly in spite of the formidable number of file drawers it contains. Similarly, a questioner can retrace the series involved in the complex choices of life.

Often the alternative is implied, not stated: Do you intend to vote in the primary? "Or not" is implied. Do you think the United States should permit pornography to be sold openly? "Or should outlaw it" is implied. In such cases, test polls have shown that the positive side generally is chosen at a slighter higher rate when the negative side is not mentioned, but usually not enough to affect the statistical validity of the result. Payne: "In any case, it is always safer to state both choices, in order to avoid the risk of the assumption implicit in giving only one."[7]

Whether the DK option is emphasized can affect the result. More answers fall in the positive/negative bins when the third option is kept out of sight. Wording that insists on "which way are you leaning at this time?" can attempt to deny the respondent the third option (although he or she can insist on it anyway). On the other hand, including "other" in the question increases its incidence.

Two-valued questions give rise to qualified answers: "Yes, but." "Maybe." "Under certain conditions." This can be incorporated into closed-ended questions by adding slots for "qualified," so that the questionnaire would be marked yes or no and qualified (with or without further open-ended explanations). Payne's example:

Are you going to the game for sure, or not?
( ) Yes, for sure.
( ) No, not going.
( ) Qualified, not sure.
( ) Don't know.

Multiplying two-valued questions into an assortment of third options is sometimes unavoidable, depending on the wording of the questions and the purposes served by the anticipated answers. The word "qualified" is not recommended for use in the question. Rather, the common terms that express the idea in a particular case are preferred, such as in between, no difference, both, neither, about the same, about right. For example: So far as you personally are concerned, has the government cut welfare spending too much, not enough, or just about right? If the direction people are leaning on the issue is wanted, it is better to leave out the middle ground; if a respondent elects it without a cue, then the schedule includes that as a possible choice.

Payne offers an interesting gradation of intensities, from mild to strong, in formulating two-valued questions. The designer can choose among them depending on his or her insight into the strength of feeling (salience and intensity) on an issue. From mildest to strongest: good idea/poor idea, prefer/not prefer, approve/disapprove, for/against, favor/oppose, would vote for/against, demand/reject.[8]

Even softer two-way choices can be fashioned by stating questions in terms of better/worst, more/less: Would you say it's better to regulate business more closely? Or would you say the less regulation the better? Do you think your family is better or worse off under Reagan than under Carter?

A good question does not load the answer. In two-valued questions, it is sometimes valuable to reverse the two parts in a question for half the interviews, to test for any distortion caused by the arrangements. In the last example, this is accomplished by switching the names Reagan and Carter. Where there are more than two possible answers included in the wording, the most substantive parts should be rearranged an appropriate number of times. Payne calls this method "split ballot."

MULTIPLE CHOICE

Multiple choice must be used when the array of substantive choices (not counting DK, and so on) exceeds two, when three or more logical gradations of a quality are pertinent to the hypothesis — Do you like your date to be very tall, tall, average height, short, very short? — or when three or more clearly identifiable options of equal logic might be chosen — Who do you think makes the best-tasting hamburger: McDonald's, Burger King, Wendy's, or Arby's?

If short open-ended questions are the most natural, structured multiple choices are the most formal. "The listing of a large number of alternatives . . . does serve to call them all to each respondent's attention and thereby puts them all on the same footing."[9]

Closed questions may be of several types: (1) Those with ordered choices, "each a gradation of a single dimension of some thought or behavior." The respondent is asked to indicate the closest answer that expresses his opinion. (2) Those with unordered choices, that is, no single logical dimension arrays the multiple answers. The respondent must consider each one and select that which best expresses her thought. And (3) those that are only partially closed, allowing the respondent to select an option of his own creation, or do so in addition to selecting from the structured menu.[10]

It has become customary with lists that exceed four or five items to have them printed on cards that can be handed to the respondent. Sometimes the options are listed in the question as well; at other times the question merely instructs the respondent to choose answers to a whole series of questions from the lists on the cards.

This is easy to do in face-to-face interviews. It is difficult, but not impossible, in mail and telephone surveys. A kit of such cards can be sent to respondents who are then telephoned, or the respondents refer to the lists when self-administering the mail questionnaire. The lists can be published in a general circulation newspaper or magazine, and respondents chosen from among the subscribers.

This procedure works well with sensitive and/or complex questions in face-to-face interviews. A card with income ranges listed (which would take forever to read aloud) is handed to the respondent. The latter, in giving his income, merely states the code letter or number of the category in which he falls. Thus the options do not have to be read and the hardy citizen does not have to whisper his income.

Like good multiple-choice exams, the lists must be exhaustive of the classes being compared in the hypothesis, or include a catchall category at the end.

Sometimes the respondent is given the option of arranging the items on the list or in the question in some rank order: first, second, third, choices, or most to least important. She might also be asked to choose more than one option: Name all of those whose hamburgers you have eaten in the last month.

In coding these, the researcher may report and compare number of respondents per rank order/item: How many picked McDonald's first, how many second? How does McDonald's compare with Wendy's on numbers of respondents who made these first, second choices? By this method, 100 percent would be the number of respondents in each category.

But the choices may be coded also in terms of the universe of total choices. Here 100 percent would be all the choices made, without regard for how many respondents made them. A response that mentioned three of the items on the lists would appear three times in the tally; one that mentioned five items would appear five times. This sounds more complicated than it is. Coding and interpreting a few examples will render the point very clear.

Multiple choices can indicate gradations within a class or question, rather than separable classes. The options can be graded for intensity of feeling or certainty about a course of action or proposition, as well as for degrees of difference in the course of action or proposition. An example of the former:

> If another company offered you a job at the same pay as you are now getting, which statement expresses best your feelings?
> ( ) I'm sure I'd take it.
> ( ) I'd probably take it.
> ( ) I don't think I'd take it.
> ( ) I definitely would not take it.
> ( ) I don't know what I'd do.

An example of the latter:

> To what extent should social security coverage be based on the contributions of employees? Or be subsidized from

general revenues?
    ( ) Mainly from contributions.
    ( ) Partly from each.
    ( ) Mainly from general revenues.

One of the most useful variations of multiple choice is the Likert Scale, named after Rensis Likert, an early pioneer of survey research.[11] Designed mainly to overcome the problem of opinion intensity, it employs a five-point scale of responses. A proposition, or series of propositions, is read by the interviewer, to each of which the respondent is asked to characterize her degree of agreement/ disagreement on the following scale: agree strongly, agree, neutral, disagree, disagree strongly.

Many elaborations are possible in which the five-point base of the Likert Scale is calibrated into a larger number of units. For example: On a scale of 1 to 10, with 1 being not at all and 10 being very much, how would you rate your dependence on television for news information? On the same scale, how strongly are you opposed to further development of nuclear power? Another variation (useful in self-administered instruments) provides a calibrated baseline, asking respondents to place a mark at the position that corresponds to the strength of their feelings.

Strongly negative   Strongly positive

\#————————————————————————————— \#

 1   2   3   4   5   6   7   8   9   10

PROBLEM OF INTENSITY

The factor of intensity is an enduring conundrum of all survey, motivation, and market research. It is clear that the social process is a dynamic one, that attitudes, values, beliefs, opinions, and behaviors do not exist in a vacuum. They are part of the constant interactions of people as they compete, collaborate, and bargain with each other. Opinions are simultaneously counters in social exchanges as well as markers at any given moment of the outcomes and status of such exchanges.

The intensity factor has to do with the deep personal equations of risk and cost associated with holding opinions in the constant interplay of influence. Some people have more influence sometimes than others; some people are willing to run greater risks and pay greater costs to persuade others, to act out, or otherwise implement their subjective and symbolic opinions.

People who are insulated from psychic costs behave differently than people who must experience the penalties of their actions. An interview setting is usually one that is highly insulated from the real impacts of holding, expressing, and acting upon opinions.

A number of psychologists, who happen to be peace activists, have pointed out that the insulation of American presidents may make nuclear war more likely. They reason that the president could be making his fateful decision while at "a psychological distance" from the victims of a nuclear exchange; that he would be in a clean, air-conditioned room, surrounded by aides talking in abstract terms about military scenarios. The reality of the extermination of millions would be pushed to the back of his mind.

A Harvard professor's solution: Put the codes needed to fire nuclear weapons in a tiny capsule and implant the capsule next to the heart of a volunteer. The president would carry a butcher knife in a sheath. If the president decided to fire the ultimate weapon, he would have to dig out the capsule with his own hands: "He has to look at someone and realize what death is — what an innocent death is. It's reality brought home."[12]

Opinions are unequal. High influence gives one person's views greater weight in public decision making. Willingness to take risks and pay costs gives persons with very intense opinions greater influence than persons with very weakly held opinions. The political process, as we have seen, is interpersonal: Who is doing what to whom with what effects? Passive or latent opinions may look the same as active and intense opinions on many polls, unless the design carefully attempts to measure this dimension.

Yet, in the real world, passive and latent opinions are disregarded as of no immediate weight. Of course, their existence may be important to know about, so that means can be taken by leaders to arouse them into intense and conscious forms or means to avoid such arousals. But weak opinions are hors de combat. They are seldom self-actuating. As ingredients in political bargaining, they are only potentials.

Likert intensity scales were invented to penetrate into the heart of the problem. They have proven very useful, making possible measurements of salience and latency. But the issue remains fundamentally unresolved. Responding to abstract verbal cues in the interview setting is usually quite different from real-world behavior.

The interviewer is not somebody with an emotional grip on the respondent, as are the people who really influence and are influenced by the respondent's real-world opinions.. There is no far-reaching prospect of personal reward-punishment in this one-sided exchange. There is no inflicting of sacrifice, effort, and pain upon the respondent to test the real power of his or her avowed thoughts. There is only the most transient and shallow love/hate in the encounter; yet only relationships with real love/hate potential have the power to make or break the subjective structures of consciousness.

Many of the critics of therapeutic counseling, like Thomas Szaz, believe that the same problem exists in the practice of psychiatric medicine — that the psychic costs and risks of such "cures" are shallow and one-sided, that they really do not work. The professional/patient relationship becomes real only if they get personally involved with each other, and that usually only intensifies the patient's problems. The decision to seek help, which is basically unassisted, is itself the cure, and the subsequent treatment is only a ritualistic expression of that fact. It can be dispensed with entirely, since it only serves to add financial stress and other possible complications.

Opinion and motivational studies are also "talking cures." The most important thing to be gained by the study of opinion would be knowledge of future behaviors, the ability to predict emerging and declining social issues, to understand the roles of various classes of people and of various value systems in future political engagements, and the ability to assess the likelihood of certain outcomes from such transactions. These processes involve real exchanges of values and can never be accurately duplicated in the airless and flat world of a survey interview. This is not to dismiss the latter as useless, but rather to recognize its limitations.

It has been suggested that one could get a truer measurement of intensity by this method: Ask the question and then run away as fast as possible. Record an answer to the question only if the respondent feels strongly enough to run after you in order to answer. Grade intensity by the distance the respondent was able to run before slowing down or giving up; then the interviewer can circle back and, panting heavily, collect the answer.

Another suggestion has been "the Don Rickles approach." The interview method would be designed as a verbal assault on respondents. The answers to the survey would be coded, not only in terms of opinions expressed, but also in terms of how they were expressed: 42 percent laughed in the interviewers' faces; 30 percent screamed and ran away; 22 percent hit the interviewer in the mouth; 6 percent called a cop.

The Lloyds of London betting odds are considered an abstract polling system that really models the real world and thus provides a more dependable basis for prediction than the views of people who are not required to put their money where their mouth is. Perhaps one can develop a polling system by which respondents are asked to bet real money on their preferences, so that reality may temper their choices.

Successful focus-group interviews have so far proven to be the best way of evaluating intensity. By re-creating a real-world milieu among the participants, focus groups are capable of releasing deeply repressed symptoms and indicators. This is one of the strongest assets of the technique. Whether researchers have the right to probe this deeply into people to whom they have no lasting commitment is a disturbing question. Pollsters and market probers are flying interlopers, inveigling unsuspecting and innocent people into their lairs, performing their magic upon them, then casting them back into the streets forever. There is little professional or personal obligation arising from the encounter. We will dig into the ethical issues in a later chapter.

In a rather new field, a number of interesting studies are currently underway aimed at measuring subjective aspects of personality, including values and opinions, by means of the indicators of body language. It is thought that, unlike verbal language, the involuntary expressions of movement and position offer a vocabulary much more informative and spontaneous. If the research discovers a Rosetta Stone to translate this language into specific meanings, then it may become feasible to add new intensity measurements to the existing tools of analysis. Videotaped interviews could be subjected to later body language reading and interpretation.

In addition to Likert Scales, traditional methods attempt to broach the problem of intensity by framing questions that emphasize the behavioral implementation of opinions as much as the opinions themselves. This is done rather straightforwardly by asking respondents to report actions as well as words. In addition to asking, From which medium do you get most of your news? one also asks, Where did you hear about the president's speech yesterday? Time diaries are especially appropriate here. One can assume that the real ways people pass their time, or the shows watched on television, provide a realistic means of measuring the relative intensities.

LIKERT SCALES

Admitting the limitations on any attempts to measure intensity, one nonetheless has opportunities and responsibilities to enlarge the concept of opinion holding by applying such scales as the human mind can devise. The most important and enduring contribution is that of Rensis Likert, the five-point scale of approval/disapproval.

> In terms of these choices, indicate your feelings about the president's proposals for a flat income tax.
>   ( ) Strongly approve.
>   ( ) Approve.
>   ( ) Neutral or not sure.
>   ( ) Disapprove.
>   ( ) Strongly disapprove.

It can also be applied in the same way to all attitudinal continuums: positive/negative, agree/disagree, support/oppose, and so on. One of the considerable advantages of the Likert Scale is that once the respondent is informed of the choices, a whole series of issues or propositions may be covered very rapidly, to each of which the same set applies.

In addition, the scale provides a wide variety of ancillary information about the public's feelings on issues, including measures of individual and group salience, the rank ordering of many different issues in terms of their relative salience, and, always of great import, a way of measuring degrees of polarization and consensus in a community about a wide variety of issues.

"Salience" refers to the level of self-conscious controversy surrounding an issue, social value, event, or personality in a given population at a given time. It refers to the level of individual and public awareness about the matter, the allocation of public attention among many such matters, the degrees and kinds of information about such matters possessed by the public (or parts thereof), and the strength of public feelings connected with them.

Certainly, salience is closely related to intensity, even if they are not identical. Any method that can generate complex data about salience invites useful inferences about intensity. The model, offered by V. O. Key, Jr., and others,[13] for the processes of political discourse is shown in Figure 2.

Issues are latent and inactive at the initial level of low salience. At this point, the dissonance is probably very large, because no process of accommodation and consensus building has occurred. Every individual and group, insofar as they may be aware of their values on the issue, tends to cultivate distinct views that have deep roots or no views at all. The issue may suddenly become joined as a matter of social controversy, either because natural conditions have thrust before the nation a new problem or because group conflicts have given it new relevance.

The accidents of political maneuver, as well as the imperatives of the objective situation, stimulate certain issues into contention. Their level of salience (public interest and awareness, as well as political engagement) rises in complex patterns throughout the society as various groups split apart, make new coalitions, bargain energetically with each other, using all the means, some fair, some foul, that society disposes. The media and the arts join in the battles and all the resources of communication become locked in the process.

Public policy, government regulations, lawmaking and enforcement, judicial determination of some aspects of the issue — all may be drawn into the rising storm as all kinds of alternate priorities struggle for resources and commitments. Arts and entertainment cannot stay out of social issues that achieve high salience, nor can many members of the public elude the winds of audacious events. At some point, latent attitudes and opinions are inflamed and alert. Salience reaches a high point and crests.

Each phase of the process may take a longer or shorter time. Some phases may endure with considerable stability for years or

FIGURE 2.
Salience Model

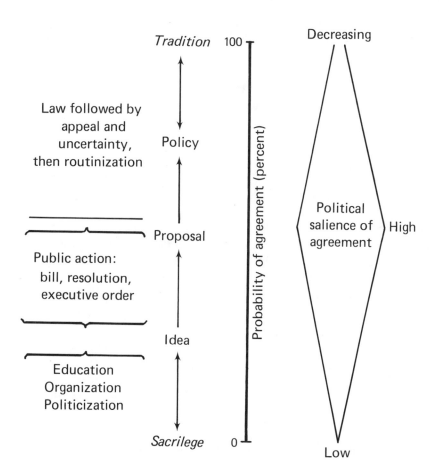

generations. Some will erupt with the suddenness of Mount St. Helens and then just as suddenly disappear back to latency, without having achieved consensus or implementation. Other issues will be driven to some change in social norms.

When a transformation of social values and institutions results from the process, a strange thing occurs. The salience falls once again, even to the vanishing point. When the smoke of political interaction clears, a new consensus may emerge, redefining social values for all participants. The old divisive values have vanished. New divisive values must take their places, as group life continues to evolve and as new markers of identity and loyalty are needed.

At each point in this process, the levels of salience may be considered roughly proportional to the "severity of the problem." In social affairs, "problem" is defined, not by any objective parameters, but according to the perceptions of the parties concerned. Social problems exist when the bargaining process is intensely joined. All the parties announce the imminent breakdown of peaceful dialogue, indeed of the social fabric itself. This potentiality, always just beneath the surface, is an important dimension in the bargaining process.

The practical option of abandoning peaceful means, resorting to violence, acts on all parties to contain the danger. The interest in reducing the risks and costs of escalation is shared by the parties and, most of the time, tends to constrain the bargaining within the limits of civility. This actually, and paradoxically, aids the process of problem solving, even while the dangerous fulminations continue.

The same paradox can be glimpsed in the latter stages of a social problem. As the issue in contention moves toward amelioration, one might hope to see a reduction in dissonance. Not so. Salience tends to increase even as the basis for consensus emerges. The very divisive elements of high salience continue to endow the parties to the dispute with political leverage right to the last moment, and even after.

The bargaining postures that characterized the most intense stages of the encounter, and which have been intensely internalized emotionally by all the parties (including their audiences), have a momentum of their own. The after-ringing of pain, the aura of catatonic posttrauma, the reflexes of combat are still present in the nation's nervous system, ready to spring back into battle like those of a punch-drunk old fighter.

Return to the condition of latency, of low issue salience, may be long delayed after substantial consensus has been reached. Students of public opinion need to be alert to the paradoxes of this phenomenon. It may be necessary to distinguish between the salience levels that mark the typical situations of pre- and postcontention, both of which may yield very similar results on the Likert Scale.

The Likert Scale assumes special significance as a means of measuring all the phases described by this model of political/social interaction. Let us examine an example.

Be so kind as to indicate your feelings on the following statements by choosing a number from this card. [Respondents are handed a card which reads:

(1) Agree strongly.
(2) Agree.
(3) Neutral or indifferent.
(4) Disagree.
(5) Disagree strongly.]

a. Teenagers seeking birth-control devices should be reported to their parents.
b. Nuclear power should be encouraged by government as the best solution to energy problems.
c. The legalization of capital punishment will deter murder.

Let us assume findings in a scientific sample poll for each proposition, in percentages.

	A	B	C
(1)	21	35	5
(2)	29	15	40
(3)	2	25	15
(4)	6	10	37
(5)	42	15	3
Total	100%	100%	100%

What do these figures mean? First, consider the raw figures themselves. On the issue of reporting birth-control requests to parents, people are pretty evenly divided, but feelings tend to be stronger on the negative than the positive side. On nuclear power, the majority of people with opinions are positive, although a substantial group are uncertain or indifferent. On capital punishment, there is a slight edge favoring it as a deterrent to murder; a large majority have opinions on this issue, but most of them are only moderately intense.

Totals of those approving/disapproving can be reported by adding (1) + (2) — total approving; (4) + (5) — total disapproving; (3) neutral would make a third category. The percentages can be calculated for the three categories, just as they were for the five. Poll A shows no significant preference either way. B shows overwhelming approval. C shows approval significantly greater than disapproval. On such a polarization analysis, the three issues can be compared with each other. A slightly stronger majority approves of capital punishment. Bare majorities approve of birth-control reporting and nuclear power.

Second, each of the three items can be tallied in terms of issue salience. This is done by adding all those on each issue that have opinions and comparing each issue on that basis. (1) + (2) + (4) + (5) = general salience. On this basis, salience is extremely high on teenage birth-control reporting, high to a slightly lesser degree on capital punishment, and considerably lower on nuclear power. The three separate issues can be ranked against each other to show their relative general salience.

Third, intensity is defined as the ratios of strongly/not so strongly expressed opinions. For each issue, the ratios can be calculated and then compared in order to determine which of the two sides of the issue is composed of the most intense feelings (note 5 over 4).

(1) / (2) = intensity of approval
(5) / (4) = intensity of disapproval

In terms of intensity, the issue of teenage birth-control reporting shows very high intensity on the negative side (7.0), more than seven times as intense as opinions favoring such reporting to parents (.72). On nuclear power, the positive side is almost twice as intense (2.3) as the negative (1.5). On capital punishment, intensities are much lower, and approval shows a higher intensity (.12) than disapproval (.08).

Four different issues can be ranked against each other in terms of high and low intensity. This is done by adding the strong opinions, both pro and con, on each issue — (1) + (5) — and the moderate plus neutral opinions — (2) + (3) + (4) — and striking ratios between the two sums. To state it verbally, we are comparing very intense opinions with opinions that are either of moderate or very low intensity (neutrality being the lowest intensity possible):

(1) + (5) / (2) + (3) + (4) = issue intensity ratio

Now the issues may be ranked comparatively in terms of their intensities. On this scale, teenage birth-control reporting is the most intense issue (1.7) of the three, nuclear power is next (1.0), and capital punishment is the least (.08).

Five, the issues can be ranked in accordance with their varying degrees of consensus/dissidence. This is done by adding neutrals with approvals, regardless of intensity, and by adding separately neutrals with disapprovals, and then by striking a ratio between the two sums. To put it verbally, we are deriving a number that represents the extent to which public opinion on various issues agrees, without regard for whether that agreement be positive, negative, or undecided.

$$(1) + (2) + (3) / (3) + (4) + (5) = \text{consensus ratio}$$

By this formula, on the results of our hypothetical poll, the issue of nuclear power shows the highest consensus (1.5) and, by definition, also the lowest dissidence. Capital punishment is next (1.09), and teenage birth-control reports the least consensus (1.04) and therefore the highest divisiveness.

Likert-scaled responses can be nicely graphed, and the resulting shape of the curve connecting the five points can be readily interpreted. Percentage of responses can be put on the vertical axis, and the five types of responses can be arranged along the horizontal axis. If a variation is used, such as a ten-point scale, then the bottom line should be calibrated accordingly.

Let us enter some typical data into the graph in Figure 3 in order to distinguish the different shapes and their meanings. Assume the following response data on a polling item:

Agree strongly	40%
Agree	35%
Neutral	13%
Disagree	9%
Disagree strongly	3%
	100%

On the graph, this would look like Figure 4. A quick glance will identify this chart as indicating a strong consensus with very intense positive preferences and very weak negative preferences. This curve is of what Key called "supportive consensus."[14] An exact reversal

FIGURE 3.
Empty Likert Graph

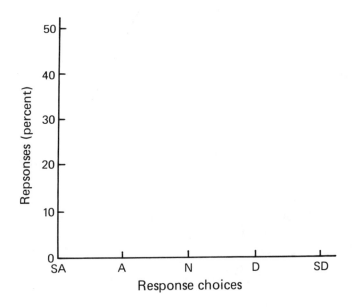

of findings will produce a mirror image of this chart, with the curve on the positive side starting very low and steeply sweeping upward. That would also indicate very high consensus, with intense preference on the negative side of the issue. In Key's terms, this would demonstrate "non-supportive consensus."

The next set of figures will generate a high degree of consensus, but with moderate or low intensities, both positive and negative. See Figure 5.

Agree strongly	9%
Agree	50%
Neutral	23%
Disagree	10%
Disagree strongly	8%
	100%

FIGURE 4.
High Consensus, High Intensity

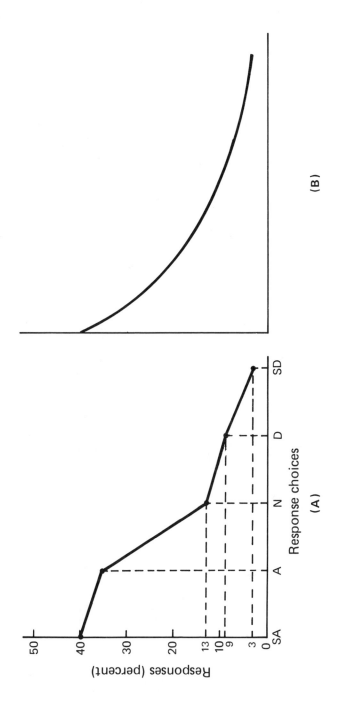

157

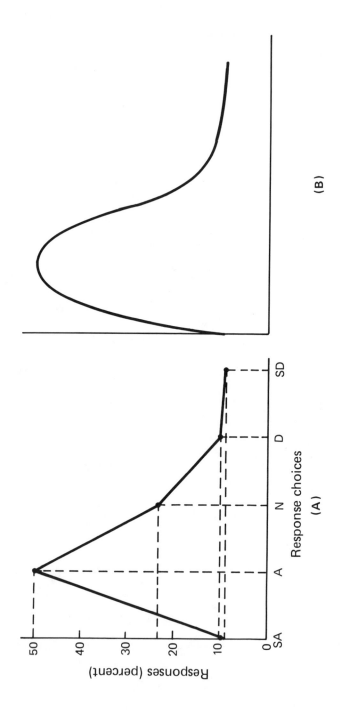

FIGURE 5.
High Consensus, Low Intensity

(A)

Response choices

Responses (percent)

(B)

Without listing the poll data, let us show three more typical graph forms. Charts showing low consensus are called "bimodal conflict models." Figure 6 shows low consensus with low intensity. Figure 7 shows low consensus combined with high intensity, that is, more or less equal numbers on both positive and negative sides, with both categories of strong feelings relatively high.

Low consensus with moderate to low intensity on both sides is graphed in Figure 8 — that is, when positive and negative views are more or less equal and when moderate intensities are relatively higher in numbers than strong intensities.

When the neutral column is substantial, greater than or close to other values, the resulting distribution of opinions is called "permissive consensus"; that is, although there is no consensus about the issue in question (both sides of the chart are evenly balanced), and intensities are generally low, there is a prevailing sense of permissiveness about the issue. Open-mindedness and indifference have the same effect upon the social dialogue. Salience will be very low, which usually goes along with permissiveness.

Finally, the last typical graph form (not illustrated) may be called the "multimodal conflict model," most difficult to classify, whose figures are ambiguous or indeterminate.

FIGURE 6.
Low Intensity Bimodal Conflict Model

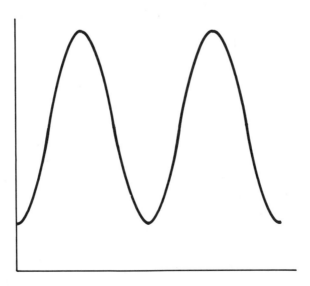

FIGURE 7.
High Intensity Bimodal Conflict Model

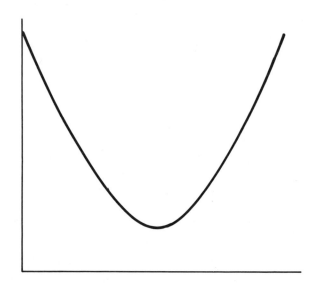

FIGURE 8.
Low Consensus Bimodal Conflict Model

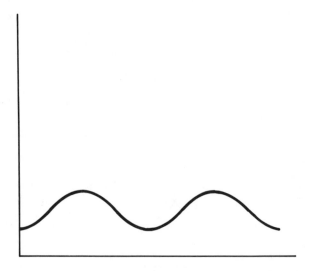

VOLATILITY

Closely related to the problem of intensity is that of volatility. The dictionary definition of volatility is "the quality of a substance to turn readily to vapor, fickle, transient, flying or able to fly." This may be regarded as the antithesis of intensity, the condition that exists when opinions are shallow and unstable, when respondents indicate an opinion, an intention to vote, whatever, with no sense of conviction. They are not attempting to mislead anyone; they are themselves as misled as their questioners.

Objective conditions may enhance public ambivalence, because the public has few illusions about the claims made by leaders, or because the issues are by nature obscure and difficult. What makes the problem very troublesome to pollsters is that such shifty attitudes are sometimes reported as highly intense, even though they may change overnight. And one cannot find any deliberate deception. Obviously, the concept of intensity requires some refinements in order to account for commitments that appear deep but cannot be counted on to endure.

We have seen that long-answer techniques are vastly superior in eliminating this distortion. Because they go deeper, probing feelings that lie beneath the surface of the personality, they tend to discover ambivalence and to identify its unique components. If one goes deep enough, one is bound to uncover elements of volatility in every kind of public opinion. However, the costs and long lead times of these techniques are prohibitive for the collection of opinion data from large national samples at timely stages of political campaigns or in the throes of policy debate. Therefore many efforts have been addressed to deal with volatility problems by refinement of short-answer techniques. If successful, such innovations would combine the best attributes of both short- and long-answer interviews — the advantages of statistical analysis combined with the advantages of depth interviewing.

One promising route is the "mushiness index" developed by Yankelovich, Skelly, and White, Inc., after the problems encountered in predicting voter behavior in the 1980 presidential election. This index would gauge the mushiness of the apparently hard numbers, alerting the users to "the likelihood that an opinion will simply change." The firm has announced that all future surveys on public policy issues will use the mushiness rating.

"The index is our professional response to the problems of measuring volatility," announced Daniel Yankelovich. In market research, "we have built-in ways of making sure our product information is not mushy," but such painstaking questioning is not possible for public policy surveys, because "news organizations aren't willing to pay the added cost and because the opportunity to report at length is not available." The firm invested "two years and a lot of money" to develop four simple questions. Mushiness is not the same as "intensity," but deals with a change in opinion not accounted for by new events or information.

The four conditions pointing to volatility are low level of personal involvement with the issue or campaign; conviction that one's information about them is inadequate; a failure to "work through" one's own inner convictions through discussions with others; and a feeling that one might easily change one's mind. In an actual survey, respondents would first be asked whether they favor or oppose something; then they would be asked four questions, each of which is rated on a six-point scale.

(1) On a scale of 1 to 6, where 1 means that the issue affects you personally very little and 6 means that you really feel deeply involved in this issue, where would you place yourself?

(2) On some issues people feel that they really have all the information that they need in order to form a strong opinion on that issue, while on other issues they would like to get additional information before solidifying their opinion. On a scale of 1 to 6, where 1 means that you feel you definitely need more information on the issue and 6 means that you do not feel you need to have any more information on the issue, where do you place yourself?

(3) On a scale of 1 to 6, where 1 means that you and your friends and family rarely, if ever, discuss the issue and 6 means that you and your friends and family discuss it relatively often, where would you place yourself?

(4) People have told us that on some issues they come to a conclusion and they stick with that position, no matter what. On other issues, however, they may take a position but they know that they could change their minds pretty easily. On a scale of 1 to 6, where 1 means that you could change

your mind very easily on this issue and 6 means that you are likely to stick with your position no matter what, where would you place yourself?

The scores are added up, resulting in a number from 4 to 24. A score of 4-10 indicates a very mushy opinion; 11-18 moderately mushy; and 19-24 firm. When fewer than 50 percent of the respondents have scores in the firm range and 20 percent or more are very mushy (4-10), the issue is deemed "mushy." The issue is deemed "moderately mushy" when fewer than 50 percent are firm but less than 20 percent are very mushy. Opinion is deemed "firm" when more than 50 percent are firm and less than 20 percent are very mushy.

This method will be used in political polls "as a more accurate measurement than the current practice of reporting undecideds."[15] A "simple refinement," not a "U-turn," one of the partners told a press conference, it will not invalidate the results of polling; but it is necessary to separate informed from uninformed opinions and to alert editors and readers of the difference and its meaning.

The mushiness index can be used uniformly, reducing cost and complexity. Because the battery of four questions can be applied as follow-ups on each of a series of favor/oppose questions, comparisons among issues can be made. The technique is equally usable in face-to-face, telephone, and mail surveys.

The creators of the index are careful to distinguish the difference between volatility and intensity. They point out that people may feel very strongly about something and still be likely to change their minds, just like those who report themselves as holding views of low intensity. "Many public policy issues, especially in the foreign policy field, are not thought through," explained Daniel Yankelovich. "Answers . . . on such issues are often top-of-the-head and subject to change."[16]

An issue generating great interest in the 1980s has been the protection of the U.S. car industry from Japanese imports. Most surveys showed a strong protectionist sentiment rising in the country. But the Yankelovich firm, using the newly developed index, found that protectionism is a "very mushy" issue for the public, discounting for policymakers the other poll findings.

Every solution creates new problems. The mushiness index is bulky, time consuming, and cumbersome. It requires careful wording by the interviewer and careful listening by the interviewee.

Its technical nature tends to weaken rapport and strain affability. Four such blunderbusses in a row, after each substantive issue question, means that it becomes unrealistic to attempt to test more than a few issues in a single survey.

More devastating is the consideration that the index items will suffer contamination by the substantive opinion question. That is, there will be a tendency for the respondent to want to support the credibility of his already stated opinion. If that has been expressed in a definite manner, he is unlikely then to tell the interviewer that he has no basis for having that opinion. In short, the mushiness index may merely amplify and conceal the volatility dimension.

We will have to wait the results of a few dozen more surveys before judging the efficacy of the Yankelovich solution to the volatility problem.

Another approach to pinning down problems of volatility is to deal more circumspectly with "don't knows" (DKs), no opinion, other, undecided, and so on. Until the cropper of the 1948 presidential election predictions, it was not uncommon to lay aside the nonresponses in electoral polls. This was based on the commonsense assumption that the nonresponders would eventually act in the same patterns and to the same proportions as the responders. If the responders gave 60/40 percent on one candidate over the other, then it was assumed this represented the average population, including those who for whatever reasons did not have opinions, refused to participate, or could not be located.

It was also assumed that of the total sample, the proportion that would actually go to the polls and vote was randomly distributed among the whole population, both responders and nonresponders. These assumptions justified using the substantive responses as representative of the whole population. Even if the real percentage of nonresponders were substantial, say 15 percent, it would be eliminated, and the rest of the responses would be treated as though it were 100 percent.

Nonresponses constitute a grave threat to poll accuracy. A survey was made of a population of 10,000 professors to find out how many are Liberals and how many Conservatives. The nonresponse rate (this was a mail poll) was about 50 percent. Among the responders, 80 percent were Liberals.

Consider all worst case assumptions: All nonresponders are liberal. This would mean that 90 percent of all professors are Liberal. Or none of the nonresponders are Liberal. This would mean that 40 percent of the population are Liberal. Thus, the range of systematic error could well be 50 percent, making utter nonsense of the entire enterprise, no matter how well designed and honestly drawn the original sample.

In this particular survey, the researchers attempted to adjust for nonresponse by weighting the returns, so that certain known distributions of rank, academic specialty, geographic location, and type of institution were represented in the final count in proportion to the known distribution of these characteristics in the total population. As one statistician pointed out in angry terms, this weighting does not correct "for fluctuations in the response rate" and does not remove the impediments to meaningful statistical analysis.[17]

Of course, in 1948, a preponderance of the nonresponders went for Truman, making the difference in the predicted and actual outcomes. Because of that sad experience, not only did Biffle and Lubell make their reputations, but all the pollsters resolved to treat nonresponses differently.

The main reasons discovered for the faulty predictions were "time of decision" and incorrect treatment of nonresponses. A large number of nonresponders made up their minds after the last polls, a fact that was missed because of the two-week lead time required in those days between taking and publishing a poll. Thereafter the technology of polling was improved to make possible polling and publication virtually up to the election eve. And thereafter margins of nonresponses were included in the final published analysis of poll findings. If the margins were large and could constitute the swing vote, efforts were made to delve deeper into these constituencies to try to see what was bugging them and whether they would in fact play a role in the outcome.

In the event that nonresponding might be systematically associated with nonvoting, greater attention was paid to probing voting intentions and past voting behavior. Finally, more emphasis was placed on forced-choice questions, which insist that respondents take a position, whether or not their minds are made up. Such questions make clear that the respondent must indicate a choice, however well considered or flimsy he perceives it to be: Which way are you leaning right now? If you had to vote today, how would you vote?

How to avoid writing dishonest questions? Don't do it deliberately. The dishonesty will be obvious and transparent, and people are smarter than they used to be. It is very difficult to rise above one's own prejudices or even to see them clearly. Get help. Pretest, pretest, pretest. Cultivate people of other points of view. Open your own mind. In studying public opinion, one tries to become a professional.

NOTES

1. Stanley L. Payne, *The Art of Asking Questions* (Princeton, N.J.: Princeton University Press, 1951).

2. Ibid., p. 14.

3. Don Dillman, *Mail and Telephone Surveys/The Total Design Method* (New York: Wiley, 1978), p. 81.

4. Payne, *The Art of Asking Questions*, p. 26.

5. See Payne's lists of basic English and problem words; ibid., pp. 151-76.

6. Ibid., pp. 177-202.

7. Ibid., p. 57.

8. Ibid., pp. 64-65.

9. Ibid., p. 76.

10. Dillman, *Mail and Telephone Surveys*, pp. 86-87.

11. Rensis Likert was a longtime Census Bureau official and later director of the Institute for Social Research at the University of Michigan. He died at 78, in 1982.

12. Roger Fisher, quoted in *New York Times*, September 7, 1982, p. C1.

13. V. O. Key, Jr., *Public Opinion and American Democracy* (New York: Knopf, 1961); Charles O. Jones, *An Introduction to the Study of Public Policy* (Belmont, Calif.: Wadsworth, 1970); and Bernard C. Hennessy, *Public Opinion*, 3rd ed. (North Scituate, Mass.: Duxbury Press, 1975).

14. For the classic presentation of intensity distributions and their meanings, see Key, *Public Opinion and American Democracy*, Chap. 2 to 5.

15. *Editor and Publisher*, June 13, 1981, p. 28.

16. Editors, *Public Opinion*, April/May 1981, p. 50.

17. Tore Dalenius, "The Ladd-Lipset Survey of the American Professoriate," *Chronicle of Higher Education*, April 23, 1979, p. 27.

CHAPTER NINE
SCIENTIFIC SAMPLING

The owner, finding a single flea on his dog, concludes that his dog has fleas and gives him a flea bath. You receive a free sample of Hickory House cheese while strolling in the shopping mall. It tastes very good indeed. With no hesitation, mouth watering, you enter the store and buy a two-pound box of the same cheese. Sampling is a universal experience, and everyone does it all the time. It is the way humankind manages to get by with imperfect and incomplete information.

Humans are limited creatures. They rely on samples of experience in order to derive universal knowledge. They conclude that their ability to do so is based on the uniformity of nature. They are confident that nature is not out to trick them. If something works in the observed sample, we expect it will work a good bit of the time.

Humans act on such assumptions with their fingers crossed. When they are disappointed, they do not blame the perfidy of nature; they blame themselves. They somehow had a bad sample. Now they must get a better one and try again. How noble is the human species, yet how ungodlike! Humans are limited in their scope. They see only a part of the whole, and they understand only part of what they see. They have no choice but to generalize from limited information. All the simple tasks of life require the use of samples in everything we do.

All art and science is based on sampling. The physical scientist in the lab works with small samples of things, yet her conclusions deal with the immensities of the universe. The social scientist works with samples of intangible human phenomena, yet his conclusions touch imponderables of the soul. All studies and experiments are small microcosms of larger realities, and they represent only a few instances of all possible studies and experiments.

Obviously, there are kinds of knowledge where sampling will not do. In any situation where one must deal with the specifics of any instance or unit, rather than with a class of instances or units, sampling is worse than useless. For example, the bank needs to know how much its depositors have in each account. It would not serve for purposes of informing them of their separate assets merely to project inferences drawn from a sample, no matter how carefully designed. Employers can't get away with paying only a sample of their workers, or basing anyone's actual paycheck on a sample of time cards.[1]

In public opinion studies, the constraints of time and resources make attempts to study entire populations impractical. In addition, the attempt may be futile, bound to be frustrated by the intrinsic difficulties of the task. Sampling may not be just necessary but also better; it permits the development of strategies and designs that use existing knowledge to yield more accurate approximations of the whole. Scientific sampling represents a quantum leap in humankind's ability to transcend the limits. Prometheus escapes his bounds to the extent that humans learn to use the gift of creative fire.

Scientific sampling is based on simple principles. A relevant population must be identified. All the members of that population must be placed into a sampling bin. Then the sample must be drawn in a random manner, which guarantees that all the elements in the bin have an equal chance of being chosen on every draw. Finally, the sample size must be large enough to create confidence that the drawn sample will be representative of the total population.

Putting all the stubs of a raffle sale in a box and, in the presence of witnesses, having a blindfolded child make the selections, being sure to stir up the contents thoroughly before each draw, and excluding from eligibility the families of the officials — how much more random can you get?[2] In commonsense terms, a properly random draw from a well-mixed bin will produce a sample that, on each additional draw, more and more closely approximates the whole population. Any characteristic distributed among all the elements in the bin can be expected to show up in the sample in roughly the same proportion as it exists in the whole population. The sample becomes a microcosm of the contents of the box from which it was drawn, permitting the inference that any description based on the sample can be applied also to the unexamined elements still in the box.

Based on the commonsense notions of chance, one understands that at any given point the sample will not be a perfect miniature, but only an approximation. But chance is pure in heart; it does not deceive in any systematic direction. If we trust ourselves to rely on its verdicts, we can have confidence in our inferences from the sample. Chance decrees that the random choices from the bin will tend to adhere to a curve of probability. If many separate samples of the same size are drawn in the same way, they will all show "a central tendency" to closely model the entire contents of the bin.

Both empirically and theoretically, such a central tendency can be formulated mathematically. If 80 percent of the elements in the box are green, all the separate samples drawn from the box will show a tendency for 80 percent of each sample to be green. The more samples drawn, regardless of the size of the samples, the stronger will be this tendency; that is, the numbers of samples containing close to 80 percent green elements will increase and the numbers of samples containing very few green elements will diminish.

Let us talk about green and red marbles in a very large barrel. We don't know how many marbles there are, nor how many of each color. We take a sample of ten marbles: six red and four green. We write down the finding, then mix them back in the barrel. We take another sample of ten: six green and four red. We take a third sample of ten: five green and five red. And so on. After taking 100 such samples, we find that two-thirds of them have seven to nine green and one-third have one to six green. We would conclude that there are more green than red marbles in the barrel. We might even reasonably conclude that the percentage of green marbles is somewhere between 70 and 90.

Note that even a very small sample can approximate the frequency of a characteristic in a large population if we draw repeated samples of the same size. Increasing the size of the sample will be of some help. Based on pure chance, repeated samples of more than ten will show the central tendency in a slightly more marked way. In the case of red/green marbles, samples larger than ten each could be expected to show slightly more than two-thirds of the samples to contain green marbles within a range of 70 to 90 percent.

Doing this kind of exercise repeatedly, one begins to see mathematical regularity in the results. Using small samples, the same central tendency will become apparent as using large samples, but there will be more of a spread of results. Using larger samples, there will be less dispersion away from the central tendency.

This is the basic notion upon which the whole edifice of statistics rests. The tendency of randomly drawn samples to cluster around the distribution of characteristics present in the whole population may be shown in a "normal distribution curve," the so-called bell curve (see Figure 9). Each point on the curve represents the frequency of green in a single sample. Taken as a whole, the curve identifies the fact that most of the samples cluster around the central tendency; that many of the samples show green to be present between 70 and 90 percent of the time, while very few samples contain less than 60 percent green marbles and even fewer considerably less than that.

FIGURE 9.
Bell Curve

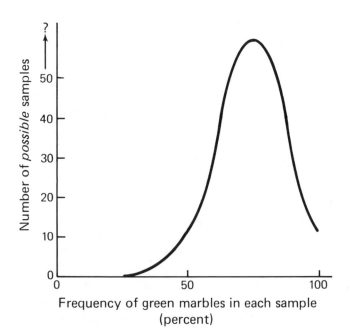

With larger sample sizes, the shape of the curve becomes more pronounced, its sides rising more steeply and its top being narrower (see Figure 10). With smaller sample sizes, the curve is much flatter in every respect. But note that the number of samples taken does not change the shape of the curve, but only accentuates that shape.

Anyone can test the empirical truth of the effects of chance. Take a coin and carry out this experiment. Decide on two sample sizes, say 10 tries as one sample size and 20 tries as the second. Now do 100 samples of 10 tries each, keeping careful records of the numbers of heads in each sample. Now do 100 samples of 20 tries each, keeping careful records of the number of heads in each sample.

Everybody knows that because there are only two practical outcomes of any single toss, there will be a central tendency for each sample to yield 50 percent heads. But one also knows that it is rare to get a single set of tosses that shows exactly that number of heads. Instead, what one will get with either sample size will be a clustering of outcomes in the range of 40 to 60 percent heads; that is, the number of samples showing a result within that range will be large. The number of samples showing a range of heads less than 30 percent or more than 70 percent will be correspondingly small.

Notice that the shapes of the two curves are different, although the central tendency toward 50 percent heads is the same. The 100 samples of 20 tries each show a slightly sharper rise and a narrower top. Try doing 100 samples of sizes larger than 20 or less than 10 each. The former will produce a curve even more pronounced and the latter even less.

Theoretical mathematicians soon noticed that it is possible to summarize the findings of these experiments in fairly simple mathematical algorithms or formulas. These make it possible to calculate in advance the expected shapes of normal distribution curves plotted for any given distribution of a characteristic in an infinite number of random samples of any given size. That exploration makes it possible for us to take only one or a few actual samples, and yet estimate, with a degree of confidence that can be quantified, the chances that the frequency of a variable in our sample would be confirmed (within a quantifiable range) if an infinite number of such samples were drawn in the same manner from the same population.

Scientific sampling is based on these principles. Social scientists do not have to retrace the footsteps of early mathematicians but

FIGURE 10.
Effects of Sample Sizes

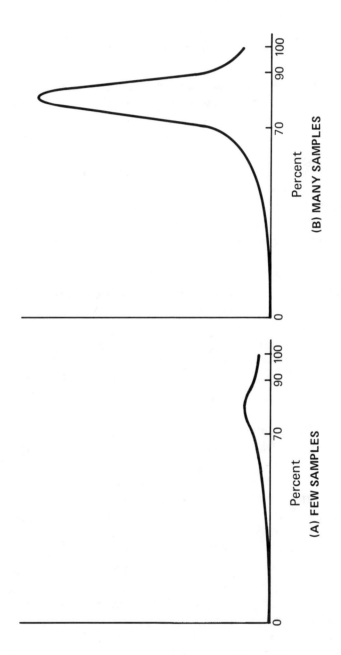

Percent

(A) FEW SAMPLES

Percent

(B) MANY SAMPLES

can apply the algorithm directly to their sample designs. They can state the results of sample surveys, quantified in terms of their degrees of confidence that the frequency of any variable in the total population lies within an acceptable range of probable error. We will see this in numbers in a later chapter.

We are entitled to apply the algorithm to measure the truth of our findings only if certain conditions are met: that our sample designs are truly random, that we defined our populations adequately, that we assembled the whole population in a sampling bin, that we drew from the bin by a method that ensured that every element of the population had a equal chance of being drawn on each draw, and that we controlled or eliminated every other source of systematic sampling bias.

Why should we want to use scientific sampling? Because it is one of the ways we can measure social phenomena. Not the only way, but one of the best. Remember the earlier discussion of methods in the social sciences. Outside the laboratory, statistical measurements are often the only means of making observations, controlling variables, and drawing conclusions from data. These are invaluable tools, in many cases irreplaceable.

Of course, one could apply the census method by making a complete count of a population. It would appear that this would produce greater accuracy than sampling, by eliminating statistical sampling error. The facts are otherwise. Quite apart from cost and time, a total canvass introduces other kinds of practical dilemmas. Did you find everybody? Is it necessary to cut back the goals of the study in order to reach the population concerned?

The only situations that lend themselves to census methods are those involving small populations, where the requirements of statistical significance set a minimum sample size that is close to or greater than the size of the whole population. Any group under 1,000 in total membership might be considered for a canvass rather than a sample survey; quantitative aggregates and parameters might be dispensed with completely in favor of depth or focus-group interviews with small, carefully structured samples. In the latter case, qualitative findings would satisfy the hypothesis, and no attempt need be made to measure sampling error or to project any findings statistically to the entire group.

In such a study the people selected to participate would constitute a nonprobability sample. No estimates of error would be possible, but the sample may be stratified judgmentally for whatever purposes the researcher has in mind.

Sample surveys are better than complete counts of a population. They are cheaper, quicker, more manageable. A well-designed sample can be more accurate than a total canvass because it will deliberately be structured to contain all the right ingredients in the right proportions, and provisions can be built in to ensure that the respondents can be located and can be interviewed. Properly done, refusals and nonresponses arising from inaccessiblity can be contained, and callbacks can reduce not-at-homes to acceptable limits.

SAMPLE SIZES

Today, with a sample size of 1,200, a national poll can provide high confidence that the sample is representative and that the range of probable error does not invalidate findings. Only 50 years ago, when scientific sampling was in swaddling clothes, it was considered safer to err on the side of big samples. George Gallup, starting out in the 1930s, sought to collect 50,000 interviews to predict the outcome of the 1936 Roosevelt-Landon race (he got it right).

The ill-fated Literary Digest poll of that year used a Leviathan sample of 2.4 million. It was assumed that size alone would correct for any sampling problems and give an accurate forecast. Using telephone directories and club lists, the Digest sent out 10 million mail questionnaires, getting back about 25 percent. The findings, tabulated at great expense, showed Landon receiving 57 percent and FDR 43 percent, almost the exact reverse of what actually happened (62 percent for FDR and 38 percent for Landon).

Rather than drowning possible bias in numbers, the Digest poll actually magnified the bias. The sample was a straw poll containing several kinds of systematic bias. Unlike today, telephones were a real luxury in 1936. In a 1936 population of 128 million, there were 11 million phones. There were almost as many unemployed, and most Americans of low or moderate means did not have phones.

In addition, there was a very high nonresponse bias. One-third of all Chicago voters, for example, received ballots, of which only one-fifth responded (about 6 percent of electorate). That is still a large number, which showed 52 percent of the respondents favoring Landon. Actually, FDR carried Chicago by 2 to 1; this reveals the extent of the self-selection bias. On top on the telephone-derived mailing list, mail surveys always overrepresent the more literate classes — accustomed to receiving and answering letters in English. In 1936, that meant mainly well-heeled Republicans.

The large numbers only repeated the built-in bias on a larger scale. A recent restudy of the Digest poll in the *American Statistician*[3] demonstrates that the pattern of nonresponses, more than sampling technique, accounts for the erroneous predictions.

In 1948, large numbers were still the vogue. Gallup's 1936 success with a 50,000 national sample set the standards for the industry. The Crossley-Hearst poll was in the same ball park. Only Roper-Fortune had cut sample size down to 15,000, but did so only to stay within budget, not having the syndication power of its competitors. All three polls predicted Dewey would beat Truman by about 5 percent — the reverse of what transpired.

The result of this learning experience led to a complete conversion from large to small sample sizes. Since 1948, samples for national polls have decreased to today's standard of 1,200 to 1,800, and the methods for structuring and selecting them have become much more sophisticated.

As election day approaches, most polling organizations increase sample size somewhat, in order to reduce the range of possible error, especially for subsamples (How will blacks vote? How will working women vote?). In both 1976 and 1980, Gallup increased sample size in his final preelection polls to 3,500, more than two times larger than the earlier surveys.[4]

Relatively large numbers are still used in election day exit polls. Samples between 30,000 and 40,000 are necessary because of the many subsample categories that are studied. In addition to the national poll, separate polls are conducted in various states where races are of special interest and which are selected as typical of their regions.

In the 1982 off-year elections, the NBC/Associated Press exit polls sought 36,000 good interviews to be used, not only as early indicators of the result, but more important, to give depth and meaning to the interpretation of actual returns. In addition to representative polling districts scattered among the 50 states, the sampling concentrated on 13 states. The questionnaire sought information about why people voted as they did, how they regarded Reagan's policies, their views on unemployment, defense spending, nuclear freeze proposals, and, in the 13 states, on a variety of state issues. In effect, the large number represented the cumulative sample size of 13 or more separate polls, each of which had about 1,500 respondents.

The proof that scientific samples are superior may not be apparent in the results. Pollsters still make mistakes. But it is apparent in the reduction of statistical error in most subsequent polls. The average error has been cut from 5 percent to about 2 percent on all election projections, which still permits wrong forecasts in very close races or in wild card upsets.

The analysis that followed the 1948 fiasco created a consensus that the errors sprang from three sources: ignoring the DKs, the long lead times between the last polls and last-minute voter decisions, and "quota sampling." We have already discussed the first two. Quota sampling belongs in a discussion of adjusting and stratifying samples.

Suffice at this point to say that the term refers to allowing interviewers to select individual respondents (in accordance with predetermined quotas) at the last stage of the carefully structured sample design, tending toward a self-selection bias. The more willing and approachable respondents, who tended in 1948 to be Dewey voters, were overrepresented. Since 1948, most quota sampling has likewise been abandoned.

Large samples do not improve the accuracy of polls. To put it more precisely, they do not improve accuracy at the same rate as they increase time and expense. Beyond a certain point, about 1,200 to 1,800 interviews, further increments of sample size improve the numbers at a rate that decreases rapidly to zero.

Samples of the correct size and design DO greatly improve the accuracy of polls, and the know-how for making such samples has greatly increased in recent decades. For the purposes of learning how to do scientific sample polls, carefully constructed samples of 100 to 500 can produce statistically significant findings with acceptable ranges of error. When a project involves a small sampling frame, such as a ward, a small city, or a university student body, the samples do not have to be extravagant in order to obtain reasonably reliable results.[5]

SAMPLING DESIGNS

We can discuss all the possiblities of scientific sampling under four headings: simple random samples, stratified random samples, area random samples, and multistage cluster samples. In all of these, it is necessary to use some form of "controlled randomization."

Drawing numbers from a hat is an obvious way to randomize the draws. That is exactly what a computer does when it generates a series of random digits. It is not difficult to write a program to print out a series of random numbers to fit any need. Most computer programs achieve this purpose by a combination of periodical intervals and random points, using the accidents of timing to provide the latter. If the researcher needs 1,000 random numbers between zero and 1,000,000, that is easily achieved; or any other pattern can be spun out instantly by the cheapest computer.

Why not draw numbers from a hat? This would be an alternative, but not a practical one. Why not just take the list of 1 million and pull some pages "at random," sticking a finger on each with your eyes closed, until you have collected 1,000 names? No good. It is impossible to get as random a selection in this way. The human brain abhors chaos and tends to systematize whatever it does. A researcher cannot trust himself to sample the list of 1 million so that every name on it has an equal chance of being drawn on each draw. Better trust the computer.

If a computer is not handy, can the researcher put together his own random digits just by writing down any numbers that pop into his head? No good. Try an experiment. After the first few numbers, you will find yourself repeating a pattern of some kind. Fortunately, almost every textbook on statistics includes tables of random digits, and lists in other forms are commercially available. These are not tailored to particular needs, but can be very easily adapted by using any parts of the lists.

If one needs 50 four-digit numbers to be the last four digits of telephone numbers in a certain area code, one can take the first four digits from any 50 numbers on the random digit list. If any of them are outside the known numbers assigned in the area code, one can substitute freely other random digits until the minimum is reached. Because the whole list is truly random, it is possible to use any parts of it in any manner.

Let us suppose we require a sample of 1,000 from a list of 150,000 names that is printed in a directory having 350 pages. Each page contains about 428 names; so we could ask the computer to supply three numbers between 1 and 428 for each of the 350 pages. Or we could ask for a single random number between 1 and 150, which we would use for our start; then we would take every 150th name. When we arrive at the end of the list, we will have 1,000 names. This procedure is called "systematic intervals with a random start." Or we could obtain 1,000 random numbers between 1 and 150,000, counting them off from the beginning of the directory to the end.

Each of these three procedures might have different advantages. If the names are in alphabetical order, we might prefer the third, which avoids the problem of periodicity. Certain names and letters are grouped according to ethnic background. Randomization based on pages would tend to undersample the Irish just slightly, because more of them are concentrated on fewer pages than other ethnic groups. The third method would avoid that tendency.

If the names were classified in other ways, for instance, geographically by town or state and alphabetically within each area, we would have to make some complex calculations. If geographic location were an important variable in our study, we would want to "stratify" our sample, that is, make sure that each area was represented in the sample in proportion to the number of people of the total list who live there.

If region is important, we would have to determine how many people are on the list from each state, then divide our sample into regional parts. If 10 percent of the total population is from the Northeast and we want to be sure not to over- or underrepresent them, then we would need 100 names from those states. We would have to see how many pages contain the 15,000 Northeasterners and design a random draw for them separately. We would do the same for other regions, ending up with a good 1,000 names for the nation as a whole, controlled for regional representation.

Similarly, if the names were classified on any other basis that we might want to consider as a variable, such as whether doctors had private or group practices, we would treat them the same as we did regions. By stratifying the sample in this way, we ensure that the sample does not over- or underrepresent a variable in which we are interested or which might unbalance our sampling mode. We could also stratify a variable that is not classified separately on the list. Hispanic background or the person's sex might be determined by merely examining the names.

We might desire to control for such variables. In that case, we would have to determine how many of each there are, and where the names are located in the directory. Then we could fashion a list of random digits appropriate to that segment of the whole list. While ensuring that 50 percent of the sample will be female, or 3 percent Hispanic, we must ascertain that, on the percentage of the draws from each subsample, every member of the class had an equal opportunity to be drawn.

These days, when so much polling is done on the phone, the computer not only spins out random digits but also randomly selects the area codes and exchanges in accordance with the sampling design and then selects the last four digits and dials the number.

Simple Random Samples

All scientific sampling is the planned use of chance to provide samples that do not contain any deliberate or subliminal bias. The sampling bin (or "frame," to use the technical term) must contain all the members of the population being studied, and all must have an equal chance of being included in the sample.

A simple random sample refers to drawing a sample by some uniformly random procedure from a homogeneous sampling frame. What particular method of random draws, or what particular series of random digits, will do the job depends on the nature of the frame that contains the population to be sampled. Examples of sampling frames are organization membership lists, mailing lists of all sorts, magazine subscription lists, names of all students matriculating at a university, all those who sign a petition, all office workers who car-pool, all Chicago taxi drivers, and so forth.

What is the population defined by the hypothesis? Is it possible to assemble a sampling frame for that population? If it is, then one need only examine the frame, decide on desired sample size, and then design a random method for drawing the particular members of the sample.

Stratified Random Samples

When a simple random sample does not guarantee that certain demographic characteristics are included in the desired proportions, then the researcher must stratify the sampling frames. The total population must be broken down into the appropriate demographic groups. Each subframe must be homogeneous with respect to the variable in question. Part of the total sample must be allocated to each subframe. The size of the total sample might have to be increased if it is found that some subsamples will be too small to permit statistical analysis.

Each part must have a sampling method appropriate to its form, and members of each subframe must have equal chances to be drawn as any other member of their own subframe.

Area Random Samples

When no directories or lists are available, area random samples may be used. Some of the most significant studies are faced with the fact that lists do not exist. This is like the task of the ecologist who wants to count the number of fish in a lake or the number of deer in a forest. He can sample the lake or forest in terms of small, accessible parts that are typical of the whole; then he can multiply the counts of each part by the number of comparable parts, which can be estimated, of the whole lake or forest.

Similarly, human area samples start with the assumption that everybody has to be somewhere on the grid of inhabited space. There are all kinds of sampling frames available of where people are located, where they live, work, and travel. The best and most comprehensive are the census tracts that are produced for the entire country by the ten-year count and by special studies in intervening years conducted by the U.S. Bureau of the Census. Other available area sampling frames are the post office zip code areas and telephone area codes and exchanges. In some places, auto license plates and social security numbers are area-coded. In addition, like the ecologist, the survey researcher can use comparable methods of assembling an area sampling frame in the wild, so to speak.

In area samples, the sampling bins contain, in the first instance, places rather than people. This includes census tracts, neighborhoods, "areas of dominant influence" (used for radio-television markets), states, counties, townships, municipalities, election districts (such as judicial or congressional districts), voting precincts, zip areas, and households. A sample may be designed on the basis of such lists or maps of such geographic entities.

A simple area sample of voting precincts could be structured by counting the total number of precincts in a state, randomly picking a certain number of precincts, then identifying a certain number of households in each precinct, where the actual interviews will be made. Random numbers can select the precincts, as well as the addresses or telephone numbers of the households in each.

Let us assume there are 5,000 precincts in the state. Voting precincts are roughly of equal population, about 500 voters. They are plotted to permit all the voters to comfortably reach a polling place and to vote without impossibly long lines during an election day of about 12 hours. Therefore all the precincts can be assumed to be equal in this respect.

It is usually better to stratify the sample. Then one breaks down the precincts according to relevant demographic data: urban, suburban, rural, average income per household, traditional party affiliation, and so on. It is necessary to specify the combination of variables to be applied in classifying the precincts.

Once that has been done, then one counts the number of precincts in each subframe, drawing randomly the correct number of precincts from each frame in accordance with the proportion of precincts with the same profile in the total population of precincts. Then one selects households within each precinct by an area random method, such as one house from each block based on a random digit. An interviewer might then go to each house and interview one adult who lives there.

What if there is no map or list of area units? It is still possible to area sample, but not nearly so well. One is placed in the position of the ecologist who must study statistically creatures whose homes do not have addresses. One can chart the number of trails in the forest, measure their lengths, and plot their locations. One can then calculate "units of trail," count the total number of such units, and apply some random means of selecting a sample of typical units. Then one can visit those units and pick a sample from the traffic found there.

Preferably, another analysis should precede this selection: ascertaining the amount of traffic passing each unit during typical parts of the day, week, or season. Then one would sample the traffic in accordance with the pattern of traffic, so that every hiker and camper in all areas at all times of the year would have an equal opportunity to be included in the sample.

In studies of public transportation use, one might prefer such a random sample of actual users, instead of using a screening device (How often have you used public transportation in the last month?) of an area sample based on telephone exchanges. Isn't this the same as a straw poll, when one stands on a random street corner and stops random passersby? It resembles it and suffers from some of the same problems; for example, self-selection or interviewer selection of ultimate responders will introduce important problems of bias. But there is a difference.

Such natural habitat area samples make possible statistical inferences from the findings. In the case of public transportation users, the researcher who carefully structures the area sampling frames can generalize about the total population and can apply measures of confidence and ranges of probable error to the results. In order for a straw poll to do this, it would have to cease to be a straw poll. The street corners would have to represent quantitatively all possible street corners in the city, state, and nation; and the people chosen would have to be proportioned quantitatively to the numbers of similar people passing similar corners at similar times of the day.

The researcher is fortunate in having a great variety of area sampling frames already at hand, so he is rarely forced to the expedients of the biologist. In addition, the latter only wants an estimate of total numbers of each species; he does not have to worry about stopping some and enquiring after their opinions. Thus he avoids the pitfalls of respondent selection bias.

Multistage Cluster Samples

The multistage cluster sample combines features of all the types we have examined. Usually starting with area samples on a broad national basis and narrowing these down into area samples of smaller size, it then applies some form of selection to identify and contact specific respondents.

The Gallup organization pioneered in this design for national samples. The whole country is divided into four geographic regions —

Northeast, South, Midwest, and West. Within each region, all population centers of similar size are grouped together:

Cities of 1 million or more
Cities between 250,000 and 1 million
Cities between 50,000 and 250,000
Suburbs of 50,000 or more
Towns between 2,500 and 50,000
Villages of less than 2,500

Using Bureau of the Census data, it is easy to determine the numbers of the population that reside in each of the six categories.

The first stage: A simple random sample of cities, suburbs, towns, and villages is drawn.

The second stage: Each population center chosen is divided into wards of comparable population. A random sample of these is drawn, structured so that the number from each class is proportional to the number of people who live in centers of that type.

The third stage: Each ward is divided into precincts, and from all the precincts (located in the selected wards of the selected population centers) a certain number are randomly drawn.

The fourth stage: Households are drawn randomly from each precinct in equal numbers.

The fifth stage: Some members of the selected households are interviewed. Even here, no discretion is allowed the interviewers. They are given instructions to ask for respondents in a certain order, interviewing the first one on their priority list who is available. Interviewers ask first for the youngest man 18 or over; and if no man is at home, the oldest woman 18 or older. What? That sounds like quota sampling, which was abandoned after the 1948 fiasco. But note the difference.

Quota sampling defines certain categories of respondents in order to structure a sample correctly in proportion to known demographics of a population. It was the means of controlling certain variables in order to get a correctly representative sample. In a national sample of 2,000, the pollster may decide to interview 1,000 men, 1,000 women, 250 farm dwellers, 900 town and small-city dwellers, 850 big-city and suburban dwellers, 450 from low-income groups, 1,200 from middle, 350 from high-income groups, 900 Democrats, 700 Republicans, and 400 Independents.

Of course, many of these categories will overlap three or four times. It is left to the individual interviewers to fill the categories with a certain number of real people, each of whom may satisfy three or four quota categories. The interviewer would set out to collect 15 respondents at the last stage of the multistage cluster design. The choice of households was based on an area random system, but the choice of respondents was left to the individual interviewers, and they could keep drawing households until the quotas were filled.

The result was found to be seriously biased toward "people who are at home, and who are very willing to be interviewed." Interviewers, left to their own judgments, would interpret their instructions to minimize callbacks and to pass over difficult or reluctant people without making a genuine effort to win their cooperation.

The experience of all polling organizations is that interviewers tend to undersample the poor, the less well educated, and racial and ethnic minorities. Quota samples are associated with voting preferences that lean to the conservative side. More Republicans than Democrats can be found at home and they are more likely to be forthcoming in a confrontation with a stranger. Even if that distortion were not based on experience, as it is, there is danger that leaving the ultimate selection to interviewers might upset "the planned use of chance."

With the abandonment of quota sampling for political polls, the priority list has taken its place. The interviewer must ask for "the youngest male over 18" first. If a male is at home, he must be the subject interviewed. No substitution is allowed. In the absence of a male, the oldest female over 18 is interviewed. If no one or no adults are at home, the interviewer must call back several times to get the mission accomplished. No substitution of the next household is allowed.

If the youngest male is busy or doesn't want to talk, the interviewer presses and even agrees to come back later; after a specified number of rejections at a single household, that unit is reported as "nonresponse" and is not replaced by another. Should the nonresponding households exceed the limits, the poll would be considered null and void and done over again with a new sample. Such events are, fortunately, rare.

The priority interview system prevents the element of interviewer discretion from upsetting the planned use of chance. The reason for using it at all arises from long experience in door-to-door poll taking. Sample designs attempt to include certain basic demographics in proportion to their known distributions in the population. Sex and age groupings are fundamental. Yet household-based samples always tend to skew the sample strongly in favor of middle-aged females.

The group least likely to be at home or to answer the door are young males. Older males are next most scarce and older females next. Because the age and sex distributions are known and show some significant correlations with voting and other behaviors, the samples are adjusted to correct for imbalance. This means that male responses will be treated as though they constituted 50 percent of the actual sample, even though household sampling always produces more than 50 percent females.

This is a legitimate and necessary adjustment. But such mathematical weighting of the results must be minimized. If the actual preponderance of middle-aged females in the sample is too great, it will begin to undermine the probability numbers assigned to the underrepresented demographic groups. To avoid this danger, without returning to the questionable practice of quotas, the priority list was developed. This has been found to bring into reasonable scope the adjustments that may have to be made to weight important subsamples so that the total sample will mirror the real world. (In Chapter 10 we will show mathematically how this is done.)

Household sampling tends to discriminate against large families. Because all households are treated as equal in the multistage sampling design, and one interview is taken from each, persons of the same age and sex may have less chance to be selected in large families than in small. This distortion can be disregarded because the planned use of chance is focused on households rather than on individuals. It has not been found to be a serious problem so far.[6]

A multistage cluster sample for telephone numbers can be constructed on the same model. For a national poll the whole country is divided into regions on the basis of certain characteristics that lend themselves to being grouped together. Such characteristics as climate, crops, patterns of industry and settlement, geographic proximity, and shared topographical features lend themselves to such regional classification.

The telephone company prints demographic data on area codes and exchanges. We know where they are, how many telephone numbers are assigned in each, and the actual ranges of assigned numbers. With these data in our sampling frames, we can go through the various stages of random selection.

We pick a sample of the area codes so that they model, in terms of the size and density characteristics of various types of population centers, the total population of area codes in each region. Then we break these down into the exchanges they contain. These are randomly sampled so as to yield a set of exchanges that constitutes a good model of the universe of all exchanges in those area codes.

Then we sample the selected exchanges with computer-generated numbers to constitute either the last two or more of the four main digits of real telephone numbers. We include in the sampling frame all assigned numbers in the exchange that at this stage compose the sample. Having set a target for a certain number of interviews, we allocate these among the exchanges in proportion to the known total households gathered in each exchange.

Most numbers are assigned consecutively in each exchange area, which contains close to 10,000 telephone/households. The turnover of numbers tends to be constant, so that the tasks of constructing sampling frames are greatly simplified. The problem of unlisted numbers, which would be very destructive if the research used as a sampling frame the ordinary telephone directory, does not exist for the multistage cluster design. That is because the unlisted numbers are included in the telephone company data, and the chance of selecting them is exactly the same as that of listed numbers.

NOTES

1. See Morris James Slonim, *Sampling/A Quick Reliable Guide to Practical Statistics* (New York: Simon & Shuster, 1960), p. 6.

2. Actually, after the first draw, each additional draw increases slightly the chances of each remaining stub being chosen. This is because there are fewer stubs in the box. To eliminate this inequality, one should return each stub after it is drawn and mix it with the others. This is known as sampling with "replacement."

3. Maurice C. Bryson, November 1976; quoted in Richard Link, "The Literary Digest Poll, Appearances Can Be Deceiving," *Public Opinion*, February/March 1980, p. 55.

4. See Seymour Martin Lipset, "Different Polls, Different Results in 1980 Politics," *Public Opinion*, August/September 1980, p. 60.

5. See Charles H. Backstrom and Gerald D. Hursh, *Survey Research* (Evanston, Ill.: Northwestern University Press, 1963).

6. See William G. Cochran, *Sampling Techniques* (New York: Wiley, 1963); and Leslie Kish, *Survey Sampling* (New York: Wiley, 1965).

CHAPTER TEN
SAMPLING FRAMES

All sorts of people use all sorts of lists for all sorts of things. The collection and publication of demographic characteristics of populations, counts of attributes and things, lists of names and addresses, maps and charts of how people and things are distributed over space are available in many forms and places.

Every encyclopedia and atlas constitute a wealth of sampling frame information. All the various annual directories and almanacs are full of data that can be used for designing scientific samples. Every membership list and every professional and industrial yearbook provide sampling frames rich in potentials for sample survey research. Every handbook of government data, *Who's Who*, lists of college graduates and alumnae, subscribers to print media, visitor books at historic shrines, collections of returned warrantee cards for merchandise, registration lists for voting — there is no end to the sampling frames available.

The best guide to sampling frames is the local reference librarian. Of course, the *U.S. Census Reports* are indispensable, most comprehensive and universal, standardized deliberately in order to enhance usefulness, and always close at hand in a good library. Conducted in every decennial year (year ending in zero), and more frequently for some areas, the data are continuously updated and improved. In 1980, giant strides were taken to enlarge the data banks by having one-fifth of the respondents fill out a long form that ventured into new demographic areas.

Aggregate data, that is, totals of things distributed over people and space, are just as important as the demographics of people. Knowing how many tons of coal are produced is just as important as knowing how many people work in the mining industry. How many bathrooms and bedrooms per family, how much income is spent on recreation, and how much on education are important parameters that permit research designs to isolate variables and to stratify samples in order to test new hypotheses. The census data are rich in aggregates and in frequency distributions useful to public opinion, motivations, and market research.

List brokers in the last 50 years have surged to prosperous careers. Business firms that in the normal flow of business compile lists have been able to realize a bonus profit through buying, selling, and trading such lists. Often a company quitting business sells its customer lists for more money than its tangible assets. Newspapers and magazines are heavily into this business, as are advertising and promotional firms of all sorts. The flood of junk mail and telephone solicitations has raised new issues of invasion of privacy and new efforts to restrict the traffic in lists.

This is not a new phenomenon. Forty years ago, anyone could buy the *Reader's Digest* subscription list for a single use for a couple of hundred thousand dollars. The addressograph plates were jealously guarded by the company, to avoid pirating or resales. Anyone who bought the list received only one set of labels, installed at the *Reader's Digest* own facilities, so that the list couldn't be copied.

The advent of the computer has made the list business more accessible to more people and more quickly and cheaply. Thus brokers are engaged not only in buying major lists but also in compiling their own. Just as public affairs and politics tend to adopt every innovation that proves itself in the marketplace, so the use of lists became just as important in the pursuit of public influence and in the work of government as it had become in business.

Lists as sampling frames for opinion study are of considerable moment. Tracking and targeting have become standard methods of planning and conducting campaigns for public influence and office, as they are in marketing products. With the development of the computer, the appetite for lists has become voracious. Enormous data base sets are being compiled for every purpose, including political tracking and targeting.

Census tapes include data by block groups, each of which contains about 1,000 people, or 325 households. There are about 2.5 million block groups in the 1980 figures, as compared with 1.7 million in 1970. The difference is accounted for by expansion of the census tract areas in the methodology. Micro data samples are included. These are individual family census reports, from which all names and other identifying information have presumably been removed to protect confidentiality. The sample of micro data represents about 1 percent of the population, but gives an excellent profile of family statistics, pinpointed by geographic area. Such national data were not available to public users before the last decade.

With these data, users can create their own sample surveys for unique population segments, or can target their audiences, and can weight the results to achieve the most perfect matches of samples and real world ever. The 1980 census provided income data for the first time for households, as well as by class of individuals and families per census tract.[1]

The interest generated by the census tapes was responsible for discovering a number of routine Census Bureau errors. In early 1983, in response to questions raised by the users, the bureau recalculated per capita income figures for 400 of the nation's 3,100 counties. There was a key error in the clerical tabulating of the long forms, which resulted in overstating incomes. In 1990, this aspect will also be automated, officials said, and a repetition would be less likely.[2]

"Crisscross" directories, put together by commercial companies, are available for virtually every community in the United States. They are of great importance for sample design. Essentially, they are lists of names, addresses, and telephone numbers classified in three axes: (1) alphabetically by last name, (2) numerically by telephone number and exchange, and (3) alphabetically by street name and numerically by address number on each street. Many of them include places of employment and whether each person owns or rents his or her housing. One can easily imagine the value of crisscross directories to bill collectors, police and fire agencies, salespeople, burglars, and politicians.

If a fire is reported at a certain address where no one is at home, the phone number next door can be looked up and that person asked where the victim may be contacted. A bill collector can, from a headquarters a thousand miles away, call up the neighbors of a deadbeat and try to get information about his whereabouts. In a day when telephone polls are replacing door-to-door polls, the crisscross can be used to translate an area sample, based on census tracts, for example, into a sampling frame of households, acquiring names and telephone numbers without the expense of hiring and training a local interviewer.

Their value is attested by the profitability of companies that publish them every year, an expensive undertaking. H. A. Manning Company of Bellows Falls, Vermont, produces directories for 60 major cities in the Northeast. Hill and Donnelly Company of New York City brings out more than 100 directories. They are not cheap, but they sell famously. Specialized crisscross directories are available that cover just commercial businesses and industries, including doctors and dentists, engineers, and so on. For pollsters who cannot afford to subscribe, many libraries are subscribers on their behalf.

Excellent sampling frames are lists of registered voters. These can be acquired with no cost from every board of elections in every city, county, and state in the country. They are generally listed alphabetically by street and numerically on each street by number. And, of course, they are organized into precincts, which are compact contiguous neighborhoods of about 500 voters each.

In states with closed party primaries, the voters are identified by party preference, a demographic of considerable interest to pollsters, permitting sample designs to test all kinds of hypotheses about political trends, the growth of independent voting, split tickets, issue salience, and so forth. Such lists are still printed on paper, but we can anticipate that they will become available on computer disks, in order to eliminate the expensive and slow human interface in the sampling routine.

Other useful sampling frames: Marquis Publishing Company of Chicago provides a host of sampling frames, including a whole family of *Who's Who* — by region, by profession, by age group (*Who's Who Among High School Students*, for example). The company also publishes annual directories of medical specialists, social workers, attorneys, mental health workers, and so on.

Burrelle of Livingston, New Jersey, puts out "special groups" media directories covering the following: blacks, European ethnics, Hispanics, Jews, older Americans, women, and young adults. It advertises: "It is a matter of audience acceptance and trust. Embed your message in a framework of culturally familiar communications.

Reach people through their favorite media. Whether you are marketing information or ideas or products, there is no better return on investment." In addition, Burrelle publishes statewide media directories in most states and provides ready-to-go pressure-sensitive mailing labels for any client.

The *Harvard Encyclopedia of American Ethnic Groups* is comprehensive and useful, but not updated often enough. The *Black Resource Guide* made its appearance in 1982. Published in Washington, D.C., it contains names, addresses, and officers of black businesses, schools, civil rights groups, associations, purchasing data, and demographics of black communities throughout the country.

Located in Chicago, National Business Lists, Inc., provides every conceivable list on businesses throughout the world. If one desires, for example, the name and address and officers of every Canadian firm that has more than 100 employees, one can get it moved from a Chicago computer to one's own computer by a telephone modem in minutes.

Every chamber of commerce and industry has a list of all business firms in its counties, available for the asking. Many of them also maintain mailing lists of fraternal service and voluntary organizations, women's clubs, organized social groups, and church-related groups. Gale Research Company of New York City brings out the *Encyclopedia of Associations* every year with 14,726 groups listed, including names and addresses of officers. The company also publishes other directories, such as *Biography and Genealogy Master Index*, *Consultants and Consulting Organizations*, *Directory of Directories*, *International Who's Who*, and a list of research centers.

The American Society of Association Executives, headquartered in the national capital, also publishes an association directory and a *Who's Who in Association Management*. Ballinger Publishers of Cambridge, Massachusetts, has newly entered the field with *The PAC Directory*, a list of 3,350 registered political action committees, including names and addresses of officers and sponsors, financial data on contributors, and political and issue alignments.

Every sampling frame has advantages and disadvantages, depending on the use one wishes to make of it. Some are not complete, some are too expensive, some are not generally available at all (for example, social security numbers in the government's computers). Those we have mentioned are mainly for purposes of illustration and do not constitute in any sense a complete inventory. It is hoped they will give the researcher a few ideas that he or she can expand with the help of the nearest librarian.

THE U.S. CENSUS

The best and most universal basis for sample design comes from the U.S. Bureau of the Census. Perhaps the reader has noted the critical role played by census data in all the lists and sampling frames we have so far examined. The researcher can go straight to the original data at no additional cost except his own labor. If he desires the original data tapes with all the unpublished materials, these are available at nominal charges. (Turning these into useful data can be costly, however.) Because they cover the whole country on a uniform basis, the census data provide the ultimate information for all kinds of sampling and is especially good for area samples.

Virtually all of the United States is now divided into census tracts for statistical purposes. Tracts are designed to be relatively uniform with respect to size, population characteristics, economic status, and living conditions. The average tract has 4,000 residents, and they have been maintained over time so that longitudinal comparisons may be made from census to census. The boundaries of each are drawn cooperatively by Census Bureau demographers working closely with local committees. Other boundaries are respected (such as municipalities, townships, counties) in order to make the data more useful for existing administrative and electoral bodies.

In each decennial census, the census tract is the smallest unit for which all parameters are tabulated. The practice of local agencies using the same units in tabulating their own data has greatly increased the value of the tract system. Local boards of election try to keep election districts coterminous with tract boundaries when reapportionments occur, although that is not always possible. Tracts are numbered in consecutive series, with separate numerical series for the central population center and for each county. Insofar as practicable, numbers are consecutive within each community and township.

The concept of census tracts was originated by Walter Laidlaw in New York City in 1906. He was convinced of the need for homogeneous subdivisions as the basis for studying neighborhoods smaller than boroughs or wards. At his urging, the bureau in 1910 tabulated data from New York and seven other cities (with populations over 500,000) in this manner. So popular did the system become that a clamor for similar data arose in the land. In the 1930 census, the number of cities was increased to 18, expanded in 1940 to 60, and by 1960 to 180. In 1970, 241 tracted areas constituted most of the inhabited urban areas of the country (and Puerto Rico).

The tracts are grouped in Standard Metropolitan Statistical Areas (SMSAs) and are today the basis for every kind of statistical use by government, academic researchers, and commercial firms. The system has proven invaluable and has been imitated to some extent by every country in the world.

Much of the credit goes to Howard Whipple Green of Cleveland, Ohio. In his capacity as chairman of the Committee on Census Enumeration Areas of the American Statistical Association, he undertook to locate "key persons" in each SMSA, a trained statistician and member of the association who took responsibility for organizing local people and bureau officials into a committee. Such committees would then undertake to define the census tracts and to maintain a census tract library. In 1955, the bureau itself took over these duties.[3]

The U.S. Census has become a central political institution in American life, invisible but potent. Billions of federal and state dollars are allocated to state and local governments in accordance with the official census counts. However difficult it is to govern these days, it is incontrovertible that governments could not function at all without the data provided by this means.

Every census opens a Pandora's box of controversy about undercounts, about systematically missing the young, the poor, minorities, illegal immigrants, and welfare families. Officials and politicians try to maintain the flow of dollars and to hold on to electoral districts and legislative seats in areas that have lost population.

The 1980 U.S. census was proclaimed by bureau officials "the most successful of all times," while critics accused it of being "a costly, futile exercise." Costing $1 billion, it has been surrounded by controversy, scandal, charges of inaccuracy and incompetence, threats by members of Congress to make their own adjustments, proposals for ditching it in favor of small scientific sample surveys, and despairing cries for help from declining urban centers.

Attempting to make 1980 a model state-of-the-art effort, the bureau introduced a number of radical innovations, including computerizing everything. It was anticipated that the raw data would be processed in record time; and indeed the first summaries began to come out within six months. But three years later, the publication of results had slowed to a crawl and had fallen behind the 1970 schedule.

For the first time the major survey was done by mail. Starting with mailing lists compiled by commercial organizations, such as the crisscross directories, checking these by computer against driver license registrations, temporary employees scoured the streets and countryside to check and complete the lists. These were loaded into computer data banks that printed out labels for mailing the two types of forms: the short form to 80 percent and the much longer form to 20 percent, the latter sampled by taking every fifth household on the lists. In addition, April 1 was a special day appointed for physical canvassing of transient areas where mailing lists could not be compiled: hotels, flophouses, college dormitories, tenements with typically rapid resident turnover, and so on.

The initial mailing achieved a return rate of 86 percent, exceeding the most optimistic projections. The nonreturns were dealt with first by mail reminders, followed by face-to-face follow-ups. "Follow-up One" sought to find 30 million people who had slipped through the net. After four callbacks, people who still had not completed the questionnaires were classified as "last resort cases," which were canvassed with more direct legal threats under "Follow-up Two."

The high return rate was greeted by huzzahs of praise for the devoted citizenship of Americans and the efficiency of the bureau. The 1980 returns showed the highest returns from suburban areas with large numbers of young families of moderate incomes. The nonreturns were higher from more affluent areas, and highest from ghettos and slums, like West Chicago, South Philadelphia, and the upper and lower East sides Manhattan.

Not cost-efficient, declared Philip M. Klutznick, secretary of commerce in charge of the census. A better head count could be obtained for a fraction of the cost: "Half a dozen demographic experts using scientific sampling could have compiled a 95% accurate reading of the population for less than $1 million."[4] The actual census is expected to have as high or higher error rate, and will have to be corrected by doing sample surveys anyway, he said. The whole thing is an expensive charade, which should be relegated like the *Spirit of St. Louis* to the Smithsonian.

In 1970, the bureau calculated an undercount of 5.3 million; this included an estimated 8 percent blacks, 2 percent whites, and close to 100 percent illegal immigrants, mainly Hispanic. In its preliminary 1980 count, the bureau came up with a total U.S. population of 230.97 million (as of early 1983), which was an adjusted figure to provide for the inevitable undercount. The predictable hue and cry arose from the land. New York City refused to accept figures that indicated a 13 percent drop in population (down a million from 7.8 million in 1970). All the older cities were alarmed by the loss of federal dollars at a time when their welfare rolls were bursting their seams. The East was dismayed to lose substantial numbers of congressional seats to the West and Southwest.

Independent research organizations were hired to conduct sample surveys to check the bureau's figures, readily establishing huge undercounts everywhere. Mayors flaunted census maps that showed people living in urban renewal areas where in fact there were only parking lots. In New York, a telephone survey of 2,030 people, including 500 blacks and 500 Hispanics, asked the question: Did you or anyone in your household fill out and return a census form this spring? It showed a 7 percent undercount, about half a million people. Penn & Schoen Associates, which did the study, placed the real figure higher, allowing for a margin of "socially desirable" answers, many respondents being presumed to want to answer the question positively.

Political and financial impacts of the count were resisted everywhere, and in 1983 most of the court challenges were still pending. An example of the impact was the fate of Occoquan, a town in Fairfax County, Virginia. It was forced to convert city hall into a gift shop when its population count went from 1,600 to 241, wiping out 90 percent of the $3,500 federal subsidy that constituted its annual budget.

The Census Bureau continued to do its own sample surveys in order to estimate undercounts, especially to get reliable data on illegal immigrants, thought to be within the range of 6 to 12 million and increasing each year by another half million. By its own reckoning, the 1980 census would end up with slightly better accuracy than any previous count. It was estimated that the black undercount was about 4.8 percent on a national basis, 7.5 percent for black men and 2.1 percent for black women.[5]

Congress moved into the act. A bill that would allow the legislature instead of the Census Bureau to adjust the figures died after a week of hearings. Many witnesses pointed to the danger of "cooking the figures" for political reasons, bringing back "rotten boroughs." Better to let the bureau cook the figures with statistical formulas, attempting to soften complaints by compromising a little and by giving the result an objective imprimatur. Better not to shift the focus from counting to haggling! Congress did authorize another national census in middecade but failed to provide any funds. The bureau said it would not move for an 1985 census unless Congress acted again.

The 1980 census may be the last universal count. Interim samplings are superior in every respect, and many predict that Congress will see the logic by 1990 and change the law. It is argued that sample surveys will not provide solid census tract data for every part of America, but surveyors reject that argument. The methodology is available to create the same impressive data banks by sample surveys, while still saving 90 percent of the agony and cost.[6]

There are signs that increasing numbers of people are no longer in a mood to give out information about themselves. To make matters worse, Andrew Hacker points out, the 1980 forms came around income tax time. The new forms attempted to increase their usefulness in terms of government's entry into so many intimate areas of life, asking all kinds of personal questions. The long form required about 320 answers from a family of four, including 30 open-ended (such as the "activities and duties associated with your occupation"). To do the job properly required maintaining household files on last year's fire insurance premiums, water bills, and interest payments on savings.

In a report, the comptroller general criticized the bureau for inadequately developing evaluation and adjustment techniques to correct census errors. He called for a formal program of applied research for statistical analysis at subnational levels.[7]

Over the past three decades, the bureau has used two techniques; the demographic method and matching studies. The former combines records of births, deaths, and net migrations to estimate true totals. The latter involves samples (ordinary random samples of selected areas and groups) who are reinterviewed, plus reverse record check samples (spot-checking information on Medicare rolls or IRS records).

Both methods were challenged. Records that are sampled are themselves incomplete, and reinterviews present some of the same problems as the census itself. The postenumeration survey of 250,000 sample households, which was part of the original 1980 plan, had to be cancelled because it would have delayed the reports required by the Constitution for congressional reapportionment. This cancellation, the comptroller general asserted, seriously "sacrifices precision in estimates of coverage error."[8]

AUDIENCE SAMPLING

Three major research organizations are involved in rating broadcast audiences. Radio audiences are measured by Pulse, Inc., and Arbitron and television audiences by Arbitron and the A. C. Nielsen Company. Each embraces different methodologies and sampling frames.

Pulse

Pulse has stuck to face-to-face interviewing, using both long- and short-answer questions and emphasizing "roster/recall," that is, the ability of respondents to look at a roster of programs and recall something about them. This approach, Pulse claims, "enables us to estimate all listening, wherever it occurs − in the home and out − plug-in or mobile."

The personal interview allows Pulse to measure "not tuning, but listening . . . not sets to which nobody may be attentive, but the attention itself . . . by all members of the family." The interview is also used to acquire qualitative information in depth "regarding audience make-up, buying habits, product use and interest" at the same time as they measure listening.[9] Pulse claims its methods avoid "the fixed panel bias" of machine or diary methods. It includes in its samples "people who have no telephones, who cannot or will not use diaries, and who refuse to permit attachment of devices to their radio and TV sets."

Using a multistage cluster sample, with the interviewers knocking on the doors of the households selected at the last stage, the "sample can be designed and executed to represent total populations." Because a different random sample is spun out each time, "no family knows in advance that its habits are of concern to anyone." This Pulse calls "natural program selection," uninfluenced by the Heisenberg effect.

Pulse samples 160 markets at least once a year each. In the larger markets, measurements are taken more often. New York, Los Angeles, San Francisco, and Chicago are measured year-round, while the next 25 markets are tested once every three months.

In each market, area clusters based on census tract and SMSA data are randomly drawn. The O. E. McIntyre Company provides a data bank of telephone households. A random set of starting points are generated. Interviewers are sent to the preselected blocks and intersections. They go to households adjacent to the ones drawn from the telephone number list. In this way the problems of unlisted numbers or no-phones, unlisted rich and unlisted young/poor, are circumvented. In each tract 12 households are interviewed.

Sampling is proportional to the known demographics of each market. The interviews are quality-checked by telephone from the central New York office. If no telephone number is listed, the checks are done by mail. About 3 percent of all the respondents are spot-checked. Pulse reports a nonresponse rate of 15 to 20 percent overall. One callback is standard practice. Statistical findings are weighted in terms of known distributions of age, sex, and ethnicity for the markets (using census aggregate data as the basis).

Arbitron

Arbitron's sampling frames are also based on 160 media markets and use census tract data to estimate aggregates. The market is defined in two ways: a Metro Survey Area (MSA), which generally corresponds to the Standard Metropolitan Statistical Areas of the census, and the Total Survey Area (TSA), which is defined to include every county within range of at least two AM radio antennas, located in an urban center, with transmitting powers of 500 kilovolts. TSAs are mapped by actual signal strength readings required by the Federal

Communications Commission as part of station keeping. Both MSAs and TSAs are adjusted somewhat from the technical basis to include adjacent cells of populations that receive listenable signals because of topographical features.

The survey areas are updated once a year, in April, based on listenership numbers during the past two spring surveys. The MSA may cover three to five counties, while the TSA typically covers ten to twenty. Counties are called metro and nonmetro counties.

Arbitron has depended on a company called Metro-Mail Corporation, the nation's leading supplier of listed telephone households, to provide the sampling frames. Arbitron then designs the multistaged clusters, which are based on telephone area codes and exchanges for each MSA and TSA.

Listed telephones in each county are sorted into order by zip codes. Business numbers are removed from the list. The computer counts the number of listings in each county and divides this number by the quota allocated to that county (in proportion to total population of entire area). This gives an interval number. Within each interval, the computer generates a random number that corresponds to a household within that interval. Example:

	Households needed	Listed Telephone Households	Interval
County X	121	25,400	210

In order to catch unlisted telephones, Arbitron uses an expanded sample frame that supplements the sample design. This system uses number series within each exchange and randomly selects numbers regardless of whether or not they are listed. Arbitron calls these "unlisted leaping lizards." This is done as follows: A telephone exchange is defined as the first five digits of the seven-digit telephone number. The number 745-1234, for example, would be listed in the bin of exchanges labeled 754-12xx. To be a complete dialing number, it requires the last two digits. Obviously, this particular set contains 100 numbers (from 00 to 99). The computer saves all the listed numbers in each set, counting the sum of all remaining numbers, which by process of elimination are the unlisted ones. A systematic random sample is drawn from this bin in exact proportion to the ratio of listed to unlisted numbers.

A letter is mailed, alerting each family in the sample that it will be receiving a telephone call from an Arbitron representative within a week. When the call comes, the purpose of the survey is once again explained, the number of persons in the household is ascertained, and then the diary is mentioned. Will the family agree to keep a diary of radio listening for one week? There is a nominal cash payment, now about $1, but emphasis is placed on the contribution to improving the medium that will result.

Up to five callbacks per household at various times of the day aim at preserving the integrity of the sample. Noncooperation or "can't be contacted" account for about 30 percent of the names in the original sample; the design allows for it. The diaries are mailed from Arbitron headquarters in Beltsville, Maryland. Just before the survey week begins, the interviewer telephones again to say "hello" and "don't forget to start keeping your diary tomorrow." The sample design takes account of the past experience that only about 55 percent of the diaries are actually returned and found usable, a serious nonresponse bias.

Sample size varies with the size of the market. The top eight markets in the country (such as New York City, Chicago, Los Angeles) use a sample objective of 1,500 to 3,000 in the MSA and 1,900 to 3,500 in the TSA. The next 23 large markets seek samples of 1,200 and 1,600, respectively. The 43 medium markets seek about 700 and 900, respectively, and the 90 smallest markets 450 and 550, respectively.

The radio sweeps of the markets are done one to four times per year. Smaller markets cannot be surveyed more than once per year because the costs become prohibitive. Larger markets contain many more stations with much greater budgets. They can afford, and their advertisers require, more current rating data. The survey period lasts for three or four weeks in each market, although a new sample is used for each week.

Arbitron believes that its method is generally better than others because the diary is personal, portable, and covers seven days of radio listening on a 24-hour basis. It is much more economical than the Pulse interview system, thus permitting larger and better samples. It can go anywhere the mail goes and can obtain a great variety of demographic and other marketing information. Some feel that the anonymity of respondents helps to avoid "social approval" bias, which is maximized in face-to-face interviews.

Arbitron is also in the TV rating business, competing directly with Nielsen in station/market research, while leaving national audience rating to Nielsen alone. The methodology is roughly the same as for radio, with diaries constituting the primary tools for data collection and analysis. About 212 markets are surveyed from one to three times during the regular season and once in the summer in the larger markets.

Because TV transmissions are governed by a different set of natural (and FCC) laws, the definition of a market has to be considerably different from radio. These are called "Areas of Dominant Influence" (ADI) and are based on measurable viewing patterns within the range of the transmitting antennas centered in urban areas. Every county in the country is assigned to one or another ADI. The term "dominant influence" refers to the fact that signals overlap geographically, so are separated in terms of the dominant signals in any given area. By definition, ADIs cannot overlap.

It is assumed that the urban center where the signals come from is also the main merchandising, social, and government center for the population within the range of its messages. ADIs are a geographic market design, Arbitron says, "which defines each market exclusive of another, based on measurable viewing patterns."[10] The ground rules require that the total viewing hours per channel for a county be measured by markets of origin. "The market of origin having the largest total percentage is deemed to be the dominant influence in the county, and that county is allocated for ADI purposes to that market of origin." Such markets are divided into MSAs and TSAs, as in the case of radio markets. The basic demographic data are based on census SMSAs and can be broken down by census tract and telephone exchange, as desired.

The rest of the procedure closely resembles that of Arbitron for radio, except that the TV diary is slightly more complicated. It aims to cover all household viewing for a week on a particular set, with entries made by the quarter hour, indicating when the set is turned on and off, what channel it is tuned to, and who is watching.

Sample sizes and methods of drawing them are identical to that previously described. The percentage of usable diaries returned from the original sample is also comparable to radio, 55 percent. The information is not as good as Nielsen's meters in providing accurate data about set use, but it is superior in testing audience composition and attention.

It is estimated that Arbitron spends $20 to $50 per household in conducting each survey. Subscription to "The Book," the confidential report published in each market for each survey, costs stations and advertising agencies (anyone may subscribe) from $12,000 (one survey for a small market) to $75,000 (for network affiliates in large markets) per year. The cost to advertisers and agencies is proportioned to their spending for commercial time in a particular market or group of markets.

"The Book," as it is known in the trade, is of considerable moment to everyone. Advertising rates are based on cost-per-thousand-per-commercial-minute (CPM/PCM), so that costs to advertisers and income for station owners are dependent on the numbers. One percentage point of audience share can mean millions of dollars per year of income won or lost. It can mean shake-ups in management and among account executives, changes in station program formats and personalities.

In the early 1970s, Arbitron piggybacked a general market research program on its radio-TV capabilities, with samples drawn from households that participated in earlier TV diary surveys. Families are asked, by mail, to complete a questionnaire on their purchases of brand-name products over a specified period. Using the same ADI sampling frames enables inferences to be drawn concerning the long-term impacts of TV advertising.

Nielsen

The Nielsen Company calls its primary sampling frames "Designated Market Areas"(DMAs). They are roughly equivalent to the ADIs in structure, definition, and purpose. When Nielsen adapted the audimeter to television so successfully, it became dominant in the field and abandoned radio rating completely. Today, it issues two rating reports, the *Nielsen Station Index*, which publishes the results of surveys in 220 TV markets separately, and the *Nielsen Television Index*, which does the same for the United States as a whole, treating it as one tremendous marketplace.

The firm maintains 13 offices around the country from which about 90,000 diaries are placed for the individual market reports. At least three times a year — November, February/March, and May — national sweeps are carried out in 220 markets by means of these diaries. Bigger markets may be measured more often.

The DMAs are sampled pretty much in the same manner as is true of Arbitron. A county is assigned to a particular DMA when 50 percent or more of the viewing involves a given urban signal transmission center. Nielsen sends diaries to all the no-answers and refusals anyway, hoping to reduce sampling error.[11]

In the early days of radio-TV rating, the test week began on Monday and ran until the following Sunday. But it was found that "diary fatigue" set in by the weekend and that figures for the last couple days were clearly fudged. Because weekend is important viewing time, both companies have moved the start of the diary week to Thursday, finding the results much more even. Young households show the poorest return rates and 35 to 49 age groups the highest. Both companies tend to oversample in low return categories, especially in low socioeconomic areas. Incomplete diaries are discarded.

The national Nielsen ratings are entirely separate and are performed mainly for national networks, advertising agencies handling national accounts, and the advertising/public relations officials of national and multinational corporations. The sample size follows the rule of all national polling designs, encompassing about 1,200 households. As we have seen, a properly designed random sample gives acceptable confidence of good numbers in about this range, whether the total population be 50,000 or 81 million. This is based on statistical inferences and the operation of pure chance.

The 1,200 are drawn by a multistage cluster sample allocated to the DMAs in proportion to total market sizes. The areas are broken into census tracts that are structured in accordance with certain demographic variables in order to ensure sample representativeness of ethnic, socioeconomic, and age factors. The area sampling eventually provides the exact locations of the households that interviewers will visit to ask permission to install one of the devices.

Cooperation is reported to be about 70 percent. Panel families are paid an honorarium of $25 (in 1975) and a pledge to pay half of any TV repair bills. There is a planned turnover rate of 20 percent to refresh the sample and guarantee that it ages overall at about the same rate as the entire population.

Until 1973, the sample households were equipped with an audimeter attached to each TV set, requiring that families mail in and replace a cartridge very two weeks. In 1974, the 1,200 homes were installed with the Storage Instantaneous Audimeter, which is wired directly to a Nielsen computer in Dunedin, Florida, and its 24-hour contents can be transferred from the entire sample twice a day.

But who is watching? To get an answer, Nielsen uses a matched sample of 2,400 households, two for each one in the basic sample, matched for all important demographic parameters. In their homes, a recordimeter is attached to the TV set that measures cumulative set use year-round. During certain specified weeks per year, the damned thing beeps every 30 minutes while the set in turned on. When that happens, the viewers are supposed to record in a diary the viewing information for that moment. The electronic record is compared with the diary as verification. By matching these data with the sample data of the Storage Instantaneous Audimeter, Nielsen can measure national program audience totals, broken down by all the identified variables (age, socioeconomic factors, and the like) that may be of importance to the clients.

The national ratings have become sort of a horse race of great public interest. People want to know how their favorite programs are doing, whether other people share their feelings about them, whether they are likely to be a commercial success and survive for another season. To nurture this general interest, all the media report the Nielsen Overnights and the sweep period ratings with the same fascination, if not more, as is accorded to presidential elections.

The firm issues two main reports: *The Nielsen Television Index National Audience Composition Reports* contains data on "average minute" audiences for all national programs. *The Market Section Audiences Reports* breaks down program viewing by the specific demographics of audiences.

Because the five major metropolitan areas represent more than 45 percent of the total U.S. population, during the past ten years Nielsen has been converting them to the Storage Instantaneous Audimeter, away from the diary method that is used for the rating of particular markets. This enables the networks and the media to get overnight readings of prime time TV shows, providing fresh grist for the mills of gossip about shows still fresh in everyone's mind, and providing network programmers with rapid feedback on the struggle for audience attention.

Counterprogramming has become a tense, quick-reaction game, moving programs around on the weekly schedule every few weeks, to maintain audience flows and to eliminate weak spots, vulnerable places where other networks may be tempted to stage a raid. The five major metro markets are rich enough to bear the added costs of this system on a permanent basis.[12]

Having described and considered the dimensions of scientific sampling design, methods and applications of randomization, selection of sampling frames, simple and complex random sampling, stratification and weighting, it remains for us to learn the statistical tools. If we design and execute a scientific sample poll, we are entitled to apply important tools that can illuminate findings and measure their solidity.

NOTES

1. See Andrew Radoff, "Census Data, New Studies Highlight NRC Meeting," *Editor and Publisher*, December 13, 1980, p. 19.

2. *Washington Post*, January 31, 1983, p. A2.

3. See U.S. Bureau of the Census, *Census Tract Manual*, 5th ed. (Washington, D.C.: U.S. Government Printing Office, 1966).

4. *Washington Post*, March 25, 1981, p. A4.

5. See Illinois Council for Black Studies, "Black People and the 1980 Census: Proceedings from a Conference on the Population Undercount" (Chicago 1982).

6. See Andrew Hacker, "Why the Big Census Is a Big Mistake," *Washington Post*, March 30, 1980, p. C1.

7. Report GGD-81-28, December 1980 (Washington, D.C.: U.S. Government Printing Office).

8. Ibid., p. iv.

9. *The Pulse Idea* (New York: Pulse, Inc.), pp. 2-3.

10. Elizabeth J. Heighton and Don Cunningham, *Advertising in the Broadcase Media* (Belmont, Calif.: Wadsworth, 1976), p. 182.

11. A fair number of these, according to Heighton and Cunningham, are returned completed.

12. An interesting comparison of diary and hardware methods in these cities indicates that the former tend to underreport daytime viewing, as well as viewing after prime time, and the viewing at all hours of nonnetwork channels.

CHAPTER ELEVEN
STATISTICS FOR POLLSTERS

The field of statistics is viewed with a jaundiced eye. There are three kinds of liars, said Mark Twain: "liars, dammed liars, and statisticians." A statistician is a person who knows the price of everything and the value of nothing; he would marry Elizabeth Taylor for her money.

Numbers stand for things that can be counted, that is, made up of similar and roughly equal units. Numbers are an invention of the mind. Nature is a hodgepodge. It is only by an act of abstraction that the properties of things can be resolved into calibrated parts. "Mathematics is a man-made artificial subject. It is not THE TRUTH," says mathematician Morris Kline. Nevertheless it makes possible remarkably accurate predictions and descriptions of the world, greatly enhancing the success of human actions. It is "the prime instrument for creating theories and deducing facts."[1]

Measurement is simply counting things and parts of things under given names. When the parts constitute unmarked subdivisions of a class, then we lay a ruler against the instance in hand. A ruler is some continuous baseline, arbitrarily divided into equal units. By creating rulers of all types, humans achieve the remarkable capability of making numerical comparisons between their artificial rulers and natural objects, thereby also enabling similar comparisons among natural objects themselves. In this way qualities that are undivided and ineffable in nature can be counted (measured) in terms of how many artificial units they contain, in terms of whether they are more or less than any other instance that can be arrayed against the ruler.

Numbers are ways of arraying, comparing, and organizing things and bits of things that have names. Things that are defined as wholes, that is, that are total and physically separable from each other, may be counted under their own class names (apples, oranges, or fruits). Properties that are not wholes and are not physically separable are called qualitative. They can be measured against some ruler that breaks down the quality into a series of identical units. Qualities can then be counted just like whole things in terms of more or less total units. It is in this manner that the mind goes from qualitative to quantitative phenomena.

In dealing with people statistically, one assumes that the things to be counted are composed of identical units. Are people really interchangeable? Are opinions, attitudes, and values that can be given the same names really the same? These searching issues must be explored if we would justify the use of statistical analysis.

Big data banks, big computers, big reliance on polling techniques are seen as part of the dehumanizing trends of modern mass societies. Some say big governments are increasingly insensitive to the human beings they serve. Alienation and anger are the inevitable result among the people. Certainly there is much lamentable about modern society. The fact that things may be "better than ever" doesn't spare us from present challenges. The uses of statistics and computers have potencies for both good and ill. New capabilities for human action spring from technique and technology. A conflicted and misguided person armed with a huge data bank and a computer can do more mischief than a lone assassin with a gun.

Human relations haven't changed that much. And the growing importance of numbers need not destroy human values. We strive to count only those aspects of human beings that can be classified together and therefore can in fact be counted. We are mindful not to lump together aspects that are different. Making fine distinctions is the main task of social science. And, in fact, statistics provides the capability for better management of our affairs, including more tender regard for the unique qualities of individuals. Statistics is the means for organizing vast congeries of data, for preventing humankind from becoming choked by overloads of information, from losing even more control over their life concerns.

The ability to improve the management of our affairs should have the effect opposite to the warnings of contemporary Luddites. The appetite for more and better information has always been construed as a powerful factor for good, enhancing humankind's ability to dream more dreams and to fulfill more of them. That is still the case. The alternative to managing information is chaos.[2]

Statistics is society's way of getting a handle on large-scale reality. The seven blind men of the old tale could have described the elephant, of which each could feel only a small part, if they had made a few measurements and put them together. The Census Bureau describes with its figures a reality about the nation, one that cannot be put together in any other way. Quantities must be plugged into all the qualitative categories in order for the big picture to emerge in all its majestic detail.

Statistics can be dangerous. They can be misused. Numbers make wonderful cudgels for winning arguments. "Even meaningless numbers can be made to ring like fine crystal, shattering intellectual resistance with pure, unassailable truth."[3] Tricky bar graphs fabricate illusions with honest numbers by adjusting the scale ratios in order to highlight a misleading fact. In a group of competing breakfast cereals, all essentially the same, the bar graph numbers accentuate small differences to appear to be of critical magnitude. Even compelling statistical correlations between two events or two variables do not prove that one causes the other. Spurious associations are endowed with great plausibility because of the authority radiated by the numbers.

There is "foolish precision" in masquerading soft facts under hard numbers, a practice too often followed. Unless every member of the class of things is really the same in the respect that is being counted, then the numbers are misleading and meaningless. False quantification is an ever-present tendency in this quantophrenic world. There is an uncritical worship of numbers that invites that dazzling third place after the decimal point that ends all argument.

Just as statisticians should attempt parsimony in the use of numbers, so we will attempt parsimony in the dose of statistics required for scientific sample surveys. This is a situation where "less is more." Students of public opinion need not be statisticians. But they must be able to generate a few standard quantitative measures for their own work and they must be able to know what the numbers mean.

We will describe and explain the basic measures that are needed in scientific sample surveys, how to apply them, and how to use the formulas to get correct answers. We will provide several examples of each. In addition, we will try to show their limitations and problems.

STATISTICAL SIGNIFICANCE

Let us assume we have been diligent in designing our sample. We put together an appropriate sampling frame, which included all the elements of the population we wish to study. We devised a scientifically random method for drawing from that frame, so that every element had an equal opportunity to be drawn on every draw.[4] We have counted the frequencies of characteristics in our sample, whether demographic or opinion variables. We tally these and write our reports.

Because we have been so conscientious in our work, we are entitled to describe our findings quantitatively. We may say: So many percent in the sample approve of Reaganomics, so many disapprove, so many had no opinion. But the purpose of the sample is to enable us to estimate the distribution of variables in the total population, not just in the sample. So on the basis of the sample findings, we may make inferences about the general population.

We have this right because we followed the procedures of scientific sampling. In addition we can measure our degree of confidence that the estimates will fall within a measurable range of error. This is extremely important for everyone to know, especially in the community of users of the report. If at an acceptable level of confidence the range of probable error is greater than differences in the distribution of a variable, then we say the findings are not "statistically significant." For example, the sample reveals:

1984 Presidential preference:

Mondale	46%
Bush	43%
DK	11%
Total	100%

Suppose we state that at an acceptable level of confidence the probable error is 5 percent. That means that the correct distribution of pro-Mondale preferences in the total population is estimated somewhere within the range of 46 percent plus or minus 5 percent, a maximum of 51 percent and a minimum of 41 percent. The correct distribution of pro-Bush voters in the total population is estimated to be 43 percent plus or minus 5 percent, a maximum of 48 percent and a minimum of 38 percent.

The correct figures for the total population, calculated by applying to the sample findings the laws of chance, may lie anywhere within those ranges. Examination of the figures reveals they overlap. There may actually be more Bush than Mondale preferences in the total population. Bush could have a maximum of 48 percent and Mondale a minimum of 41 percent.

Given these sample findings, a statistician would be forced to conclude that the results are inconclusive, too close to call. The difference in voter preferences found in the sample is less than the range of probable error. Technically, we would say that the findings at an acceptable level of confidence are not "statistically significant."

If the sample findings had shown a large enough difference in voter preferences, then, at the same probable error of 5 percent, we might have been able to declare "statistically significant" estimates for the total population of all voters. This would require a finding that Mondale was at least slightly more than 10 percent ahead of Bush, so that subtracting the maximum error from his count and adding it to his rival's would leave him still ahead. Mondale 51 percent, Bush 40 percent, at a 5 percent probable error range (both plus and minus), would mean that the estimate projection to the total population would show Mondale with a minimum of 46 percent and Bush with a maximum of 45 percent – Mondale still ahead.

Returning to original sample findings, we might still make "statistically significant" estimates of total voter preferences if the range of error at an acceptable level of confidence could be reduced below 1.5 percent, let's say 1.4 percent. That would calculate out to a minimum Mondale preference of 44.6 percent and a maximum Bush preference of 44.4 percent, with Mondale ahead. With these figures, we would report the statistically significant estimate that all American voters probably prefer Mondale, by a slight margin.

We could reduce our range of probable error by increasing our sample size. However, as we will see, very large increases in sample size will mean only minuscule reductions in the range of error. Given the expense of very large increases in sample size, which will not materially remove the error, we may opt for merely reading the sample results as "too close to call" and let it go at that.

Of course, if the sample findings had shown a greater disparity between Bush and Mondale, then even without increasing the sample size we would be able to make a statistically significant estimate for the entire population. How large should a sample be? Apart from the element of cost, the sample must be large enough to ensure that the results are within the limits of chance error that satisfy the researcher and/or the sponsor.

CONFIDENCE INTERVALS

We have been using the phrase "at an acceptable level of confidence." The commonsense meaning of that phrase may have made it sound harmless enough. But it has an exact statistical meaning, and it is not harmless at all — but central to our ability to measure the range of error in estimates of a total population that are based on small scientific samples.

Introduced as a standard parameter of statistical inference about a generation ago, the phrase refers to the chances that our specific sample might resemble other such samples drawn from the same sampling frame. It is a calculated number, representing a ratio between the number of samples that might be drawn (of the same size, from the same sampling frame, drawn in the same manner) that (1) show a frequency distribution of a given variable within the predicted range of error, as compared with (2) samples that show a frequency distribution of the same variable outside the predicted range of error.

Another way of putting it: We are entitled to have confidence that our estimates of the total population are within the range of error in direct proportion to the chances of drawing another sample that confirms those figures. If we were to draw many, many samples of the same size, from the same bin, by the same method, we would gradually gain confidence that our particular sample is a good one. In addition, we could quantify our confidence in direct proportion to the ratio between confirming and disconfirming samples.

If after drawing many such samples, 100 percent of them were within the range of predicted error, we would naturally feel 100 percent confident that we have a good sample. We would feel 100 percent justified in jumping from the sample findings to estimates of what we could find if we counted the whole population. If after many samples, we found that half of them were outside the interval of predicted error, we could naturally begin to doubt the quality of our first sample.

We could express this doubt by saying that our confidence has dropped. It is not 100 percent, but considerably less. If we wanted to give it a number, we couldn't express it more vividly than by using the actual percentages of confirming/disconfirming samples. So we might say our confidence is 50 percent that further samples drawn would, in terms of the frequency of a given variable in the samples, show numbers within the predicted range of error. This is the same as saying that, on the basis of past experience, one can expect that one out of two of any future samples (of the same size, drawn from the same bin, in the same way) will be within the range of error.

Levels of confidence are expressed in percentages and have been standardized at levels that correspond to certain typical normal distributions, which we will discuss later. At this point it will be useful to know that standard levels of confidence are 68 percent, 95 percent, and 99.6 percent. One could calculate levels in between, but in most cases that is not necessary. For most statistical inferences, that is, estimates of whole populations based on scientific samples, a 95 percent level of confidence is sufficient. The highest level of the three is considered "virtual certainty" and is often achievable in sample surveys. The 68 percent level may be all one can muster for a particular finding, and may occasionally be useful, but it is too low to be seriously considered in most cases.

A statistical inference, accompanied by a stated margin of error, is reported in this fashion: "The poll found that American voters preferred Mondale over Bush by 46 percent to 43 percent. This result, plus or minus 1.4 percent, is accurate 95 percent of the time." Sometimes the caveat is ended with the phrase "in 95 percent of the cases." Or sometimes: "At the 95 percent level of confidence, the result would be expected to fall between plus or minus 1.4 percent if all Americans had been interviewed." This language may be translated as follows: An infinite number of samples of the same size, drawn from the same population, in the same manner, would show results 95 percent of the time within the stated margin of error; or, of all the samples thus drawn, statistical theory tells us that 95 percent of them would show results within the stated range.

Confidence levels make essential statements about statistical data. Without them, the data themselves would be inadequate and even deceiving. A common misunderstanding arises. Many assume that the range of probable error refers directly to the frequency of the variable in a population. They are tempted to say that the range of "plus or minus" 1.4 percent means that 95 percent of the people interviewed accurately reported their preferences and that the cumulative errors in their reports added up to plus or minus 1.4 percent.

The range of error of an estimated distribution of a characteristic in a population refers to the likelihood that a certain percentage of identically designed samples will confirm a frequency within that range. The percentage of such confirming samples constitutes the quantitative level of confidence. Probable error and confidence refer to sampling chance, not to the likelihood that people will accurately report their preferences between Bush and Mondale.

The chances of validity and reliability in self-perception and interviewing, including nonresponse, mistaken understanding of questions, hostility toward the interviewer, and practical difficulties of locating and reaching people indicated by the sample design, add additional sources of survey error. But these are not measurable by the laws of chance.

One has to say that these sources of error will probably increase the range of probable error by an uncertain amount. Of course, every attempt is made to control such variables; most of the time such attempts can be regarded as successful — as can be seen in the range of normal deviation between forecast and actual election results, which generally is smaller than the range of error given in the confidence interval.

FIGURING PERCENTAGES

Before demonstrating how to calculate these numbers, we must cover preliminary mathematical steps. We take nothing for granted and begin with changing raw totals into percentages.

A percentage is a ratio of two numbers to each other on a base of 100 (literally, that is what the word says — "per centum"). It amounts to saying: If I had 100 of these (instead of the number one actually has), how many of that 100 would share any given characteristic?

A number that is twice the size of another number is 200 percent of that number. A number that is half of another number is 50 percent of that number. To calculate percentage parts, one adds the raw numbers of all the parts to get the base number, and then divides that total into each of the parts that compose it, as follows:

	Raw sample results:	
Mondale		644
Bush		602
DK		154
Total		1,400

Going from raw numbers to percentages requires dividing a number by the base. In the above example, each raw number must be divided by 1,400. The decimal can be removed by multiplying the result by 100, which is the same as converting the base number to 100. Going from percent back to raw totals merely requires reversing the operation, dividing the percentage figure by 100 in order to reintroduce the decimal, then multiplying the product by the raw number of the base.

There are three standard measurements of central tendency: average, median, and mode.

Average (or arithmetical mean) refers to loping off differences in order to equalize a set of numbers that make a certain total. Everyone already knows how to calculate an average. You simply get the sum of all the parts and divide by the total number of parts. Put another way: An average of a list of numbers equals their sum, divided by how many numbers there are.

Median refers to the middle number of a set if all the numbers were arrayed according to their values, from lesser to greater, and the array were sliced in the center. Half of the numbers in the set would have lesser values than the median number, and half would have greater values than the median number.

Calculate the median of a series of numbers by counting the number of separate items (not values), dividing by 2; now count that number of items in order of value, beginning with either the lowest or highest, until you find the middle item. The value of that item is the median. If there are an even number of items, then find the average of the two middle numbers to determine the median value.

If the values of the greater and lesser items are in balance, then the median coincides with the average. However, if they are skewed, then average and median will diverge. Skewing means that values of the items, not how many separate numbers there are, tend to be out of balance; that is, while higher and lower parts are equal in how many items each contains, the divergence of their values from the mean is unequal.

A normal distribution curve is symmetrical. The separate numbers and their values are in balance. In common language, that means the distribution tails off from the central tendency equally, both above and below. For each number below the median number, there is one above it that departs from the median by about the same amount. The average departures from the median, both above and below its value, are equal. Average and median coincide (see Figure 11).

FIGURE 11.
Normal Distribution

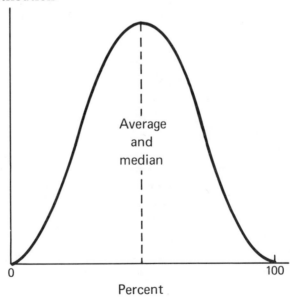

Percent

An asymmetrical curve indicates a distribution that is skewed away from the median. If the average falls to the left of the median, this indicates that the larger numbers diverge farther from the median than the smaller numbers. If the average falls to the right of the median, this indicates that the differences between the smaller numbers and the median are greater than those between the larger numbers and the median. There are the same totals of items on each side of the median in a skewed as in a normal distribution, but the values of the items do not balance each other off.

Mode refers to the highest point on a bell curve, the number or value that occurs most often in a series. It may not coincide with either the average or the median. It has very little significance in a flat distribution, but becomes more pronounced when the central tendency is strong.

The laws of chance can be expressed in mathematical form. Formulas have been worked out which enable us to calculate standard deviation and confidence intervals. These algorithms are based on the simple principle that things can be expected to happen by chance in inverse proportion to the number of potential outcomes that are equally likely.

A coin has two sides; there are two possible outcomes of a toss. The inverse is therefore one out of two. That states that the chance of throwing either a head or a tail is 50 percent. On two or more throws, the fraction is multiplied by itself once for each additional toss.

Chance of heads on a single toss = 1/2
Chance of two heads on two tosses = 1/4
Chance of three heads of three tosses = 1/16

This simple example illustrates an important point: The chances of getting any given series of results from repeated tries vary inversely as the square of all the possible outcomes to each try. If the chance of getting a head on one try is one out of two, then getting two heads on two tries it will be one out of four and so on. In a series of acts governed by chance, in which the number of possible outcomes remains the same, the chance of getting a given series of outcomes varies as the square root of the total possible outcomes.

Similarly, we can readily determine that the probability of getting two heads in one toss of two coins is 1/4, or .25, or 25 percent. If the probability that an event will happen is 1/4, then the chances that it will not happen is "one minus 1/4" or 3/4, or .75, or 75 percent.

This is the law of square root, which governs virtually all probability theory. In the case of a six-sided die, the chance of getting any of six numbers on a single toss will be one out of six. The chances of getting the same number twice in a row will be one out of 36. Notice the number of possibilities on each toss is squared for each additional toss. The inverse of a square is a square root.

Whether you want to look at the odds for or the odds against any given outcome, it is much easier to resort to the right mathematical formula than to enumerate the possible outcomes. In this way complex probabilities, like rolling 16 dice or tossing 30 coins at a time, can be readily calculated. But the principles in these complex calculations will be exactly the same as those described here for the simpler events.

Random sampling is based on the laws of probability. Each draw is a toss of the coin with the same number of possible outcomes as there are elements in the sampling frame or members of the population.

STANDARD DEVIATION

Attempts to estimate the characteristics of a total population from a sample are bound to stray somewhat from the figures obtained by making a 100 percent count. The difference between the two numbers is the sampling error. In order to find the sampling error, we must first calculate a "standard deviation," or SD.

The SD is the average deviation from the arithmetical mean. If we take an average of a group of numbers, then list the differences between that number and all the original numbers (both minus and plus), and then average those — we will have the standard deviation. For example, to calculate the average age of a classroom of 30 people we add together all the ages and then divide by the number of people. Let's say we find an average age of 27. Now we add and subtract all the ages to this number, listing only the differences. For a person age 22, we will list 5; for a person age 42, we will list 20; and so on. Now we add all the figures on the list (as absolute numbers) and divide the total by the number of figures on the list. The result is the average deviation from the average or mean.

In a large number of chance draws from a bin, we apply the square root law to get the SD. We multiply the fractions of the total sample by each other (*P* for those draws that contain the parameter, *Q* for those that do not), divide this by the number in the sample (*n*), and take the square root of the product.

What happens if we double the sample size? With each increase in sample size, the sampling error goes down. We can also see another implication of the square root law, that it only goes down at a rate that is related to the increased sample by the inverse of the square; or, in other words, that continued increments to the sample size bring about rapid diminution of improvement in sampling error. Very quickly, further increases in sample size lead to improvements in sampling error that are microscopic, hardly worth the investment.

Multiplying the size of the sample by some factor divides the sampling error by the square root of that factor. In order to reduce the error by half, the sample size must be quadrupled.

In a real-world situation, we do not know the actual distribution of a variable in a population; to find out is our reason for sampling it. Therefore, we cannot figure a standard deviation from the total numbers of red and green marbles. Instead, we do it in terms of the sample itself, using the formula:

$$\text{SD (in \%)} = \sqrt{\frac{P \text{ (\% of green)} \times Q \text{ (\% of red)}}{n \text{ (number in sample)}}}$$

Let us assume that we randomly draw a sample of 100 from the barrel, finding 52 percent green and 48 percent red in our sample. For future discussion, let us consider *Q* to stand for the absence of *P*, or *Q* = not *P*. Whatever variable whose frequency in a population we seek to measure we shall call *P*. In percentage figures the whole population is 100 percent. So *Q* will always be equal to 100 minus *P*. The formula looks like so:

$$\text{SD (in \%)} = \sqrt{\frac{52 \times 48}{100}} = 4.9\%$$

Just to drive the procedure home, let's try it with different numbers. Let green marbles constitute 67.5 percent of the draws in a sample of 1,500:

$$SD = \sqrt{67.5 \times 32.5 / 1,500} = 1.20\%$$

Remember that the SD is the average difference between the mean sample result and all other possible sample results. The operations of chance are working to give us a sample with measurable variations from the results of an infinite number of samples of the same size, drawn in the same manner, from the same sampling bin.

The counts of green marbles in an infinite number of identical samplings would yield a normal distribution curve with a mode or mean close to the range of the actual distribution of green marbles in the barrel. If we know the barrel has 67.5 percent green marbles, we would expect most of the samples of 100 each to have about that number of greens. However, we know that this will not happen. There will be samples with hardly any green marbles and samples almost entirely made up of green marbles. If we draw a curve of green marbles in many samples of 100 each, it will look like Figure 12.

Let us return to the previous set of findings. We do not know the actual proportions of red and green marbles in the barrel; our sample however contains 52 percent green specimens. In estimating the actual percentage of green in the barrel, we may broaden the mean of all hypothetical (possible) samples by the value of one standard deviation, plus or minus, to account for sampling error. This will include about two-thirds of all the possible samples that could be drawn. With a sample size of 100, the value of one SD is 4.9 percent, or 5 marbles. If we include all samples within the range of 52 plus or minus 5, or all samples that contain a count of green marbles between 48 and 57, we will have accounted for about two-thirds of all possible samples.

Thus, we could say, using the earlier definition of confidence intervals, that based on a sample showing 52 percent green, we are about 68 percent confident that the real distribution of the characteristic in the whole barrel is a figure somewhere between 48 and 57 or, to put it simply, about 52 give or take 5.

If we enlarge the range of error by two times the SD, we will be including about 95 percent of all possible samples of the same size, drawn in the same way, from the same barrel. See Figure 13. Thus we could state at a 95 percent level of confidence that

FIGURE 12.
Green Marbles in Samples

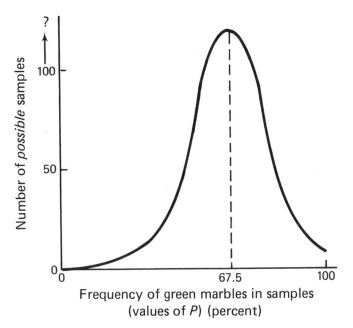

Small numbers of the samples will show high or low divergence from the known value of P.

the actual percentage of green marbles in the barrel lies between 42 and 62 percent. If we enlarge the interval by three times the SD, we are able to say with virtual certainty (99.6 percent confidence) that the actual count of green marbles in the barrel is somewhere between 37 and 67 percent (see Figure 14).

In order to calculate the SD for distributions that have more than one P and Q, one finds the SDs for all the variables in the population and figures an average in terms of the proportional frequencies of each. Let us take as an example the results on a question: Whom do you consider the most effective member of Congress? In a sample of 1,000, six congressmen were invariably mentioned:

FIGURE 13.
Confidence Intervals, 68% and 95%

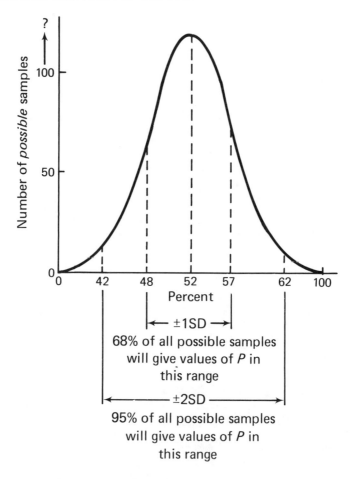

± 1SD: 68 percent of all possible samples will give values of P in this range.
± 2SD: 95 percent of all possible samples will give values of P in this range.

FIGURE 14.
Confidence Interval at Virtual Certainty

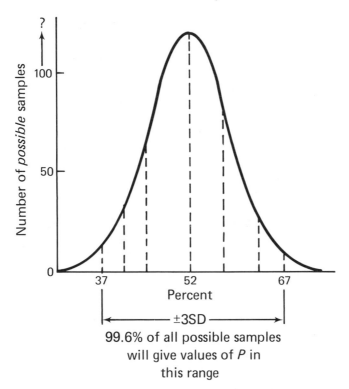

Congressman X	32%
Congressman Y	23%
Congressman Z	16%
Congressman A	15%
Congressman B	9%
Congressman C	5%
Total	100%

To calculate an SD for this question, one derives a separate SD for each result, treating it as *P*, and adding the rest together as *Q*. One should get SDs for each finding: X, 1.4; Y, 1.3; Z, 1.1;

A, 1.1; B, 0.9; and C, 0.7. In order to average these in proportion to their frequencies, one must multiply each by its frequency percentage, add them together, and divide by the base of 100. This will yield a derived SD (in this case, 1.2) for the entire poll item:

$$SD = \frac{(1.4 \times 32) + (1.3 \times 23) + (1.1 \times 16) + (1.1 \times 15) + (.9 \times 9) + (.7 \times 5)}{100}$$

Obviously, one can't have everything both ways. Probability is a trade-off of values. The greater the degree of certainty, the wider the range of the prediction; the more precise the prediction, the lower the degree of certainty. Such a wide range of possible error may vitiate the main purpose of our statistical projection. If we require a better basis for confidence, or if we need to know whether there are really more green than red, none of the sampling results may please us.

We can increase the size of the sample. Some early increments will reduce the standard deviation usefully. As we have seen, the increments lose efficacy rapidly after one passes approximately the 1,000 mark. Look at some of the relationships that exist in the formula. Assuming we want statistically significant results — that is, the difference between P and Q in the sample is greater than the range of probable error — then

- The lower the SD, the higher the stated level of confidence may be for the findings, and vice versa.
- The higher the number in the sample, the lower will be the SD, and vice versa.
- The greater the skewing between P and Q, the lower will be the SD, and vice versa.
- The higher the level of confidence that can be stated, the larger the sample, the greater the skew in the parameter, and the lower the SD, or the reverse.

All these propositions are contained in the formula for confidence level, which may be written thusly:

Where $SD = \sqrt{P \times Q / n}$, then
Confidence 99.6% = $P \pm (3 \times SD)$
Confidence 95%   = $P \pm (2 \times SD)$
Confidence 68%   = $P \pm SD$

We will invent a number of poll examples to demonstrate the calculations. Let's start with a simple two-value question. A poll is taken among registered Democrats. Which of the following two candidates, Gary Hart or John Glenn, would you like to see win the 1984 Democratic nomination? Results: Hart 54 percent, Glenn 46 percent.

The sample size is 1,400. We calculate SD = 1.3 percent. We can report the results of our poll. At a level of 95 percent confidence, estimates based on the sample indicate that Hart's support among all registered Democrats is somewhere between 51.4 and 56.6 percent (that is, 54% ± 2 × 1.3%); Glenn's between 43.4 and 48.6 percent (that is, 46% ± 2 × 1.3%). Because Hart's minimum is still greater than Glenn's maximum, we can report that the results are statistically significant at the 95 percent level of confidence. That is, even allowing for chance sampling error, Hart wins the poll.

Another three-value question. Sample size 850. Results: for nuclear freeze, 58 percent; against nuclear freeze, 22 percent; not sure, 20 percent. The SD for the largest response is 1.7 percent For each of the other responses, the SD is about 1.4 percent. The average SD for the item as a whole is 1.57 percent.

The responses make it very safe to report the positive response, which is loud and clear. Even at 99.6 percent confidence, this estimate is significant. However, the division between those opposed and unsure is within the range of sampling error; the researcher would have to note this fact and report that a very large minority, 42 percent, were unwilling to endorse the freeze, but the division between these two responses was inconclusive.

A two-valued question, with results too close to call. Sample size is 555. For handgun registration, 52.2 percent; against, 47.8. The SD = 2.12 percent. At 95 percent confidence, the sampling error range is 4.24 percent. If we add that figure to against and deduct it from for, the results overlap. The result therefore is inconclusive. We should report this interesting and revealing fact. And next time increase the sample size.

If we designed a question with more alternative responses, we would proceed in the same manner. Calculate the SD for all the options and then state each with ± 2 × SD. That would permit us to state our findings at 95 percent level of confidence.

How does the survey researcher state the levels of confidence and SDs for a long complex questionnaire? Taking sample size and the results on the major items on the poll, one can take the coward's way out: Consult a nomogram, a chart provided in statistical handbooks. These will yield the desired index. Or we can figure it out ourselves with a pocket calculator and the above formulas. Which items on the poll should be rated by a confidence level/ sampling error statement? The most substantive and central issues of the poll — following the example of the *New York Times* and mentioning in a methodological note that the error may be larger for smaller subsamples.

WEIGHTING AND ADJUSTING

It is customary for a syndicated poll to print a methodological note along with the poll results, usually under the heading "How this poll was conducted." This follows rules adopted by polling organizations in order to enable readers to distinguish between good and shoddy work. Typical is a 1982 survey conducted by the *New York Times*. The note says in part:

> Based on telephone interviews conducted March 1-6 with 1,530 adults. . . . The sample was selected by a computer from a complete list of exchanges . . . chosen in such a way as to insure that each region was represented in proportion to the numbers in the population. For each exchange, the numbers were formed by random digits, thus permitting access to both listed and unlisted residential numbers.
>
> In 14 percent of the households a second member of the household was also interviewed to obtain factual information when the initial respondent did not feel knowledgeable.
>
> In theory, it can be said that in 95 cases out of 100 the results based on the entire sample differ by no more than 3 percentage points in either direction from what would have been obtained by interviewing all adult Americans. The error for subgroups is larger, depending on the number of sample cases in the subgroup.[5]

Note how carefully this disclaimer is worded. Readers are now in a position to understand the full implications of the language. Note especially reference to the 14 percent households where the sampling rule was apparently violated — but, no! Only to get factual information verified. The note ends with mention of the professional pollster responsible for design and conduct of the poll: "Assisting the *Times* . . . is Dr. Michael R. Kagay of Princeton University."

Also included in the note are the following words we wish to highlight:

> The results have been weighted to take account of household size and to adjust for variations in the sample relating to region, race, sex, age, and education.

What does this indicate? Can a pollster change the numbers in the sample after the fact? Doesn't this look a bit sneaky? Yes, it does look suspicious. If it were done to accomplish a preconceived distortion of the results, it would be dishonest and dastardly. If done correctly, with dedication to truth and without insidious unconscious intent, adjusting and weighting are justifiable; indeed, they are necessary to improve the accuracy of the poll.

Adjusting and weighting indicate that parts of the sample have been increased in numbers and parts decreased in numbers, so that, in regard to certain variables, the overall sample is structured as an exact microcosm of the whole sampling frame. These are the methods used to control certain variables in the sample after the fact. Based mainly on parameters of aggregate data from the census, this is often necessary to correct for slight imbalances in the sample actually drawn.

No new interviews or cases are introduced into the sample. All the cases already there as a result of the original research design are kept intact. They constitute the scientifically randomized draw and are not to be changed. However, the accidents of the draw may result in over- or underrepresentation of known attributes. There may be too many women as compared with men, too few blacks as compared with whites, too many retired people as compared with young and middle-aged.

If such discrepancies are overly large, then weighting cannot be used. To stretch the already too-short blanket will not help the situation. It will only increase the problems of sampling error for these subsamples. Then adjustments are inadmissible. But, on the other hand, if the confidence intervals for such subsamples are within an acceptable range, then no harm and much good may be accomplished by adjusting the overall sample to make it a better replica of the overall population.

Because no new interviews are added, weighting means that each significant part of the total sample is multiplied or divided by a fraction that will give the poll results for that part more or less weight in the overall results. If there are 10 percent too many women, then those interviews are treated in the overall tallies as though there were 5 percent less; by the same token, the gross figures of male respondents are treated as though there were 5 percent more.[6] The actual breakdowns of responses for each group remain the same; there is no tampering with the integrity of the interviews and the sample design.

We have seen that the problem of representing important variables in the sample can be addressed in a variety of ways: by providing interviewers with a priority list in asking for specific respondents in a door-to-door or telephone household selected by a multistage cluster method. "May I talk to the oldest male over 18?" Or by stratifying the sample design itself before the sample is drawn. In this case each important subgroup is sampled separately from different subsampling frames — in accordance with the numbers of each subgroup in the general sampling frame. Lists of census tracts composed of 90 percent black people can be drawn from separately, in order to get the right percentage of black respondents. This is carried out in the same scientifically random way.

However, some important variables are difficult to stratify. With area samples and multistage cluster samples, it is easier to weight and adjust for sex, age, and education variables after the fact, providing the adjustments are not overlarge. Information on these factors is provided by the poll itself, and it is no formidable task to program the computers for the simple calculations required to bring all the actual subsamples into alignments that replicate the known universe.

We have noted another method used until the 1948 presidential election for solving the representation problem, quota sampling. In this method, the subsamples were built into the sampling design ahead of time, and the interviewers were assigned the job of filling the interview slots with the right respondents. As we have seen, this method was found seriously wanting because it undermined the principle of randomization.

Quota sampling is no longer used in sample surveys, although it still enjoys a respectable place in depth and focus-group interviews. In these techniques statistics takes a place second to qualitative hypotheses; and it is important to design and recruit the samples to represent certain constituencies. This is done by telephone "screening" interviews, aimed mainly at tagging recruits in order to fill representation quotas. This is entirely honorable and necessary for the purposes at hand. The eclipse of quota sampling in sample surveys should not be confused with quota recruiting in depth and focus interviewing.

Election polls are increasingly weighted in terms of a "probable electorate" in order to reduce volatility errors and improve forecasts. The sample is drawn by the usual multistage cluster methods. The polling instrument contains added questions dealing with voter registration (Are you registered to vote this year?), past voting behavior (Did you vote in the last presidential election?), and current voting intentions (Will you vote next Tuesday?).

These are not screening questions, and the interviews are not aborted in the event of negative answers. All the responses are tallied, including those that respond negatively to these questions. The positive responses indicate the "probable electorate." The results of both probable and improbable voters are then weighted in accordance with the known percentage of Americans who actually turn out and vote on election day.

In an analysis of the 1936 Literary Digest poll, one writer claims that such a weighting would have produced a correct forecast of the Roosevelt-Landon race, even though the sample design left much to be desired. "A modest amount of data analysis could have saved . . . a great deal of embarrassment and mythical notoriety."[7] Richard Link points out that the original poll included information on how the respondents reported their 1932 votes. The 1932 actual voting returns might have been applied to adjust the 1936 findings, awarding the electoral voters of each state to the candidate with the higher adjusted percentage.

Two kinds of adjustment are used in modern election polling: adjustment by swings and adjustment by ratio.

Adjustment by swings =

$$1936 \text{ poll } \% - (1932 \text{ poll } \% - 1932 \text{ actual vote } \%)$$

Adjustment by ratio =

$$\frac{1932 \text{ Actual vote } \%}{1932 \text{ Poll } \%} \times 1936 \text{ poll } \%$$

Take the case of California. In 1932, the *Digest* found that 46.8 percent of voters planned to vote Democratic; actually, California went that way by 61 percent, 14 percent higher than indicated. In 1936, the *Digest* found 46.3 percent saying they planned to vote Democratic. If the 1932 experience had been applied to adjust the figures, using either method, the state would have been listed in the Democratic column, as it was in the actual voting returns.

By the same methods, Link points out, a total of 19 states would have been moved to the FDR side in the 1936 projections, and the results would have pointed to a Democratic landslide, which it was. The editors of the *Digest* had a conscious policy of not adjusting data, simply telling the story of results. The 1936 poll is always held up as an example of poor sampling. Perhaps, Link opines, it should rather be held up as an example of the fact that "failure to adjust bad data can also be fatal."

The mathematics of weighting are not formidable. In essence, we take the results of any given item on a questionnaire and tally the results separately for each of the subgroups intended for adjustment, changing them into percentages (which we will represent with the symbol Z). Now we have all the separate subgroups figured on the same basis of 100, without regard for how much of the collective result we wish each part to constitute. We multiply each set of figures by the fractions of the population (in percent, which we will designate with the symbol D) that we wish each part to constitute and divide by 100 to return to the original percentage basis. The formula:

$$Z \text{ (adjusted result)} = \frac{(Z_1 \times D_1 \%) + (Z_2 \times D_2 \%) + \ldots}{100}$$

To work it out for the easiest example, male/female ratios, let us take a 1980 poll between Reagan and Carter. The sample size was 1,000, of which 400 were male and 600 female. The raw figures were the following:

	Men	Women	All Respondents
Reagan	240	270	510
Carter	160	330	490
Total	400	600	1,000

We were to report the result for all respondents (whether in raw figures or changed into percentages), we get Reagan — 51 percent,

Carter — 49 percent, a very distorted and wrong picture of feelings about the candidates. We know that women are present in the population at the 50 percent level, and we also know — our raw results show it — that feelings about these candidates tend to be somewhat sex-linked. Therefore, we must weight the sample to reflect the real world, and we must recalculate the results for all respondents in accordance with the actual percentages of male/female.

First we recalculate the breakdown of each group on the basis of 100 percent:

	Men	Women
Reagan	60%	45%
Carter	40	55
Total	100%	100%

Using the above formula, in which Z is the raw finding in percentage as shown above, and D is the demographic for each subsample (in this illustration 50 percent each), we insert the figures:

$$\text{All Reagan voters} = \frac{(60 \times 50) + (45 \times 50)}{100} = 52.5\%$$

$$\text{All Carter voters} = \frac{(40 \times 50) + (55 \times 50)}{100} = 47.5\%$$

If the weighted result for all respondents is compared with the raw result for all respondents, it is apparent that Reagan's edge has been increased from 2 points to 4.5 points, changing the poll results from "too close to call" to a forecast of a Reagan victory.

Taking a somewhat more complicated example, Black/White ratios, let us return to the 1980 poll between Reagan and Carter. The sample size was 1,000, of which 160 were Blacks (16 percent) and 840 white (84 percent). The raw figures were the following:

	White	Black	All Respondents
Reagan	462	30	492
Carter	320	112	432
Other	58	18	76
Total	840	160	1,000

Were we to report the result for all respondents, either in raw figures or changed into percentages for the total sample (Reagan — 49.2

percent, Carter — 43.2 percent, other — 7.6 percent, we would have considerable overrepresentation of strongly Carter blacks. But we know the black population is actually only 10 percent. So in the interests of professional standards, we feel compelled to make an adjustment in order that the results will reflect the total population better than does our sample. We must weight the sample to reflect the real world, and we must recalculate the results for all respondents accordingly.[8]

First we recalculate the breakdown of each group on the basis of 100 percent:

	Whites	Blacks
Reagan	55 %	18.7%
Carter	38	70
Other	6.9	11.2
Total	99.9%	99.9%

Using the above formula, in which Z is the raw finding in percentage as shown above, and D is the demographic for each subsample, in this instance, 90 percent for whites and 10 percent for blacks, we insert the figures:

$$\text{All Reagan voters} = \frac{(55 \times 90) + (18.7 \times 10)}{100} = 51.3\%$$

$$\text{All Carter voters} = \frac{(38 \times 90) + (18.7 \times 10)}{100} = 36.1\%$$

$$\text{All other voters} = \frac{(6.9 \times 90) + (11.2 \times 10)}{100} = 12.6\%$$

If the weighted result for all respondents is compared with the raw result for all respondents, it is apparent that Reagan's edge has been increased substantially over Carter, once again changing the poll in the direction of icing the Reagan victory. The reason the Reagan edge increased substantially is that black voters, who strongly favored Carter, were overrepresented in the sample. When blacks were accorded their proper place in the sample, in proportion to their real numbers in the electorate, Carter lost this apparent advantage. No dirty trick has been played on anyone. The sample has been merely brought back into alignment with reality.

ADJUSTING AUDIENCE RATINGS

Radio-TV ratings weight and adjust their samples after the fact, as well as stratify the designs before the fact. All types of surveys confront the dilemma of reaching blacks and Hispanic minorities. Perhaps this fact speaks eloquently of the need for renewed efforts to create a just multiracial society. The absence of real communication between dominant institutions and minority people is demonstrated by these polling problems, even during a time of relative tranquility.

Arbitron attempts to avoid the distortions caused by such barriers in three ways: special interviewing procedures in high-density ethnic areas, identification of the race/nationality of respondents, and weighting audience estimates by race. We will describe these approaches in some detail because of their applications in all kinds of surveys.

Arbitron initiated this technique in 1967 and now applies it in 60 metros. The objectives are to find the minorities and get them into the sampling frame. If that proves to be imperfect, then the method corrects the figures in terms of known demographics.

Special ethnic interviewing is used in metro areas with 20 percent or more black or Hispanic population, using corrected census data (that is, the numbers of minorities are increased by the estimated undercount). If the areas have stations programming 50 percent or more of their broadcast time to such minority audiences, then the criterion is lowered to 15 percent for the metro to qualify for special interviews.

When a market qualifies for ethnic measurement, each county within the metro is examined. Census tracts are combined into zip code areas. If a zip contains 35 percent or more black or Hispanic population, it is designated a control area for special interviewing.

The main ingredient is that the interviewer calls the sample population on the telephone each day for seven days in a row. On the basis of information given by respondents, the caller himself, rather than the respondents, keeps diaries for all members of each household. This procedure is followed for all households in the control areas, regardless of race/nationality characteristics.

Respondents are called ahead of time and asked to cooperate in the proposed series of later telephone calls. "There is no attempt," Arbitron says, "to ask people what they listened to seven days ago.

People who are contacted daily about their listening can be more accurate."[9]

In Spanish-speaking areas, the daily telephone call is not considered necessary. The technique employs personal face-to-face placement, follow-up, and pickup of bilingual diaries by bilingual interviewers. During the middle of the survey week, a second personal visit is made to encourage continuation with the diary.

Diaries obtained by these methods are processed along with those placed by telephone in nonethnic areas, which are returned by mail. These methods improve data collection dramatically. Of course, they are very expensive, but have been deemed essential in order to maintain the integrity of the rating system, especially at a time when black/Hispanic populations are now major components of urban America, with black majorities in 18 important cities and large Hispanic minorities in more than 25.

In 1972, Arbitron tested a variety of ways of getting people to indicate their race and nationality. In the past, the issue had always been somewhat delicate. Many respondents did not like being asked. However, the issue seemed to be less sensitive in the "let it all hang out" era of the 1970s. It was determined that a simple checkoff in all face-to-face and telephone interviews was sufficient. Arbitron was at first tentative about such identification, fearful that it would be resented and damage rapport. However, it was found to be much less delicate than anticipated. So the item has become standard for all households in the metro.

The process of weighting occurs after retrieving all the diaries. Census data tell the analyst how many people there are in each group that composes the market, by age, sex, and race/nationality. If the sample diaries in each age bracket, for example, do not represent the same proportion in the sample as that age group does in the whole population, then it is adjusted. The results of the diaries are not modified, of course, but they are weighted more if their numbers are light and weighted less if their numbers are heavy. Arbitron calls the method, basically the same as we have described, the Sampling Balancing Technique.

CONCLUSIONS

Statistical methods are a remarkable achievement of the human mind, and they are inescapable in the modern world. Numbers are a language. Stripping away their mysteries reveals a set of essential tools that all can use. Such understanding is needed in order to take full advantage of the great potentials that survey research holds as a means of getting new knowledge. At the same time, it is just as important to be critical, to understand the limitations of statistical tools, to appreciate the problems that inevitably are generated by unsatisfactory statistical designs and/or inadequate implementation.

Data collected and compiled by public and private agencies constitute the sensory inputs of gargantuan mass societies. They often cannot be seen and felt in the concrete, but they are real. Abstract and insubstantial entities can really exist and must be grasped and managed by means appropriate to their scale.

NOTES

1. Interview in *U.S. News and World Report*, February 22, 1981, p. 63.
2. See Fred Fallik and Bruce L. Brown, *Statistics for Behavioral Sciences* (Homewood, Ill.: Dorsey Press, 1983).
3. Malcolm W. Browne, "When Numbers Just Don't Add Up," *New York Times*, April 22, 1980, p. C1.
4. We will dismiss the issue of replacement. Just keep in mind that replacement is necessary for equal operation of chance. Without replacement, there is a slight increase in favor of those picked later.
5. *New York Times*, March 29, 1982, p. A5.
6. It doesn't matter how you slice the cake, as the total results are reported in percentages. You might say the male contingent remains the same, while the female is cut 10 percent; or that the female is kept the same, while the male is increased 10 percent.
7. Richard Link, "The Literary Digest Poll: Appearances Can Be Deceiving," *Public Opinion*, February/March 1980, p. 55.
8. It should be noted that sample size in this example is a problem. The number of blacks is too small to do much with in any case, because the sample size needs to be larger. We are ignoring this point in the interests of illustrating adjustments.
9. Arbitron, Inc., *How Arbitron Measures Radio* (1979), p. 36.

CHAPTER TWELVE
PROTECTION OF HUMAN SUBJECTS

Along with the new politics of the 1960s came every variety of demand for government to protect the people from exploiters and manipulators, and many of these demands were implemented by law or policy. During this period the Department of Health, Education, and Welfare issued its famous rules on the rights of human subjects in all federally funded research, social as well as physical.

The counterculture movement burned behavioral science labs and computers along with ROTC offices in the late 1960s. Behaviorist conditioning was a favorite target. As occurs during cultural transformations, whatever had been formerly positive became negative. The idealized version of the white-coated scientist in his lab fighting polio, selflessly searching for truth, was turned upside down.

Horror stories about scientific abuse of human subjects became standard news items. Concern for the abuses of science was long overdue. Apart from the senationalistic attacks that brought the subject into public debate, there was a genuine issue. Overvaluation of science had too long endowed some very dubious projects with virtual immunity. A worshipful public attitude had permitted real abuses to be hidden by a conspiracy of silence. The issues raised by the early attacks tended to find appropriate levels of realism through an arduous process of trial and error.

The moral and ethical principles were codified in the Nazi war crimes trials at Nuremburg. Yet many Western researchers showed a lack of sensitivity to these principles and were guilty of abuses in their research. One celebrated case was the Tuskegee syphilis experiment, which was brought to public notice in 1972. For 40 years the U.S. Health Service had deliberately withheld medical treatment from 400 syphilitic black men in rural Alabama. The experiment sought to determine the harm the disease would do if left untreated. The sample of cases was matched with 400 men living under similar life conditions but without the disease.

The Health Service told the infected men they had "bad blood" and promised them free treatment. In fact, they were given deceptive treatment — aspirin, spring tonic, and spinal taps, the latter as the means of measuring the progress of the disease. The men were deliberately denied appropriate therapy, their names on a list to prevent other fieldworkers from treating them with antibiotics. As the men died off during the 40 years of the experiment, elaborate autopsies were performed to get data.[1]

This case is far from unique. The scientific community has too often exacted the price of progress from those for whom health care has only been available at experimental risk. It has been a common practice for physicians and medical students to learn their trade at the expense of indigent patients. The poor, students, the imprisoned, blacks, women and children, and the aged have contributed disproportionately to the march of medical knowledge. In 1981, the seven survivors of the Tuskegee group divided a $9 million settlement.

Along similar lines, a noted doctor at the University of Chicago was charged with injecting live cancer cells into helpless brain-damaged inmates in public care facilities, possibly hastening the deaths of dozens. For this work, he received the Nobel Prize.[2] In the battle against humanity's most perfidious enemy, no methods could be ignored. It appears to be routine practice to test cancer cures on unsuspecting patients.[3]

Shock therapy was routinely administered to troublesome mental patients in public hospitals, and to otherwise healthy prison inmates as well. As part of the patients' rights movement, these practices came under attack. Many psychiatrists challenged their therapeutic value and the American Civil Liberties Union charged that their use was mainly a form of coercive behavior control and experimentation. Ken Kesey's novel, *One Flew over the Cuckoo's Nest*, popularized the attack on mind control in mental health facilities, including as well the use of group counselling.

In the social sciences, the same issues emerged, combined with concern for invasion of privacy, confidentiality of research records, research fraud, faked results, plagiarism, and deliberate misrepresentation to consenting subjects. Psychological screening tests, IQ tests, and all institutional testing programs came under a shadow. Sunshine laws were passed, opening confidential letters of reference in academic credentials for review by the persons involved. Truth-in-testing laws spread throughout the nation, giving individuals the right to see their papers and check the grading.[4]

In addition, U.S. social science research was attacked as an instrument of espionage and social control in foreign countries and within American radical movements. Led by the faculty of Harvard University, professors throughout the country adopted guidelines for research aimed at disclosing and preventing participation in intelligence and propaganda activities that involved "lending their names and positions to gain public acceptance" for activities and materials they know to be misleading or untrue.[5]

Questions were raised about the work of psychologist Stanley Milgram on the impact of role authority on individual ethics. In a series of well-known experiments, those hired as lab workers were the real test subjects. They were instructed to inflict electric shock on the "subjects" (who were really lab workers) and to ignore their screams of pain and pleas for surcease. In fact, there were no real shocks; the "subjects" were acting. Milgram discovered that most people hired to perform a job put aside their own moral feelings and carry out instructions, what might be termed the "Eichmann syndrome." Deception was the heart of the experiment.

The debate over the Milgram study clearly illustrated the ethical trends. A decade before it was hailed as a brilliant if disturbing experiment, Milgram received the American Association for the Advancement of Science award for social psychology in 1964. Now it is regarded as raising serious ethical questions; the dominant view is that to conduct such a study is wrong. Herbert Kelman, Harvard psychologist, noted: It involved "entrapment and degradation, . . . I don't think unsought self-knowledge is morally defensible."[6]

THE HEW INITIATIVE

In 1974, the Department of Health, Education, and Welfare (HEW) issued the first national set of regulations for the protection of human subjects in research. Although these were mandatory only for institutions receiving HEW funds, and the only sanction was the cancellation of grants, they had a universal impact. Others federal agencies and departments, including the National Science Foundation and the Department of Defense, endorsed the code. In 1977, Congress adopted the National Research Act, which embodied the same approach. Virtually every research firm and institution, profit and nonprofit, was receiving some federal money and so fell under the regulations.

The code made no major distinctions between behavioral and physical research. Injecting drugs into veins was on exactly the same footing as survey research into opinions. The central requirement was that all subjects involved in research give their informed consent in advance in writing. To implement this, every institution was required to establish an Institutional Review Board (IRB), with community representation, to approve the methods contemplated in all projects using human subjects, including the research design itself and the adequacy of proposed advance written notifications to subjects.

The HEW guidelines evolved into a elaborate attempt at precision and uniformity, the regulations getting ever more complex, with monthly revision sheets flowing from Washington into loose-leaf binders in every institution. The work loads of the IRBs became extremely heavy, and research proposals, most of them still unfunded and maybe unfundable, were getting backlogged everywhere. From some typical materials:

> The University is responsible for safeguarding the rights and welfare of human subjects involved in any research activity, whether the research is supported by external funds or not. To provide for adequate discharge of this responsibility, the Human Subjects Review Committee reviews and approves all applications for projects involving human subjects. The HSRRC determines in each case that the rights and welfare of the subjects are adequately protected, that the risks to an individual are outweighed by the potential benefits to him or her or to society as a whole, by the importance of the knowledge to be gained, and that informed consent is obtained from the subject by appropriate and adequate methods.

The review process was mandatory for all proposed research before written proposals could be submitted to funding agencies. There were dozens of aspiring proposals being generated by people whose futures depended on success at "grantsmanship." For each serious proposal, the review process has to consider 20 or 30 others, hardly avoiding getting into the relative merits of proposals under the broad guidelines of risks outweighed by potential benefits to society as a whole.

One instruction warned: "It is important to emphasize that review and approval by the HSRRC must be completed before the research can begin." Some universities also insisted that student research, even that conducted as classroom exercises, be similarly reviewed.

And the IRBs always contained leading private citizens in the community — ministers, wives of bankers, welfare activists. No provisions were made for paying the board members, whose duties soon swelled to major proportions. At one university, a student wanted to study how well actors responded to suggestions from directors. The IRB insisted that he get an informed consent from everyone involved. He abandoned the project.[7]

Where observation and interviewing were the primary methodologies, shortened procedures appeared everywhere to unblock the normal research activities somewhat, but to little avail. Even these became more burdensome and legalistic. Some examples quoted directly from an IRB package:

> Relevant characteristics of subjects. Please specify remuneration, if any, to be received. If this proposal involves subjects who are minors, incompetent persons, mentally disabled persons and/or prisoners, and it is deemed by the HSRRC not to place human subjects at risk, will legally effective informed consent still be obtained? The basic elements necessary for "informed consent" include: Statement of the general purpose of the study — a fair explanation to the individual of the procedures to be followed and their purpose. . . . A description of any attendant discomforts and/or risks to be expected . . . aspects of confidentiality . . . an instruction that the individual is free to withdraw his consent . . . at any time without prejudice to him.

A researcher in child behavior at the University of Illinois wanted to study the medications being administered to children in a mental institution. "I sent my plans to two committees. After a year and a half, I filled out 25 pages of forms, but I hadn't seen a single child."[8] An anthropologist who had been working with an Indian tribe for ten years was suddenly required to get informed consent forms signed by every member of the tribe.

In addition to the cumbersome administrative routine, the new rules discarded all the traditional safeguards of professionalism. Peer review, publication, professional ethics, education and self-discipline, example, and the evolution of standards and procedures already embodied in traditional practices were treated as of no value. In their place was a policing procedure dominated by nonscientists or by professionals with outside fields of competence, based on the assumption that every proposal was to be considered guilty and was required to prove its innocence.

In 1977, the Privacy Protection Study Commission developed a bill on confidentiality of research sources, which President Carter strongly endorsed. Relating to all research records, medical, historical, social scientific, survey, and the like, permission would have to be explicitly granted by every source for every person to be granted access the the records. Such persons would have to take a sort of reverse Miranda warning: "I am prohibited by law from releasing information about you to anyone except those that I tell you about. If I should break the law, I will be subject to a $5,000 fine and you will have the right to sue me." Scientists would be barred from recontacting subjects of earlier research without the approval of an IRB.[9]

A storm of controversy ensued. The catalog of issues raised began with impossible conditions imposed on carrying out many kinds of research. The confidentiality of medical records, for example, would make population-based health research (epidemiology) — the use of demographic health data to identify agents and factors that cause disease and to identify high-risk areas and persons — impossible. Such studies are usually conducted many years after the information is recorded.[10]

There is a requirement in many experimental designs for "naive subjects," that is, subjects whose behavior will not be distorted by the conditions of the experiment. This requirement holds for both mice and men. A mouse that has already been used in maze experiments gets cagey and acts differently from one that has never seen a maze. This introduces variables that the researcher cannot always control, thus upsetting the experiments. Psychoanalysts used to ask their patients not to read Freud during the period of their treatment, because to do so might induce symptoms that fit pre-conceived diagnoses.

Much of the effectiveness of public opinion polling would be impaired by too much palaver up-front about all the risks and pur-poses of the poll. People would be frightened off by lengthy warn-ings and would be reluctant to sign any legal-looking documents in advance. In addition, stating the hypotheses of the research would motivate many respondents to want to argue with them and give the answers that they perceive to serve their arguments.

Institutional lawyers all too often dictate the consent forms, designed to protect the institution, not to inform the individual. "One has only to read a few such forms to note the legal language, the requirement for witnesses, and the obvious intent." The harm may take the form of "suggested symptoms, induced anxiety, panic-related accidents, or serious psychological reactions." Such effects cannot be considered "rights of human subjects."[11] It was suggested that "full access to the information" should be substituted in the law for "full disclosure."

Something known as the "placebo effect" could distort all experimental results. In many research designs, groups are matched in terms of characteristics, with one factor being isolated by being applied to only one of the groups. In this way, the effects of that factor can be determined.

The placebo is the negative of that factor, a substitute known to have neutral effects which the control group gets in place of the real thing. If control groups were informed whether they received an real input or a placebo, two results are likely: Those who get the real thing will show positive indications based not on the input but on knowledge of the input, and those who receive the placebo will show the anticipated absence of the response, also based on psychogenic effects. In other words, the advance information upon which consent is based will in fact be the active variable, and the effects of the real variable will be disguised or hidden.

What of the morality of using a placebo at all? Should subjects be given a right of choice as to which experimental group they wish to be in? In public opinion research, should subjects be given the right to review stratification and weighting decisions?

When people were told of possible dangers, no matter how slight the chance, large numbers of symptoms always occur among the con-senters. The placebo effect invariably increases the incidence of harm being reported by those in the experiment. An editorial in *Science* was titled: "Informed Consent May Be Hazardous to Health."[12] If in addition they are told that compensation is available if they suffer any physical or psychological ill effects, what impact will this have on the results?

The legal and ethical issues are particularly thorny in studying problems of aging. How does one obtain informed consent from patients already senile, who must be studied if any progress is to be made in fighting diseases of aging?[13]

High on the list of issues raised by the HEW code are those of academic freedom. By creating an outside authority to weigh the researcher's rights against those of research subjects, the scientist is effectively deprived of the inherent freedom to follow her or his own judgment and vision in the search for truth. The process obviates the traditional, and probably more effective, reliance on the researcher's own sense of responsibility and the canons of science.

There are some things that cannot be achieved by formal administrative rules, organizations, and procedures. Much of what society defines and recognizes as "professional responsibility" falls in this category. Certain functions must be performed, and in order to be performed, authority and jurisdiction must be granted to some individuals.

Outside review is not practical at every step, so society grants the benefit of the doubt to learned men and women and allows them to exercise judgment within the bounds of their professional integrity and learning. Ultimate accountability comes through peer bodies at a later stage or through the normal processes of law. Doctors, lawyers, and social scientists can be censured by their professional organizations. They can be sued in any court for civil wrongs.

Why, many researchers asked, where they subject to prior review? Were they not true professionals? What about doctors, lawyers, and journalists? In addition to academic freedom, what about their ordinary First Amendment rights as citizens? Didn't they have the rights under freedom of speech and association to do research without interference? They saw a species of prior censorship in the IRB procedure between them and funding agencies.[14]

The issue of ethics in social science is complicated by real ambivalence in social values. Journalists use "sting" techniques and win Pulitzer prizes. Reporters join cults and extremist political groups to get their stories and are honored for doing so. Participant observation as a social research technique, on the other hand, violates the principles of informed consent and thus would be barred. Much of sociology and anthropology would be outlawed.

The research community is itself ambivalent about the issue. The editorial board of the *Journal of Applied Behavioral Analysis* was the subject of a study of the article referee process. Without the benefit of informed consent in advance, members were asked to review a series of articles, doctored to treat favorably and unfavorably works and concepts associated with the known views of individual board members. The pseudo-paper experiment indicated that referees tended to recommend publication of papers that supported their own views on issues of theory, while they nitpicked to death those that disagreed. The subjects, who had endorsed the journal's strong views on IRB overreaching, were outraged over the treatment accorded them.

In addition to bureaucracy, delay, and the attendant personal mortification endured in the process, researchers complained about the unevenness of the results. Some projects were passed with minimal difficulty and others could not satisfy the board's concerns. Not only did community representatives have their own political motivations and axes to grind, but the academic representatives injected faculty politics into proceedings. The broad mandates on the merits of projects opened the door to making the IRBs another forum for continuing battles over academic budgets and clashes of personalities – with the community people acting as judges, not so much on the proposals themselves, but on issues of university politics.

A 1978 study of the performance of IRBs revealed that about 60 percent of the proposals processed were biomedical. Behavioral research, based on interviews, testing, questionnaires, and observation, accounted for one-third and behavior modification accounted for about one-fifth. The average IRB considered 43 projects per year, expending about 760 member-hours on the work. Average meeting time per proposal was 38 member-hours.

The majority of members in the sample were biomedical scientists (50 percent) and behavioral scientists (20 percent); the remainder included administrators, lawyers, nurses, and members of the clergy. All the boards contained some community members, who were usually a minority. Research investigators who were interviewed for the study charged that "the review procedure is an unwarranted intrusion on the investigator's autonomy, that the IRB gets into inappropriate areas, that it makes judgments it is not qualified to make, and that it impeded research." Behavioral researchers had the least favorable attitudes.[15] Fear was expressed that researchers and research dollars would begin to flow overseas in order to escape such restrictions. The same process had already occurred in the development and testing of new drugs.

REFORM ATTEMPTS

Writing in *Science*, Frederick Mosteller, president of the American Association for the Advancement of Science, noted that the proposals worsened existing rules by applying them not only to consenting subjects but also to identifiable subjects who are dead: "A political scientist collating *New York Times* stories about individual politicians, a sociologist studying sports, a statistician intent on identifying the authors of the *Federalist Papers* could not proceed without an IRB's consent."

Mosteller noted that the risks of research were not all the same, but range from "the possibility of sudden death to that of faint embarrassment." Government intervention should "be closely tied to the reality of the risk," not generalized out of a false piety. An earlier commission found "harmful effects" in only 79 of 2,384 social science projects studied, and these were found to be "trivial or only temporarily disabling."[16]

The ethical problems facing the social science researcher differ from those of biomedical research, even as these differ from field to field. In social psychological research, Mosteller said, "There is often a question of use of deception." In documentary research, "the question of privacy of records arises." In interview research, "the major problem is protecting confidences." Each requires a different approach. Institutional review boards may be inappropriate for interviewing and library research. "Indeed, clearing procedures with a review board makes it harder . . . to protect confidences."

The major professional associations urged HEW to abandon its dragnet methods and to concentrate on areas where specific and documented harm exists. "In research, as in other walks of life," Mosteller concluded, "risk exists in interactions that consist of nothing more than open exchange of information." To attempt to prescribe for every conceivable evil could create remedies worse than the disease.

With a National Science Foundation grant, the American Statistics Association addressed itself to the rights of respondents in survey research, attempting to evolve a balanced set of principles that would preserve the value of such research without sacrificing ethical and moral principles. There is, its report said, a "necessity for being aware of what might be called the morality of survey operations as well as the refinements and improvements of technique."

ASA President Lester Frankel declared: "Perhaps, we are not treating the respondent with respect as a human being. There is a tendency among statisticians to regard the person as only incidental to the information about the person." Said Mervin Field: "One of the remarkable things is the willingness of the public to participate. It is a very precious thing. We are concerned that it is not abused or diluted."[17]

On the basis of its report in 1978, the Health and Human Services Department (formerly HEW) established an Ethics Advisory Board, and the president appointed another commission to come up with revised guidelines. In early 1981, the Health and Human Services Department issued new guidelines, listing categories of research that henceforth would require only "brief review," as well as categories that would be exempted entirely. "These regulations," the document said, "constitute a major de-regulation from rules in force at the present time." Much social science research could be excluded from IRB jurisdiction.[18]

The new rules specified that studies of educational practices conducted in established educational settings would be exempt, including studies of the effectiveness of instructional techniques and curricula. Also exempt would be studies involving the use of educational tests, if data are kept in such a way that protected the identity of research subjects. Surveys, interviews, and observational techniques would not be reviewed unless respondents could be identified from the data; their responses could subject participants to criminal or civil liability or damage their employment or financial standing; or the topics dealt with such sensitive topics as illegal conduct, drug use, sexual behavior, or use of alcohol. Interviews or surveys dealing with elected or appointed public figures and candidates for public office need not be reviewed.

Quick review procedures should be implemented for "minimal risk" studies, such as those involving voice recordings made for research purposes, studies of speech defects, those involving the use of existing data, documents, records, and demographic materials, and those involving individual or group behavior or characteristics where "the investigator does not manipulate subject's behavior and the research will not involve stress to subjects," such as studies of game theory, test development, and perception.

The department said it was still considering final regulations for use of such specialized groups as children, the aged, and the mentally handicapped. In cases of disputes in applying the regulations, the secretary of HHS would have the final authority to determine if projects must be reviewed by IRBs.

On the issue of compensation and insurance for research subjects, the Presidential Commission for the Study of Ethical Problems in Medical, Biomedical, and Behavioral Research made recommendations in late 1981 that tended in the opposite direction. Reluctant to endorse the demand that the federal government insure researchers against claims, the commission instead recommended the strengthening of mechanisms of informed consent and enforcement. All institutions, in addition to IRBs, should have specific units to receive reports of alleged misconduct, investigate them promptly, and report formal findings to IRBs and to sponsoring government agencies. Governmentwide procedures should be instituted to bar or suspend researchers from other research grants, and principal investigators should submit, as part of their annual reports, data on "the number of subjects who participated in each project, as well as the nature and frequency of adverse effects."[19]

The new rules won praise from most of the research community, but demands were voiced for even more relaxation. Ithiel de Sola Pool of MIT said that while the regulations were "entirely reasonable for research funded by the department, the same regulations applied to social science research generally would be unsatisfactory."[20] "If an anthropologist or political scientist is proceeding, as many do, without special funding, it would be quite improper to tell him that he could not conduct his normal . . . processes without first filing for permission" with an IRB. "Many . . . develop lifetime relationships of trust with special groups of subjects. We should not accept the notion that universities should monitor and police these relationships."

IMPACTS AND SEQUELS

The immediate impact of the new rules was to induce greater moderation into the behavior of IRBs, whose authority had grown as they were deluged with work. More researchers took it upon themselves to interpret the rules so as to exempt themselves from review; and there was less disposition for IRBs to challenge those interpretations. In practice, the new rules excluded almost all social science research, because the loss in confidence of the boards and the gain in confidence among the researchers spontaneously led to that consequence.

The debate on the rights of human subjects in research led to a much greater sensitivity among all researchers. There is now considerably less inclination deliberately to mislead anyone, even in the most minimal risk category of public opinion surveys. Interviews always begin with a brief general statement about the purpose of the interview, something about confidentiality, and a polite request for cooperation. No deliberate misrepresentation, although neither are there any elaborate preliminary statements that might trouble the waters.

The "informed consent in writing in advance" has been unceremoniously dumped for most social science projects it would appear.[21] The debate shifted to biomedical fields, where HHS set the rule that each institution, not the grant or contract agency of government, would have to pay damages to subjects who claimed injuries in projects financed by government; and to such ethical issues as when life begins, abortion, genetic screening, and DNA experiments.

In his AAAS presidential address, Frederick Mosteller called for more research on research before these difficult ethical questions be resolved. Society must have better information before it can decide the issues at stake. One cannot rely solely on informed consent. People will consent to things that society may deem unworthy of their sacrifice or unfair to other nonresearch subjects.[22]

The issues are not easy. In one form or another they have engaged the best work of philosophers throughout time and have never been resolved. The relativistic "consequentialist view" (cost/benefit) sometimes gives way to the absolutistic view that actions are either moral or immoral and must be defined with no middle ground.

It is easy to say that research that directly benefits a subject is permissible; that research that is likely to injure a subject, even though it may benefit others, is forbidden. What about research that holds no direct benefit to the subject and involves little risk? Most difficult is to strike an equation for research that cannot benefit a subject, though it may benefit others, and that places him or her at risk. What about the shaded areas of these equations, where the benefit and the harm are indefinite? Or marginal? Some of the most grievous injuries are inflicted because research is not done at all, or where deleterious effects are not discovered until too late because of ignorance. What about the right of human subjects not to be deprived of the benefits of research?

Obviously, if there is "reasonable risk," research should not be undertaken without the subject's understanding and consent. But such equations are full of imponderables and pitfalls. All the items of the equation are hard to measure, and ethics and morality depend on small differences. On the other hand, the experience of the last decade suggests that government rule making is an unpromising route. The solution to every problem, as the old saw says, creates a new problem. The removal of one injustice creates a new injustice.

Professionalism is not to be despised as a means of protecting the public weal. In the performance of tasks where trust and confidence are prerequisites, no amount of oversight can replace the integrity and self-discipline of the professional. In so many situations where human beings serve each other's needs, ultimately there can be no one in control but the individual and his or her conscience. To respect that fact sometimes means refraining from seeking assurances that cannot as a practical matter be secured by more regulations and more officialdom.

But some messages are strong and clear. Survey researchers must return to the original issues, maintain their sensitivity to the impact of survey research on human subjects, and continue to question and study the obscure effects of research on all concerned. People deserve honesty, forthrightness, and good manners. Without the basic courtesies, how long will opinion analysts be able to pursue their craft?

NOTES

1. See James H. Jones, *Bad Blood: The Tuskegee Syphilis Experiment* (New York: Free Press, 1981). In their defense, the doctors thought they were improving the health care of the poor by learning something about an affliction that strikes the poor with great severity.

2. Charges were made that during the 1960s cancer patients received unnecessary doses of gamma rays at Oak Ridge National Laboratory in an experiment aimed at learning how much radiation astronauts could tolerate before becoming ill and choking in their oxygen masks. Charges made by Howard Rosenburg, in *Mother Jones* magazine, were denied by Oak Ridge officials (reported in *Science*, September 4, 1981, p. 1093). The 200 patients in the experiment were misled as to the purpose of whole-body irradiation and many of them died during the period of the research.

3. In chemical tests, the starting dose for humans would be one-tenth of the amount that kills only 10 percent of the mice. Beginning with what is known as Phase I, researchers would continually raise the doses to see how much of the drug humans could tolerate, in order to observe side effects. The primary purpose is to determine toxicity, not to treat the patients. *Washington Post*, October 18, 1981, p. A16. The National Cancer Institute examines about 15,000 chemical compounds this way each year.

4. See Herman Schuchman, Leila Foster, Sandra Nye, et al., *Confidentiality of Health Records* (New York: Gardner Press, 1981).

5. See Recommended Interim Guidelines, State University of New York, Binghamton, September 11, 1978, p. 2.

6. Constance Holden, "Ethics in Social Science Research," *Science*, November 2, 1979, p. 538.

7. Cheryl M. Fields, *Chronicle of Higher Education*, March 12, 1979, p. 5.

8. Ibid.

9. *Science*, April 20, 1979, p. 1033.

10. See Leon Gordis and Ellen Gold, "Privacy, Confidentiality, and the Use of Medical Records in Research," *Science*, January 11, 1980, p. 153.

11. James F. Fries and Elizabeth Loftus, *Science*, August 17, 1979, p. 647.

12. April 6, 1979, p. 233.

13. Gina Kolata, "Alzheimer's Research Poses Dilemma," *Science*, January 1, 1982, p. 47.

14. See B. Barber, J. J. Lally, J. Makarushka, and D. Sullivan, *Research on Human Subjects* (New York: Russell Sage Foundation, 1973).

15. Bradford H. Gray, Robert A. Cooke, and Arnold S. Tannenbaum, "Research Involving Human Subjects," *Science*, September 22, 1978, p. 1094.

16. "Regulation of Social Research," *Science*, June 13, 1980, p. 1219.

17. Quoted by Robert Reinhold, *New York Times*, October 26, 1975, p. 1.

18. *Federal Register*, January 26, 1981. Rules to take effect July 27, 1981. See also the rules published in the *Federal Register* of August 14, 1979, Part II.

19. *Chronicle of Higher Education*, December 2, 1981, p. 1.

20. Ithiel de Sola Pool, quoted in *Chronicle of Higher Education*, February 16, 1981, p. 9.

21. The author has canvased about a dozen colleagues on various campuses; their experience consistently supports this observation.

22. Rules banning voluntary drug testing on prisoners in 1981 were challenged by prisoner groups themselves, who opposed the meddling of civil rights activists in their business. Frederick Mosteller, "Innovation and Evaluation," *Science*, February 27, 1981, pp. 881-84.

CHAPTER THIRTEEN
SEARCHING FOR POLLING STANDARDS

French law forbids the publishing of polls in the last week before election day, on the theory that they might unduly influence the outcome. New York State has a law that any use of private poll data in a campaign requires full disclosure of the poll's origins and findings. United States law imposes a fine of $2,000 on anyone seeking to poll members of the armed forces on their voting preferences.

After the 1948 elections, the House of Representatives held hearings on proposals to establish a public commission to regulate all syndicated pollsters. After the 1980 elections, when Carter conceded before the polls closed on the West Coast, Congress debated whether to outlaw election day projections based on exit polls.

Any institution that acquires real power in a political system becomes the center of controversy. Claims and counterclaims are made for public control, and the result is usually some combination of self-regulation, designed to preempt outside interference, and public regulation. The areas of survey, motivational, and market research have witnessed an active interplay between self- and public regulation that has been debated for years. So far, self-regulation and reliance on the marketplace have triumphed, although the tides of battle have swept back and forth over the years.

EARLY PROJECTIONS

After the 1980 election, great concern was expressed for the impact on the voters of preelection forecasts, exit polls, and computerized TV projections based on fragmentary returns. There was widespread feeling that the real election was being rigged by overeager attempts to scoop the competition in picking the winners.

"Bandwagon" is the term used to describe the tendency of people to accept the verdict of the public opinion polls as unchangeable, leading voters to support the trend or to sit out the election, and causing trailing candidates to become defeatist and desist in their efforts. This creates a self-fulfilling prophecy. Possible also is the opposite effect of "counter-bandwagon." This occurs when the polls generate overconfidence in the leading camps, causing efforts to slacken and voters for the leaders to feel that their votes are not needed and the trailing candidates to redouble their efforts to overcome the reported trend. This becomes a self-negating prophecy.

In either case the poll prediction itself is a disturbing element and may affect the election outcome. This was viewed as especially pernicious if the polls were wrong about the facts, if some of them were of dubious quality, or if they were objective and proper but deliberately used as election propaganda.

In the most thoroughly polled country in the world, there has always been concern for these issues. But the concern always flares up like November chimney fires after a spectacular goof or a brazen scam. Then the issue fades into the background and is forgotten until the next time.

There is concern that competition among the television networks, plus the improved technology of information processing, will eventually bring about a reductio ad absurdum of earlier and earlier, better and better forecasts. A bill establishing a 12-hour simultaneous national election day was passed by the Senate in 1972. In 1974, the Senate passed a bill barring disclosure of election results before midnight Eastern Standard Time. Both measures died in the House.[1]

The 8:15 P.M. EST projection of Carter's defeat in 1980 was thought to have discouraged many Democratic voters in the western states from going to the polls. This wouldn't have changed the presidential race but may have pulled down state and local Democratic candidates in close counts. It was thought that the outcome of the California governorship would have been reversed if defeatism about the presidential election had not been thrown at the voters four hours before the polls closed in that state.

Senator S. I. Hayakawa declared: "Voters believed that voting on the way home from work was a useless exercise. They had been disenfranchised by a system that allowed an election to be called while the polls were still open."[2] California Secretary of State March Fong Eu testified that voter turnout dropped suddenly after 5:15 P.M., California time after NBC projected Reagan the winner.

Both the House and the Senate held extensive hearings. Representatives of the three major networks agreed in their testimony that no studies have proven that early projections affect the outcome of elections. They argued that polls and projections, like other vehicles for expressing opinion, have indeterminate effects, generating renewed efforts to vote or to campaign as well as defeatism and overconfidence. The role of election predictions cuts both ways, and should not be controlled. Imponderables determine whether the impacts go one way or the other, and whether or not the forecasts weigh heavily or lightly along with all the other factors of influence.

William J. Small, president of NBC News, conceded that the projections had "generated an emotional response and a great deal of conjecture." But, he insisted, "there is no hard evidence . . . that the projections contribute to declining voter turnout."[3] Small pointed out that voter turnout was actually up over 1976 in 9 of the 13 states in the Pacific and Mountain time zones, including California, where 75.6 percent of registered voters went to the polls, much higher than the national average (53.9 percent). "It would be wrong to adopt solutions for what may be a phantom problem."

Evidence was mustered to support the network claims:

- In 1964, a "landslide year," four separate studies, including surveys done at the Universities of California and Michigan, reported no significant changes in voting behavior resulting from election broadcasts.
- In 1968, a "close year," an NBC-sponsored study by a professional polling organization concluded that projections had no measurable impact on voting.

- The Los Angeles County Registrar concluded after a month-long study that "the early network projections and the president's concession had little, if any, impact on the turn-out."
- The national drop-off in voting between 1976 and 1980, continuing a 20-year trend, showed no special pattern in the western states. The percentage of voting was lower than the national average in Washington and Wyoming but higher than the national average in California, Arizona, and Idaho.
- The widely scattered reports of people leaving the voting lines after hearing the news have not been substantiated.[4]

The network spokesmen pointed out how difficult and dangerous it is to control news judgment. Congress should not attempt to blank out the news of what has already happened in the East from reaching the western time zones. This could have mischievous effects because the news would spread anyway by all the other channels of information and through rumor. Once a government body begins to censure the news, there is no end to the process.

"I would like to go on record as expressing the vehement opposition of CBS News to any proposals which would require any news organization to suppress information in its possession, or would deny us access to any information that would otherwise be available," said William A. Leonard, CBS News president. He said the causes for falling voter turnouts in the last 20 years are springing, not from poll predictions, but from "the complexity and frustrations of modern life, a growing disrespect for institutions, a sense of alienation and despair about the value of the vote, impatience with the political process, lack of faith in and respect for the candidates."[5]

The network executives suggested instead that other means be contemplated, such as setting national simultaneous voting hours. A plea from the League of Women Voters, the Committee for the Study of the American Electorate, and 32 other organizations, including the National Education Association, church groups, and labor unions, that the networks voluntarily refrain from election projections was rejected.

The Committee on House Administration ended its hearings by passing a resolution asking broadcasters "to voluntarily refrain from projecting elections prior to the close of the polls" and to adopt guidelines restricting the use of exit polls. The report found that "early projections may well have affected voter turnout"; that by decreasing voter participation, they may have "affected the outcome of close state and local elections"; and that early projections "undermine people's belief in the importance of their vote, a belief essential in a democratic society."[6]

The report endorsed none of the bills submitted by various members of Congress. The idea that election day be declared a national holiday was rejected as "too costly," and as not a real solution: "Testimony indicated that low voter turnout is not due to time constraints but rather to other less tangible factors." The idea that all election returns be sealed until the last polling place closes was rejected because "it would create an artifical vacuum . . . and force the networks to increase their use of exit polls." The only effective solution, "short of an outright prohibition," the report said, "is through a voluntary agreement between the networks."

The media have since then demonstrated a willingness to be responsive, but without giving up any basic rights. ABC Chairman Leonard H. Goldenson declared in a major address at Harvard's Kennedy School that his company would join an effort to reverse the trend of lower voter turnouts. He called for repeal of "equal time laws," which cripple broadcasting's ability to cover political campaigns in having to accord the same attention to obscure candidates, and for Public Broadcasting to take over gavel-to-gavel coverage of national conventions, paid for by the three networks. ABC has been trying to avoid the coverage since 1980, when it was seen as ratings poison.[7]

George Gallup, Sr., dean of American pollsters, echoed the call for network restraint. "By using exit polls, it would be fairly simple to call the national election by 11 A.M. on election day, except in the very closest election," he said. "That will be the inevitable urge if the networks do not show some restraint."[8]

SETTING STANDARDS

Many other areas of survey research and polling have been viewed as public policy problems over the years. After the 1948 elections, Congress seriously debated proposals to set up a national regulatory commission to license and police all syndicated and private polling organizations. The move was narrowly averted by the leading polling organizations undertaking to police themselves.

Given the important role polls have acquired, they have difficulty keeping their heads out of the field of fire. Leaking private poll data is a fairly common phenomenon. If a national party gives a candidate the results of a poll in time for them to be of any use, this is counted as a campaign contribution against the limits imposed on the candidate. However, because of the 1974 Campaign Spending Act amendments, private groups and political action committees (PACs) escape this stricture. Thus financing polls has become a legal method of contributing to races.

Many groups, like the American Medical Association, routinely pay media consultant bills for candidates as an indirect method of campaign contribution. In 1982, AMPAC, the AMA's political action committee, spent $381,000 to hire pollsters in 36 congressional races. The polls cost an average of $10,600, twice the legal limit on direct PAC contributions to candidates.[9] The loophole has been widely exploited. The District of Columbia, under local laws that model the federal laws, permitted the three candidates for mayor in 1981 to accept polling services that exceeded campaign contribution limits by factors of 1,000 and permitted the donors to remain anonymous.[10]

Leaking the results of polling can be an effective means of campaigning. Except in New York and California, each camp can be selective in leaking only those things that support its side and damage the enemy, without the necessity to provide all the supporting evidence about the poll's objectivity. Leaking can help intimidate the other side by trying to establish a bandwagon effect and to impress the world with the unbounded resources and momentum of the heavy polling side.

Archibald M. Crossley publically attacked the 1967 campaign of Lyndon Johnson after the latter leaked private Crossley data to show himself doing better against the foreseeable opposition than syndicated polls were reporting. "I did not approve of the leaking of the reports," Crossley declared, "and did not give sanction for them to be released." The results themselves had "all sorts of cautions on their use that were not observed."[11]

In the 1976 New York race for the the U.S. Senate seat held by James Buckley, a typical clash occurred in the many-sided primary for the Democratic nomination; it went something like this: Leak No. 1 – A poll performed by Penn-Schoen for the state Democratic committee reportedly showed (in a leak to the *Times*) that Bella Abzug would be handily defeated by Buckley in the general election. "Foul," screamed Abzug. Hence, Leak No. 2 to the *News* to show further evidence supporting Leak No. 1. Once again, "Foul." So the Abzug camp began leaking in return, not only results of its own polls, but information on the "amateurish college kids who had done the committee poll," and word that a Conservative party poll had Abzug beating its own candidate.[12]

"Everyone winks when the staff [of a PAC or private interest group] calls the candidate at night and gives him information" on their independently conducted polls. Lynn Nofziger: "I wouldn't have any problem getting that done. There's no way in the world . . . I'm not going to get the information I need, or get Dick Wirthlin's data, . . . or whatever. . . . I could go on the attack in a way that [the official] campaign might not be comfortable doing."[13]

Because of this tendency, New York State adopted a polling law in the mid-1970s forcing full disclosure of any polling data used for promotional purposes in a political campaign. The law requires that the entire poll be released, including data of how it was conducted, by whom, the questions asked, and the size and method of sampling. The only invocation of the law came in a 1980 congressional race in the 27th District. The incumbent, Matt McHugh, filed charges with the state election board against his opponent after the latter had publically stated that "a recent in-depth poll showed that people don't know McHugh's record or philosophy."[14]

During the entire history of polling, informal codes of standards and good practice have existed. In the beginning, each organization evolved its own. All responsible firms share an interest in maintaining the credibility and honor of the craft; this is especially important in view of the swelling numbers of new companies in the field. Whenever they have been caught conspicuously wrong, as in 1948, they have assembled to examine the sources of error and to conspicuously refine their methods to avoid a repetition. During the last decade, whenever events have conspired to cast discredit on the profession, the various associations have rallied behind a conspicuous restatement of principles.

There are three national associations of pollsters: the National Council on Public Polls, the Council of American Survey Research

Organizations, and, most broadly based, the American Association for Public Opinion Research. The American Statistical Association has also played an active role in this area.

Albert H. Cantril, president of the National Council of Public Polls, has been a leading conscience of the industry as well as an effective public relations spokesman on its behalf. In 1972, while the House of Representatives was conducting hearings on the subject, the American Association for Public Opinion Research adopted a code that had been under study since 1969.

Polling was no longer a jokey industry, but a wealthy and powerful establishment. It was clear by the 1970s that something more substantial had to be done to polish its ethics, to reduce the number of shoddy, trivial, and unscientific surveys, to ensure respondent confidentiality, and to be sure that information supplied by the public is not used in harmful or devious ways. The code attempted to mark the difference between professional and nonprofessional efforts. Every poll published by members must contain the following methodological information:

- The name of the sponsor. Too often this was not revealed at all, or was concealed behind the name of the polling organization.
- The exact wording of the questions, and the findings of the whole poll. Obviously, this is the area of greatest loading and therefore most important.
- Definition of the population that was sampled: the concept used to identify the sampling frame and the means by which the frame was assembled for sampling.
- The size of the sample and the method of sampling.
- The size of nonreturns and nonresponses and the reporting of don't knows.
- The calculation of sampling error within a stated, usually 95 percent, level of confidence, with some information on the range of error of subsamples and with notice given of weighting and adjustments.
- How the interviewing was carried out, whether by telephone, face-to-face, mail, or other method.
- When the actual interviewing was done.

In the summer of 1975, the National Science Foundation awarded a $95,000 grant to the American Statistical Association to assess the quality of survey research and try to draw up uniform standards acceptable to all workers in the discipline. At the same time, the Council of American Survey Research Organizations, composed of the leading commercial firms, was organized. This was partly to evolve their own standards, which, according to Albert E. Goldman, the group's president, could not be the same as those for published polls. His organization would try to combat the proliferation of surveys "by encyclopedia salesmen" and others seeking entry into homes.[15]

As the world leaders in the field, Americans led the way for other nations. Under the initiative of Humphrey Taylor of the British Opinion Research Centre, a similar code was adopted by the U.K trade association. *The Economist* called also for adoption of a code by users, newspapers, and other clients. "For them there could also be a code of conduct, one that would go beyond the requirements which the polls themselves seek to impose." Suggested were the following: "Always give details of date of fieldwork, sample size, type of sample. Do not write or tolerate misleading headlines" in newspaper poll reports. "Give a clear indication of how the don't knows are dealt with. State whether a turnout filter has been applied, and whether and in what way the figures have otherwise been adjusted. Do not exaggerate small changes in party support. State the expected margin of error."[16]

A 1976 study found American newspapers to have a very poor record in this regard. The study, conducted by the Gannett Urban Journalism Center, targeted 30 leading city papers for the entire year. It found that "horse race journalism" was the primary focus of interest in 61 percent of the stories; 20 percent were concerned with poll findings on attributes of candidates; and only 8 percent dealt with public opinion on issues. Less than one-third of the stories reported the exact wording of the questions. In 52 percent of the cases there was not even a paraphrase of the words used. In most coverage of polls the articles did include such basic information as who was surveyed (99 percent), who sponsored the poll (90 percent), method of obtaining interviews (77 percent), and sample size (83 percent).

Commenting on the study, Burns Roper objected to the way sampling error was reported, because it tended to give a sense of "undue precision" to the results. "It is used to imply unwarranted accuracy, rather than the potential inaccuracy that it is intended to convey," obscuring "the considerable human judgments involved in the surveys." He pointed out that there "are far more important factors than sampling error to throw polls off." The largest sources of error (that is, who is likely to vote and how to measure preferences) was not mentioned in more than 90 percent of the newspaper reports.[17]

Because of misreporting, the Canadian Daily Newspaper Publishers Association sent out a checklist in 1978, which deserves to be mentioned on several points. In addition to the eight points of the 1974 code, the checklist asked: "Who did the interviewing? There is a vast difference between trained interviewers for a professional polling organization and volunteers assembled to conduct a survey for a political candidate. Do the headline and introductory paragraphs accurately reflect the poll results? Temptations to oversimplify or overreach for meaning are great and often succumbed to." Finally, "Has the whole story been told? There is no way for news consumers to answer that question for themselves."[18]

Because of these problems many newspapers in recent years have added professional pollsters to their editorial staffs, not merely to design, organize, and conduct scientific polls for the paper, which many of them do, but also to write and edit all stories that cover polling data. Increasingly, newspapers find that polls are news, especially those that they originate themselves. "The prestige value is enormous. Every finding is an exclusive. . . . People quote you and use your name when mentioning your poll," declared I. A. Lewis, poll editor of the *Los Angeles Times*. "The *Times* poll is copied in 40 or 50 papers . . . but an awful lot's at stake. You can do more damage with a bad one than help with a good one."[19]

In 1979, a stronger code was adopted by the National Council of Public Polls, occasioning the first public split among major polling organizations. The new code was under consideration since the founding of the organization in 1969 and had been contentious both before and after its formal adoption.

Pat Caddell's Cambridge Survey Research, Inc., and NBC News broke the usual unanimity and refused to endorse the code, resigning from the association rather than be bound. Both said they agreed with the principles, but not the procedures, for implementation and enforcement. Unlike the codes of the two other trade associations, this one had teeth, providing for charges, hearings, and possible probation or explusion for members violating its provisions.

The code closely follows the points of the earlier code. But, in addition, it specifies that although a privately commissioned survey might be kept confidential, the polling organization would have an obligation to release the eight items of required information in the event that a client attempted to make public use of the poll findings. This is a sensitive and important innovation.

Caddell's firm could not accept that requirement. "We're not happy to get into the role of policing our clients," said John Gorman, company treasurer. Current contracts with clients, he said, did not permit such disclosures against the clients' wishes. It did not intend to change its ways of doing business, and the company has many private clients both here and abroad.

The code also provided for "binding arbitration" of charges made under the code against association members. A spokesman for NBC strongly objected to this quasi-legal infringement on "the editorial independence" of the network. NBC felt that it could not subject its news judgments to review by any outside body, even the polling peers of the industry, who would not be likely to act too arbitrarily against one of their own. The provision was mainly to offer an alternative to grievants, thus avoiding resort to civil action in the courts.[20]

Michael Wheeler, writing in *Public Opinion*, attacked the NCPP for taking so long to agree to enforce simple disclosure standards. He pointed out that the association's former president (Cantril) told Congress that efforts had been "puny," and that he did not have faith in the efficacy of the code. Cantril had testified: "Pollsters can hardly be expected to judge each other's work. Thus the emptiness of calls for self-regulation." Wheeler concluded: "There is little prospect that the organization will ever discipline members for shoddy work."[21]

Cantril took strong exception to the pessimistic outlook. "As any professor of law is aware, procedures are only as strong as their ability to protect due process. . . . We reject the implication that the National Council had to drag its reluctant membership to adopt a set of procedures and the conclusion that our Principles of Disclosure will not be taken seriously by members."[22]

In response to the announcement of the new code, many non-member polling organizations publicly declared their observance of most of the rules. The *New York Times* announced that its polls done with CBS News already routinely gave all of the data required except for "the complete wording of all of the questions asked." The *Los Angeles Times* announced that it always printed "an abbreviated version" of polling methods, but sent out the full information to news service subscribers. Associated Press, whose poll is combined with NBC, noted that it always included the data in its releases. The *Washington Post* noted that it only gives some of the information, but would carefully consider how to better comply with the code.

A pollster's best weapon against the misuse of his work is "to quit working for a client who abuses the material."[23] Contrariwise, the best weapon for the client against bad polls is to change pollsters. There is so much competition in the marketplace that a process of comparison shopping is inevitable on the part of all participants. Whether they will use this process better to inform and educate the public remains to be seen.[24]

Although newspaper polling is not nearly as profitable as market research, it has high visibility and opens up the door to much profitable new business. Wheeler is probably right in his charges that very few people are going to bite the hand that feeds them; that self-regulation in this area may not prove itself equal to the challenges; and that stronger methods may once again be contemplated. In view of this, it is all the more remarkable that the industry has adopted the strong enforcement rules of 1979.

The mere existence of a problem is not an irrefutable argument for government intervention. Sometimes formal regulation by law and public agencies is an unnecessary and awkward expense. If left alone, the results will often be just as salubrious, without getting a lot of lawyers, congressmen, and fixers into the act and without the concomitant expense of supporting new bureaucracies and converting every transaction into a hassle of political and pressure tactics.

The story of self-regulation and the setting of standards by pollsters has been one of the bright spots in the history of an industry. Professionalism is not to be despised as a means of protecting the public weal. In the performance of tasks where trust and confidence are prerequisites, no amount of government oversight can replace the integrity and self-discipline of the professional.

The essence of professionalism is dedication to standards of performance and service that overcome parochial and partisan interests. The first duty of a professional is to her or his craft, its credibility and improvement. Lacking that, one cannot serve the best interests of anyone. The pursuit of excellence means seeking to achieve skills and knowledge whose values transcend passions and ends of the moment; it means craftsmanship whose honor endures and is recognized for its own sake; and it means husbanding capabilities for all the proper uses of humankind, capabilities in whose conservation all share a common interest.

NOTES

1. Many considered the night of the Carter-Reagan debate a low point when ABC asked viewers to dial a 900 number to vote for the winner of the debate. Despite the fact that the survey was a simple straw poll, ABC treated the result as newsworthy, and most newspapers carried the story that Reagan had won the debate 2 to 1. This made responsible pollsters cringe.

2. *Washington Post*, May 8, 1981, p. A8.

3. *Editor and Publisher*, July 11, 1981, p. 17.

4. Lester M. Crystal, NBC News producer, letter in *The New Republic*, January 3 and 10, 1981, p. 2.

5. *Washington Post*, June 11, 1981, p. A3.

6. Quoted in *Broadcasting*, September 27, 1982, p. 90.

7. *Broadcasting*, December 20, 1982, p. 23.

8. Quoted by Alvin P. Sanoff, "The Perils of Polling 1980," *Washington Journalism Review*, January/February 1981, p. 32.

9. *New York Times*, September 24, 1982, p. B5.

10. See Michael Isikoff, *Washington Post*, October 1, 1981, p. A1.

11. *New York Times*, September 8, 1967, p. 37.

12. Geoffrey Stokes, *Village Voice*, October 20, 1975, p. 26.

13. Quoted by Elizabeth Drew, *The New Yorker*, December 13, 1982, pp. 91-92.

14. *Sun-Bulletin* (Binghamton, N.Y.), March 13, 1980, p. 7A.

15. Cited by Robert Reinhold, *New York Times*, October 26, 1975, p. 1.

16. "Polls Watcher Wanted," *The Economist*, January 13, 1979, p. 5.

17. Deirdre Carmody, *New York Times*, November 13, 1976, p. C21.

18. Charles B. Seib, "Poll Time Again," *Washington Post*, May 4, 1979, p. A21.

19. Quoted in *Editor and Publisher*, November 10, 1979, p. 82.

20. Reported in *New York Times*, December 18, 1979, p. B15.

21. Michael Wheeler, "Reining in Horserace Journalism," *Public Opinion*, February/March, 1980, p. 42.

22. Letter, *Public Opinion* June/July 1980, p. 57.

23. Wheeler, "Reining in Horserace Journalism," p. 43.

24. In 1978, the Research Information Center of Arizona withdrew from the Minnesota poll that it conducted for the *Minneapolis Tribune* because it

claimed the editors had revised the findings of a poll without its permission. The dispute had to do with sample adjustments, and the editors for their part challenged the quality of the work. That such a dispute should be publicly ventilated was highly unusual.

CHAPTER FOURTEEN
THE FUTURE OF PUBLIC OPINION

According to Northrup Frye, what primarily distinguishes Western civilization is the "revolutionary and prophetic element of confrontation with society. This element gives meaning and shape to history by presenting it with a dialectical challenge."[1] This process of dialectical rigor is a continuing one, and it has been our intention in this book to pull together the state of the art, to find and explore all the new currents of thought and social/technological innovations that impact on the study of public opinion, to offer the best evidence available, old and new, that the passion of these disciplines burns as brightly as ever, and that nurturing that flame is a duty of considerable value.

Let us speculate about some of the trends facing America:

• We are moving from an industrial to a postindustrial (postindustrious?) society, in which information and services become more important than goods. More people work for McDonald's than in the entire U.S. steel industry. In June 1982, for the first time in history, that fact was true of the whole labor force.

• Almost from the beginning of its history, the U.S. economy has been predominantly internal; our home markets consumed most of what we produced, and vice versa. We are now deeply and irretrievably tied into the world market.

• America has become a "bottom-up" society, much different from the "top-down" hierarchical society we were as late as the 1950s. Social change comes from unexpected sources and is always to some degree unmanageable. Those charged with managing it cannot plan or contain its surprises. Social, political, and even industrial institutions are being restructured.

• We are moving from a representational democracy to a participatory one. We no longer depend on elected representatives to get things done; we do it ourselves in vast droves by going to court, placing initiatives on ballots, mounting media-targeted news-theater demonstrations, even unleashing the mentally unhinged into media-targeted acts of madness.

• We are moving toward high tech and high touch. Every increase in the complexity of technology brings a new challenge to the existing forms of institutional life. As robots are introduced in factories, for example, both challenge and response have impact on patterns of work and attempts by workers to protect themselves against change.

• All systems of communication are experiencing a convergence. The microchip and the achievement of cheap and virtually infinite storage capacity of information have meant that telephone, two-way television, libraries, newspapers and magazines, the post office, office work, shopping, trading, much of business of the downtown office world and the central business district, and who knows what else, can now be collapsed into a console that everyone can readily afford, indeed, will not be able to do without. The society can turn into the "Global Village," in which every living room will be a master control room (like NASA's Houston Space Center) and information production may return to cottage industries.

• As a result of these impacts, informal networks and self-programming may replace old chain-of-command and centralized institutions in business, communications, politics, and home life. "Now-casting," the ability to assemble good information on where the society is at any moment in the present, in contrast to fore-casting, has become practical and accessible in large societies.

Self-knowledge for abstract entities like the nation and the world approaches what was previously possible only for small systems. The segmentation of audiences does not necessarily imply the fragmentation of the nation. It is apparent that a complex dialectical relationship exists between trends that hold groups together and those that tear them apart. What must be addressed are the new parameters of affinity that are emerging, and are fulfilling many of the functions previously performed by vanished institutions.

- Self-help may have to replace institutional help in areas ranging from exercise and nutrition to diagnosis and treatment of disease, counseling of all types, and education.

- People in this country will continue to move away from the "slowly sinking cities of the North." The declining urban areas will continue to be the new poorhouses of the welfare state, increasingly turned over to the permanent underclasses of society.

- We will need to begin approaching problems from a longer term perspective because, in spite of the wonders of technology, resources will be more and more constricted. The wasteful halcyon days of inexhaustible resources are over forever. While probably avoiding the dead sea of a sum zero game, we will face sharper conflicts that can only be moderated by building consensus capable of surviving over a longer term than in the past.

- Finally, we will be increasingly caught between the new challenges with their wider options of choice and the heightened tensions of constricted resources. This may sound like a contradiction of terms, but it is likely to become a fact of life, with implications now hardly foreseeable.[2]

POSITIVE CHALLENGES

One surprising development of modern communication networks is the return to interpersonal linkages. The prognosticators of doom did not anticipate that a mass audience could spontaneously segment itself into differentiated parts. So wedded are they to the homogeneous mass audience that arose over the last hundred years that they see its decline as a decline of civilization itself. They did not foresee that all forms of communication, from the most primitive to the most technological, could flourish simultaneously at different levels of complex relationships. Not that new technology doesn't transform the functions and meanings of the old; but that new functions and meanings emerge that discover ways of preserving fundamental values and usages.

Just as there are differentiated audiences for different communicators, so there are differentiated responses to all communications. Each receiver of a message exercises a spate of critical faculties, including his degrees of receptivity and reactivity, his discrimination between levels of meaning in the message, his choices in finding occasions and modes of acting out a response.

Completion of the act of communication is not controlled by the communication itself. Humans are not passive devices at the end of a telegraph wire; they are complex and creative organisms, frequently perverse and unpredictable, always able to inject a new element into the networks of which they are a part. They are capable of weighing psychic costs against psychic benefits and accepting or rejecting the results of the calculation, of reaching into the complex structures of intensity in the emotive galleries of memory, coming up with things that surprise themselves as much as they startle or dismay others.

People are capable of sudden conversions and sudden apostasies; they are always active parts of the communication process and not merely its objects. No matter how unilateral are mass media, the audiences retain full sovereignty and means of ultimate feedback. This specifically includes the popular as well as the high culture audiences. Whatever may be blamed on the media must be blamed on the whole society and culture!

Is there a danger that the breakup of the national audience into fractional and specialized parts will jeopardize the unity of the nation-state itself and imperil the future stability of global institutions? Many are concerned with the decline in HUTs (homes using television). Since 1978, network TV viewing has declined about ten points. Some of the factors seen as responsible for the decline are the predicted end of the three major national TV networks, the explosion of new technologies and the vast expansion of small communicators, including self-programming, the reduced interest in national news, the economic squeeze on the print media, and the growing distrust of the news product by all audiences.

These trends do seem to be happening, but it is hard to believe that the functions presently performed will not continue to be performed, one way or the other. It seems that national and global audiences will continue to exist for some purposes, and some media will serve their needs; while local and specialized audiences will maintain their own networks, supporting the commercial media that they find necessary.

The tribal village reemerges on a global scale, with all the linkages of face-to-face relationships being revalidated at all levels. There is a return to cottage industries as interactive computer networks make every home an independent producer and processer of information.

The so-called "mass audience" is not disappearing; but its forms and functions are becoming highly specialized. It exists for certain purposes and disappears for other purposes. It cannot be mobilized automatically just because the technological connections are in place and operational. When the technological connections are brand new, their ultimate impacts are disguised. A flood of new messages suddenly becomes possible. This possibility generates high sensitivity on both ends. Both the message makers and receivers are transfixed and fascinated. They cannot leave the linkage alone, inventing situations and meanings that justify their use.

The cooling off of the media means the segmentation of the national audience for some of the most salient purposes of individual and social life. It also means that old communication networks are resuscitated for both new and old purposes and thrive along side each other.

The audience fractures into all kinds of pieces. Every person builds up an elaborate set of differential receptivities. He attends to the inputs from this or that linkage for this or that purpose, defined and selected through a complex set of values and loyalties. His subjective screening devices change as he lives and grows in a structured cultural environment.

The next five to ten years will be fascinating for pollsters, audience analysts, and media researchers. The decline of the three TV networks is already happening. The HUTs continue to waffle precariously. Cable penetration is now more than 36 percent of national households, and up to 120 channels of programming and services are becoming standard. The old standard of 30 percent audience share for a successful network program may never return with independent stations, superstations, pay channels, videotext and teletext, low power drop-ins, direct satellite home antennas spreading like mushrooms throughout the suburbs, cellular mobile telephones, and so on. Magnetic tape and disks will tie together all varieties of group networks.

It means that options for self-programming will be extended as never before; that the media environment will for the first time in history be a library of infinite choices; that everyman will now be a learned monk within sacred vaults of cultural history. Accessibility and vanishing cost will make all the treasuries of civilization instantly available in every living room, programmed, not by a secret brotherhood of professional programmers, but by every independent individual. To browse and enlarge his tastes, he will surely discover rewards and interests that no one can anticipate.

The differences may not be soon apparent. Much of the opportunity will no doubt be expended on the kind of content that has dominated the age of mass audiences. Indeed, the producers and writers will be challenged to offer materials that will rally and hold the attention of the largest numbers possible. But if the histories of other media are any indication of what may happen, the trend toward diversification and differentiation will continue in television and related media, as it has in newspapers and radio.

The demographers of the future will have to become even more sophisticated. Mass audience communications will continue to lose salience. Tracking and targeting will become increasingly important in every kind of promotion, persuasion, and reading of the national spirit. Measuring public opinion, media, and audiences will require more complex techniques. Target audiences must be defined more precisely — not only demographics, but life style and behavior. Research must examine attitudes and opinions in greater depth. "Creative treatments will become more varied to meet the needs of new, more specific audiences — longer commercials, info-mercials, multiple-page treatments, integration of program and editorial materials. De-massification will require more time, more effort, more creativity, but more media opportunities to produce better results."[3]

These speculations can only suggest the changing nature of society and the evolutions we can anticipate. Most of these trends are already self-evident and do not require a prognosticator's magic ball. But these trends also contain seeds of their own deflection, oppositions that could abort any tendency and accomplish an utterly different outcome. Indeed, that is the record of most attempts to read the future. In any case, it is clear that America is facing important challenges and changes, and that the old ways will no longer serve. Thus in every area it is time for a new synthesis.

Inquiry into the volitional dimensions of society will play an even more critical role. Tracking and targeting will bring every citizen into the new two-way multitudinous dialogues of the emerging orders. The survey equivalent of CAT scanners may be lurking just over the horizon, with implications at once promising and portentious.

Hardware revolutions now occur every three years or so. We are still in the infancy of the convergence of communications and information processing. It is not unrealistic to assume continuation of the impact of discovery. Interactive home computer networks are just beyond our noses. The classic phase of discovering the uses and potentials of this development has not yet begun, but it is now rushing upon us.

These futuristic signs confront public opinion researchers with a special responsibility. The changes seem aimed directly at their speciality, converting their work from advisory information that is a passive adjunct to the practices of governing and politics into a active and official means of input into the apparatus of the state and all the institutions of society. This is a challenge that cannot be taken lightly, nor can it be avoided. If present trends continue, the new ways of doing things will grow like uncultivated weeds whether or not we approve, and someone must attempt to keep the gardens of democracy well groomed and habitable.

The study of public opinion provides this emerging reality with the indispensable tools to temper and moderate the uses of the new communication networks. More than ever the skills and dedication of public opinion researchers will be needed to tame the technologies and to make the future work for everyone.

NOTES

1. Frye, *The Great Code, the Bible and Literature* (New York: Harcourt Brace Jovanovich, 1982), p. 133.

2. See John Naisbitt, *Megatrends: Ten New Directions Transforming Our Lives* (New York: Warner Books, 1981).

3. *Editor and Publisher*, March 20, 1982, pp. 18-19.

INDEX

ABOUT THE AUTHOR

Harold L. Nieburg is a professor of political science at the State University of New York at Binghamton. Among his seven books are *In the Name of Science* (1965), a study of research and development and economic concentration; *Political Violence* (1969), which came out of his work for the Eisenhower Commission on the Causes and Prevention of Violence; and *Culture Storm* (1972), a study of the emerging youth culture in the 1960s. He is the author of more than 60 articles published in *The American Political Science Review*, *The American Economic Review*, *Dissent*, *The Nation*, and the *Bulletin of Atomic Scientists*. Nieburg's interests are far-ranging, and he has written on subjects as diverse as nuclear strategy and popular culture. This present work springs from 30 years of teaching and professional involvement in polling and audience studies. He previously taught at the Universities of Wisconsin and Chicago.